COMPUTER BOOK SERIES FROM IDG

SGML For Du...

M000310133

Common SGML terms and acronyms

Term	Definition
attribute	Information associated with an element that provides extra data about its purpose or content.
content model	A description of the characters, entities, and other elements that a specific SGML element can contain.
DTD	**Document Type Definition**. A definition of the elements and entities that can be used in that SGML document, the context in which they can be used, and what characters or other elements they can contain.
document instance	The content (data) and markup that comprises a specific SGML document that conforms to a DTD.
element	A structural component of an SGML document as defined by the DTD to which that document conforms. Elements are the basic building blocks of SGML documents.
entity	An SGML variable stored in a location outside of an SGML document instance, representing some content that can be included in an SGML document by including the name of that entity. There are two types of entities: **general entities** and **parameter entities.**
general entity	An entity that can be used in an SGML DTD or document instance by specifying its name in the form **&*entity-name*;**
internal declaration	Any SGML markup declarations provided inside square brackets in the document type declaration.
markup	Portions of a document that provide information about its content.
parameter entity	An entity that can only be used in an SGML DTD by including its name in the form **%*entity-name*;**
PUBLIC identifier	Used in entity or document type declarations, a PUBLIC identifier gives the name which an SGML application must look up in a centralized repository to find the content of a specific entity or DTD.
SGML Parser	A software application that provides applications with easy access to the content and markup of an SGML document, determining whether a specific SGML document instance conforms to a specified DTD and whether the content models specified in an SGML DTD are unambiguous.
SYSTEM identifier	Used in entity or document type declarations, a SYSTEM identifier means that the SGML application itself knows how to locate the content of that entity. For example, a SYSTEM identifier often gives the full pathname of a DTD or set of entities in your computer's file system.
tags	The beginning and ending notation that identifies the boundaries of an element in an SGML document, for example, the <KEYWORD></KEYWORD> tag. <KEYWORD> is the *beginning, start,* or *opening tag* for an instance of the <KEYWORD> element. </KEYWORD> is the *ending* or *closing* tag for this instance of the <KEYWORD> element.

IDG BOOKS WORLDWIDE

Copyright © 1997 IDG Books Worldwide, Inc. All rights reserved.
Cheat Sheet $2.95 value. Item 0175-5.
For more information about IDG Books, call 1-800-762-2974.

...For Dummies: #1 Computer Book Series for Beginners

SGML For Dummies®

The three parts of an SGML Document

Note: SGML declarations and DTDs are typically stored in a separate file from document instances because they are typically associated with many different SGML documents.

Component	Contains . . .
SGML Declaration	Settings used by the SGML parser, controlling the length of element and literal names, and activating or deactivating SGML features such as tag omission and minimization. The default SGML declaration is known as the **Reference Concrete Syntax**.
SGML DTD	The Document Type Definition that defines the structure of that particular document.
Document Instance	A particular document, marked up using the elements and entities defined in the DTD used by that document.

Symbols used in SGML DTDs

Symbol	Description	Example	Explanation
SGML Connectors			
|	One element or the other	paragraph | list	Either a paragraph or a list is valid at this point.
,	Elements must be present in the specified order	paragraph, list	A paragraph must be present, followed by a list.
&	Both elements must be present, in any order	paragraph & list	Either a paragraph followed by a list, or a list followed by a paragraph, must be present.
SGML Occurrence Indicators			
*	Any number (including zero) of this element can be present	paragraph*	Any number of paragraphs (including zero) can be present.
?	Element is optional	paragraph?	A single paragraph could appear at this point.
+	One or more of this element must be present	paragraph+	At least one paragraph must appear at this point.
SGML Grouping Indicators			
( )	Used to group associated elements	((paragraph | list), paragraph+)	A paragraph or a list, followed by any number of paragraphs, must appear at this point.

®

COMPUTER BOOK SERIES FROM IDG

References for the Rest of Us! ®

Are you intimidated and confused by computers? Do you find that traditional manuals are overloaded with technical details you'll never use? Do your friends and family always call you to fix simple problems on their PCs? Then the *...For Dummies*® computer book series from IDG Books Worldwide is for you.

...For Dummies books are written for those frustrated computer users who know they aren't really dumb but find that PC hardware, software, and indeed the unique vocabulary of computing make them feel helpless. *...For Dummies* books use a lighthearted approach, a down-to-earth style, and even cartoons and humorous icons to diffuse computer novices' fears and build their confidence. Lighthearted but not lightweight, these books are a perfect survival guide for anyone forced to use a computer.

"I like my copy so much I told friends; now they bought copies."

Irene C., Orwell, Ohio

"Quick, concise, nontechnical, and humorous."

Jay A., Elburn, Illinois

"Thanks, I needed this book. Now I can sleep at night."

Robin F., British Columbia, Canada

Already, millions of satisfied readers agree. They have made *...For Dummies* books the #1 introductory level computer book series and have written asking for more. So, if you're looking for the most fun and easy way to learn about computers, look to *...For Dummies* books to give you a helping hand.

™

IDG BOOKS WORLDWIDE

5/97

SGML
FOR
DUMMIES®

SGML FOR DUMMIES®

by Bill von Hagen

IDG
BOOKS
WORLDWIDE

IDG Books Worldwide, Inc.
An International Data Group Company

Foster City, CA ♦ Chicago, IL ♦ Indianapolis, IN ♦ Southlake, TX

SMLG For Dummies®

Published by
IDG Books Worldwide, Inc.
An International Data Group Company
919 E. Hillsdale Blvd.
Suite 400
Foster City, CA 94404
http://www.idgbooks.com (IDG Books Worldwide Web site)
http://www.dummies.com (Dummies Press Web site)

Copyright © 1997 IDG Books Worldwide, Inc. All rights reserved. No part of this book, including interior design, cover design, and icons, may be reproduced or transmitted in any form, by any means (electronic, photocopying, recording, or otherwise) without the prior written permission of the publisher.

Library of Congress Catalog Card No.: 97-72406

ISBN: 0-7645-0175-5

Printed in the United States of America

10 9 8 7 6 5 4 3 2 1

10/RX/QX/ZX/IN

Distributed in the United States by IDG Books Worldwide, Inc.

Distributed by Macmillan Canada for Canada; by Transworld Publishers Limited in the United Kingdom; by IDG Norge Books for Norway; by IDG Sweden Books for Sweden; by Woodslane Pty. Ltd. for Australia; by Woodslane Enterprises Ltd. for New Zealand; by Longman Singapore Publishers Ltd. for Singapore, Malaysia, Thailand, and Indonesia; by Simron Pty. Ltd. for South Africa; by Toppan Company Ltd. for Japan; by Distribuidora Cuspide for Argentina; by Livraria Cultura for Brazil; by Ediciencia S.A. for Ecuador; by Addison-Wesley Publishing Company for Korea; by Ediciones ZETA S.C.R. Ltda. for Peru; by WS Computer Publishing Corporation, Inc., for the Philippines; by Unalis Corporation for Taiwan; by Contemporanea de Ediciones for Venezuela; by Computer Book & Magazine Store for Puerto Rico; by Express Computer Distributors for the Caribbean and West Indies. Authorized Sales Agent: Anthony Rudkin Associates for the Middle East and North Africa.

For general information on IDG Books Worldwide's books in the U.S., please call our Consumer Customer Service department at 800-762-2974. For reseller information, including discounts and premium sales, please call our Reseller Customer Service department at 800-434-3422.

For information on where to purchase IDG Books Worldwide's books outside the U.S., please contact our International Sales department at 415-655-3200 or fax 415-655-3295.

For information on foreign language translations, please contact our Foreign & Subsidiary Rights department at 415-655-3021 or fax 415-655-3281.

For sales inquiries and special prices for bulk quantities, please contact our Sales department at 415-655-3200 or write to the address above.

For information on using IDG Books Worldwide's books in the classroom or for ordering examination copies, please contact our Educational Sales department at 800-434-2086 or fax 817-251-8174.

For press review copies, author interviews, or other publicity information, please contact our Public Relations department at 415-655-3000 or fax 415-655-3299.

For authorization to photocopy items for corporate, personal, or educational use, please contact Copyright Clearance Center, 222 Rosewood Drive, Danvers, MA 01923, or fax 508-750-4470.

LIMIT OF LIABILITY/DISCLAIMER OF WARRANTY: AUTHOR AND PUBLISHER HAVE USED THEIR BEST EFFORTS IN PREPARING THIS BOOK. IDG BOOKS WORLDWIDE, INC., AND AUTHOR MAKE NO REPRESENTATIONS OR WARRANTIES WITH RESPECT TO THE ACCURACY OR COMPLETENESS OF THE CONTENTS OF THIS BOOK AND SPECIFICALLY DISCLAIM ANY IMPLIED WARRANTIES OF MERCHANTABILITY OR FITNESS FOR A PARTICULAR PURPOSE. THERE ARE NO WARRANTIES WHICH EXTEND BEYOND THE DESCRIPTIONS CONTAINED IN THIS PARAGRAPH. NO WARRANTY MAY BE CREATED OR EXTENDED BY SALES REPRESENTATIVES OR WRITTEN SALES MATERIALS. THE ACCURACY AND COMPLETENESS OF THE INFORMATION PROVIDED HEREIN AND THE OPINIONS STATED HEREIN ARE NOT GUARANTEED OR WARRANTED TO PRODUCE ANY PARTICULAR RESULTS, AND THE ADVICE AND STRATEGIES CONTAINED HEREIN MAY NOT BE SUITABLE FOR EVERY INDIVIDUAL. NEITHER IDG BOOKS WORLDWIDE, INC., NOR AUTHOR SHALL BE LIABLE FOR ANY LOSS OF PROFIT OR ANY OTHER COMMERCIAL DAMAGES, INCLUDING BUT NOT LIMITED TO SPECIAL, INCIDENTAL, CONSEQUENTIAL, OR OTHER DAMAGES.

Trademarks: All brand names and product names used in this book are trade names, service marks, trademarks, or registered trademarks of their respective owners. IDG Books Worldwide is not associated with any product or vendor mentioned in this book.

is a trademark under exclusive license to IDG Books Worldwide, Inc., from International Data Group, Inc.

About the Author

Bill von Hagen has been a technical writer and documentation tools developer for over ten years. In a past life, he was a musician (well, he was actually a drummer), appearing on several CDs and LPs for garage rock heavies "The Cynics." He is part owner of Get Hip, Inc., a record label and international distributor of indie, punk, and garage music, where he wrote the software that currently runs the business. In whatever time is left, he actively collects old computer hardware and software, owning more than 150 computer systems. Bill's wife is patient indeed. . . .

Contact Bill at wvh@gethip.com, or check out his Web page at http://www.city-net.com/~wvh.

ABOUT IDG BOOKS WORLDWIDE

Welcome to the world of IDG Books Worldwide.

IDG Books Worldwide, Inc., is a subsidiary of International Data Group, the world's largest publisher of computer-related information and the leading global provider of information services on information technology. IDG was founded more than 25 years ago and now employs more than 8,500 people worldwide. IDG publishes more than 275 computer publications in over 75 countries (see listing below). More than 60 million people read one or more IDG publications each month.

Launched in 1990, IDG Books Worldwide is today the #1 publisher of best-selling computer books in the United States. We are proud to have received eight awards from the Computer Press Association in recognition of editorial excellence and three from *Computer Currents'* First Annual Readers' Choice Awards. Our best-selling *...For Dummies®* series has more than 30 million copies in print with translations in 30 languages. IDG Books Worldwide, through a joint venture with IDG's Hi-Tech Beijing, became the first U.S. publisher to publish a computer book in the People's Republic of China. In record time, IDG Books Worldwide has become the first choice for millions of readers around the world who want to learn how to better manage their businesses.

Our mission is simple: Every one of our books is designed to bring extra value and skill-building instructions to the reader. Our books are written by experts who understand and care about our readers. The knowledge base of our editorial staff comes from years of experience in publishing, education, and journalism — experience we use to produce books for the '90s. In short, we care about books, so we attract the best people. We devote special attention to details such as audience, interior design, use of icons, and illustrations. And because we use an efficient process of authoring, editing, and desktop publishing our books electronically, we can spend more time ensuring superior content and spend less time on the technicalities of making books.

You can count on our commitment to deliver high-quality books at competitive prices on topics you want to read about. At IDG Books Worldwide, we continue in the IDG tradition of delivering quality for more than 25 years. You'll find no better book on a subject than one from IDG Books Worldwide.

John Kilcullen
John Kilcullen
CEO
IDG Books Worldwide, Inc.

Steven Berkowitz
Steven Berkowitz
President and Publisher
IDG Books Worldwide, Inc.

**Eighth Annual
Computer Press
Awards ≥1992**

**Ninth Annual
Computer Press
Awards ≥1993**

**Tenth Annual
Computer Press
Awards ≥1994**

**Eleventh Annual
Computer Press
Awards ≥1995**

IDG Books Worldwide, Inc., is a subsidiary of International Data Group, the world's largest publisher of computer-related information and the leading global provider of information services on information technology. International Data Group publishes over 275 computer publications in over 75 countries. Sixty million people read one or more International Data Group publications each month. International Data Group's publications include: **ARGENTINA:** Buyer's Guide, Computerworld Argentina, PC World Argentina; **AUSTRALIA:** Australian Macworld, Australian PC World, Australian Reseller News, Computerworld, IT Casebook, Network World, Publish, Webmaster; **AUSTRIA:** Computerwelt Osterreich, Networks Austria, PC Tip Austria; **BANGLADESH:** PC World Bangladesh; **BELARUS:** PC World Belarus; **BELGIUM:** Data News; **BRAZIL:** Annuário de Informática, Computerworld, Connections, Macworld, PC Player, PC World, Publish, Reseller News, Supergamepower; **BULGARIA:** Computerworld Bulgaria, Network World Bulgaria, PC & MacWorld Bulgaria; **CANADA:** CIO Canada, Client/Server World, ComputerWorld Canada, InfoWorld Canada, NetworkWorld Canada, WebWorld; **CHILE:** Computerworld Chile, PC World Chile; **COLOMBIA:** Computerworld Colombia, PC World Colombia; **COSTA RICA:** PC World Centro America; **THE CZECH AND SLOVAK REPUBLICS:** Computerworld Czechoslovakia, Macworld Czech Republic, PC World Czechoslovakia; **DENMARK:** Communications World Danmark, Computerworld Danmark, Macworld Danmark, PC World Danmark, Techworld Denmark; **DOMINICAN REPUBLIC:** PC World Republica Dominicana; **ECUADOR:** PC World Ecuador; **EGYPT:** Computerworld Middle East, PC World Middle East; **EL SALVADOR:** PC World Centro America; **FINLAND:** MikroPC, Tietoverkko, Tietoviikko; **FRANCE:** Distributique, Hebdo, Info PC, Le Monde Informatique, Macworld, Reseaux & Telecoms, WebMaster France; **GERMANY:** Computer Partner, Computerwoche, Computerwoche Extra, Computerwoche FOCUS, Global Online, Macwelt, PC Welt; **GREECE:** Amiga Computing, GamePro Greece, Multimedia World; **GUATEMALA:** PC World Centro America; **HONDURAS:** PC World Centro America; **HONG KONG:** Computerworld Hong Kong, PC World Hong Kong, Publish in Asia; **HUNGARY:** ABCD CD-ROM, Computerworld Szamitastechnika, Internetto online Magazine, PC World Hungary, PC-X Magazin Hungary; **ICELAND:** Tolvuheimur PC World Island; **INDIA:** Information Communications World, Information Systems Computerworld, PC World India, Publish in Asia; **INDONESIA:** InfoKomputer PC World, Komputek Computerworld, Publish in Asia; **IRELAND:** ComputerScope, PC Live!; **ISRAEL:** Macworld Israel, People & Computers/Computerworld; **ITALY:** Computerworld Italia, Macworld Italia, Networking Italia, PC World Italia; **JAPAN:** DTP World, Macworld Japan, Nikkei Personal Computing, OS/2 World Japan, SunWorld Japan, Windows NT World, Windows World Japan; **KENYA:** PC World East African; **KOREA:** Hi-Tech Information, Macworld Korea, PC World Korea; **MACEDONIA:** PC World Macedonia; **MALAYSIA:** Computerworld Malaysia, PC World Malaysia, Publish in Asia; **MALTA:** PC World Malta; **MEXICO:** Computerworld Mexico, PC World Mexico; **MYANMAR:** PC World Myanmar; **NETHERLANDS:** Computer! Totaal, LAN Internetworking Magazine, LAN World Buyers Guide, Macworld Netherlands, Net, WebWereld; **NEW ZEALAND:** Absolute Beginners Guide and Plain & Simple Series, Computer Buyer, Computer Industry Directory, Computerworld New Zealand, MTB, Network World, PC World New Zealand; **NICARAGUA:** PC World Centro America; **NORWAY:** Computerworld Norge, CW Rapport, Datamagasinet, Financial Rapport, Kursguide Norge, Macworld Norge, Multimediaworld Norge, PC World Ekspress Norge, PC World Nettverk, PC World Norge, PC World ProduktGuide Norge; **PAKISTAN:** Computerworld Pakistan; **PANAMA:** PC World Panama; **PEOPLE'S REPUBLIC OF CHINA:** China Computer Users, China Computerworld, China InfoWorld, China Telecom World Weekly, Computer & Communication, Electronic Design China, Electronics Today, Electronics Weekly, Game Software, PC World China, Popular Computer Week, Software Weekly, Software World, Telecom World; **PERU:** Computerworld Peru, PC World Profesional Peru, PC World SoHo Peru; **PHILIPPINES:** Click!, Computerworld Philippines, PC World Philippines, Publish in Asia; **POLAND:** Computerworld Poland, Computerworld Special Report Poland, Cyber, Macworld Poland, Networld Poland, PC World Komputer; **PORTUGAL:** Cerebro/PC World, Computerworld/Correio Informático, Dealer World Portugal, Mac*In/PC*In Portugal, Multimedia World; **PUERTO RICO:** PC World Puerto Rico; **ROMANIA:** Computerworld Romania, PC World Romania, Telecom Romania; **RUSSIA:** Computerworld Russia, Mir PK, Publish, Seti; **SINGAPORE:** Computerworld Singapore, PC World Singapore, Publish in Asia; **SLOVENIA:** Monitor; **SOUTH AFRICA:** Computing SA, Network World SA, Software World SA; **SPAIN:** Communicaciones World España, Computerworld España, Dealer World España, Macworld España, PC World España; **SRI LANKA:** Infolink PC World; **SWEDEN:** CAP&Design, Computer Sweden, Corporate Computing Sweden, Internetworld Sweden, it.branschen, Macworld Sweden, MaxiData Sweden, MikroDatorn, Natverk & Kommunikation, PC World Sweden, PCaktiv, Windows World Sweden; **SWITZERLAND:** Computerworld Schweiz, Macworld Schweiz, PCtip; **TAIWAN:** Computerworld Taiwan, Macworld Taiwan, NEW ViSiON/Publish, PC World Taiwan, Windows World Taiwan; **THAILAND:** Publish in Asia, Thai Computerworld; **TURKEY:** Computerworld Turkiye, Macworld Turkiye, Network World Turkiye, PC World Turkiye; **UKRAINE:** Computerworld Kiev, Multimedia World Ukraine, PC World Ukraine; **UNITED KINGDOM:** Acorn User UK, Amiga Action UK, Amiga Computing UK, Apple Talk UK, Computing, Macworld, Parents and Computers UK, PC Advisor, PC Home, PSX Pro, The WEB; **UNITED STATES:** Cable in the Classroom, CIO Magazine, Computerworld, DOS World, Federal Computer Week, GamePro Magazine, InfoWorld, I-Way, Macworld, Network World, PC Games, PC World, Publish, Video Event, THE WEB Magazine, and WebMaster; online webzines: JavaWorld, NetscapeWorld, and SunWorld Online; **URUGUAY:** InfoWorld Uruguay; **VENEZUELA:** Computerworld Venezuela, PC World Venezuela; and **VIETNAM:** PC World Vietnam.
3/24/97

Dedication

To my wife, Dorothy Fisher, for all her love, patience, and support while I wrote this book — and, now that I think of it, always! This book is also for my parents, Wolf and Jane von Hagen, who showed me the magic that you can find between the covers of a book. Maybe all those overdue library books were worth it — thanks, Mrs. Connors!

Author's Acknowledgments

This book couldn't have happened without significant input and support from folks at IDG Press. Thanks to Jill Pisoni for the opportunity to write this, and to Bill Helling, Michael Simsic, and John Fieber for their expertise, suggestions, enhancements, and patience.

Gregg, I'm getting you a copy of this book so that you can put it on the shelf beside *Patton!*

Publisher's Acknowledgments

We're proud of this book; please send us your comments about it by using the IDG Books Worldwide Registration Card at the back of the book or by e-mailing us at feedback/dummies@idgbooks.com. Some of the people who helped bring this book to market include the following:

Acquisitions, Development, and Editorial

Project Editor: Bill Helling

Senior Acquisitions Editor: Jill Pisoni

Product Development Director: Mary Bednarek

Media Development Manager: Joyce Pepple

Associate Permissions Editor: Heather H. Dismore

Copy Editor: Michael Simsic

Technical Editor: John Fieber

Editorial Manager: Mary C. Corder

Editorial Assistant: Chris Collins

Production

Project Coordinator: Debbie Stailey

Layout and Graphics: Angela F. Hunckler, Jane E. Martin, Brent Savage, Michael Sullivan

Proofreaders: Christine Sabooni, Christine Berman, Nancy Price, Robert Springer

Indexer: David Heiret

Special Help: Access Technology; Joell Smith, Associate Technical Editor

General and Administrative

IDG Books Worldwide, Inc.: John Kilcullen, CEO; Steven Berkowitz, President and Publisher

IDG Books Technology Publishing: Brenda McLaughlin, Senior Vice President and Group Publisher

Dummies Technology Press and Dummies Editorial: Diane Graves Steele, Vice President and Associate Publisher; Judith A. Taylor, Product Marketing Manager; Kristin A. Cocks, Editorial Director

Dummies Trade Press: Kathleen A. Welton, Vice President and Publisher

IDG Books Production for Dummies Press: Beth Jenkins, Production Director; Cindy L. Phipps, Manager of Project Coordination, Production Proofreading, and Indexing; Kathie S. Schutte, Supervisor of Page Layout; Shelley Lea, Supervisor of Graphics and Design; Debbie J. Gates, Production Systems Specialist; Tony Augsburger, Supervisor of Reprints and Bluelines; Leslie Popplewell, Media Archive Coordinator

Dummies Packaging and Book Design: Patti Sandez, Packaging Specialist; Lance Kayser, Packaging Assistant; Kavish + Kavish, Cover Design

◆

The publisher would like to give special thanks to Patrick J. McGovern, without whom this book would not have been possible.

◆

Contents at a Glance

Cartoons at a Glance

By Rich Tennant

"Hey Dad- guess how many elements fit inside your SGML DTD."

page 181

"AAAAH - HE'S NOT THAT SMART. HE WON'T CHECK HIS SYTAX, FORGETS TO DECLARE HIS ENTITIES, AND DROOLS ALL OVER THE KEYBOARD."

page 235

AFTER SPENDING 9 DAYS WITH 12 DIFFERENT VENDORS AND READING 26 BROCHURES, DAVE HAD AN ACUTE ATTACK OF TOXIC OPTION SYNDROME.

page 339

And this is Bud Mellnick who writes all of our SGML.

<PAR>Hello. </PAR>

page 35

"I FOUND THESE TWO IN THE COMPUTER LAB REUSING AND SHARING INFORMATION IN THEIR DOCUMENTS."

page 7

"NO THANKS. BUT I WOULD LIKE ONE MORE CHANCE TO SEE IF I CAN CONVERT SOME EXISTING DOCUMENTS INTO SGML."

page 277

Okay young man, it's time to wash your hands, brush your teeth, and parse your SGML.

Awwww, Mom.

page 321

"QUICK KIDS! YOUR MOTHER EXPRESSING THE VALUE OF AN SGML PARAMETER ENTRY."

page 141

Fax: 508-546-7747 • E-mail: the5wave@tiac.net

Table of Contents

Part III: Defining the Appearance of a Document 141

Chapter 9: Introducing SGML Document Formatting 143

Chapter 10: How to Include Specific Formatting Instructions 157

Chapter 11: SGML Tools That You Probably Already Know 165

Part IV: Developing a Document Type Definition 181

Chapter 12: Developing a DTD — It's Not for Everyone 183

Introduction

. . . .

*W*elcome to *SGML For Dummies*, a friendly and sometimes irreverent introduction to SGML, a new approach to documentation that's sweeping the nation. "Sweeping the nation" may be a slight exaggeration, but I always wanted to say that. That's lesson one about this book — let's have some fun! SGML is a interesting and useful way of approaching and resolving many issues in technical writing, documentation development, and electronic publishing, but that doesn't mean that we have to look serious, dress alike, and seem thoughtful the whole time we're discussing it. Of all the classes I took years ago when I was in college, the ones I remember best are the ones that were entertaining. I hope to do the same sort of thing in this book.

The next lesson is that we both know you're not a dummy. After all, you were smart enough to buy this book! So why the title of this book and the related series? First off, because it's funny. The *...For Dummies* books are useful reference books that explore their subject matter in detail, but that doesn't mean that they can't be entertaining as well as insightful. Another reason for the *...For Dummies* series is that the pace at which the computer field (and related topics, such as SGML) is changing is enough to make anyone feel like a dummy sometimes. It certainly has for me . . . .

No worries, mate! By the time you finish this book, you'll have a clear idea of the documentation and business issues that SGML is designed to solve. Hopefully, you'll also have had some fun in the process of learning about SGML, which is the best feedback I could ever get.

About This Book

This book is intended for use by writers, editors, documentation managers, business people, and anyone else who has ever heard the FLA (Four-Letter Acronym) SGML and wondered more about it. Using SGML as a documentation solution is mandatory in some industries, but (more important) it can make your life easier and can save you and your organization money and time. Using SGML also makes it easier for you to re-use your documents and other information in many different ways, such as on the Internet or through other forms of electronic publishing. Sound interesting?

Some sample topics I discuss in this book are

- ✔ The origins and history of SGML
- ✔ The documentation problems that SGML can help you solve
- ✔ Good business reasons for moving your documents to SGML
- ✔ How (and whether) to create your own SGML document types
- ✔ How to convert existing documents into SGML
- ✔ How SGML and electronic publishing are related

You may find that thinking about SGML causes you to change the way you think about how you write and organize documents, but that's a good thing! Focusing on the content and structure of your documents is an investment in the future of those documents.

What You Should Know Before Reading This Book

The only real prerequisites for reading and enjoying this book are a sense of humor and some curiosity about SGML. I assume that you have some basic interest in, or knowledge of, how one writes documents using a computer. Beyond this, you don't even have to know any documentation buzzwords — wherever I use them, I try to explain them.

What You'll Find in This Book

Part I: Introduction to SGML

This part introduces SGML, explains how SGML can benefit both writers and business people, and provides background information about the differences between SGML and format-oriented approaches to documentation.

Part II: Defining the Structure of a Document

SGML is a structured approach to documentation, focusing on the organization and content of your documents rather than the specific fonts and paragraph styles used when they are printed. This part discusses how you define the structure of a document and examines the building blocks of an SGML *document type definition* (DTD). It also discusses ways in which SGML can help you re-use information between different documents, provides a *Weekly World News* expose of HTML, and provides some locations on the Web where you can find some popular SGML document definitions.

Part III: Defining the Appearance of a Document

While SGML lets you focus on the structure and content of your documents, it would be fairly worthless without some reasonable way of formatting and printing them. This part discusses various standard ways of associating formatting information with an SGML document type and explains some tricks for including application-specific formatting (a conceptual no-no). This part also analyzes some standard documentation software that supports SGML and discusses how they've integrated SGML into their applications.

Part IV: Developing a Document Type Definition

The *Document Type Definition* (DTD) is the coat hanger on which the rest of SGML is suspended. This part discusses whether you should consider creating your own DTD, or whether you should just use one of the standard DTDs that are already in popular use. This part discusses the factors in selecting a DTD and provides suggestions for analyzing your existing documents to see whether they need a custom DTD. This part provides suggestions for designing a DTD and also discusses how to adapt a standard DTD to meet your specific needs.

Part V: Using SGML in Business

This part discusses various ways in which SGML can benefit your organization — and provides background information about popular topics such as electronic and Internet publishing. This part also discusses software that can make it easier for you to work with SGML documentation in a business environment, such as document management systems and databases.

Part VI: How Do I Get There from Here?

Assuming you've seen the light, this part covers the different types of SGML tools that are available and how you can select the tools that are right for your organization. It also discusses different approaches to converting existing documents into SGML and lists additional sources for information about SGML.

Part VII: The Part of Tens

All IDG Books Worldwide ...*For Dummies* books include a "Part of Tens" section, which provides summaries of various interesting points about their subjects. This "Part of Tens" section summarizes business reasons for moving to SGML, hot topics in creating an SGML Document Type Definition, and common mistakes in moving to SGML and creating a DTD.

Part VIII: Appendixes

This part provides appendixes that list sources of public-domain and commercial SGML software. Another appendix also contains information on what you'll find in the CD and what you need to do in order to use it.

Icons Used in This Book

The ...*For Dummies* books use standard icons to identify certain types of information in the books. We've also added a few for this book that specifically relate to SGML. You'll see the following icons sprinkled through this book:

A reminder of prerequisites for a specific task, or other factors that you should consider related to the task at hand. You may also want to keep this stuff in mind.

Basic information about some fundamental aspect of SGML, an SGML keyword, or about using SGML.

Advanced information about SGML, or fancy, convoluted suggestions that will impress your fellow SGML wizards.

A warning that a specific paragraph is especially nerdy. You can often skip such paragraphs if you're not interested in low-level details about implementing SGML or how certain SGML tools actually work. These paragraphs almost always contain computer jargon, which can make them more fun to read or more worthy of avoidance, depending on your perspective.

A specific detail about using or implementing SGML that you may find especially useful.

Typestyles in This Book

SGML is designed for use by writers, emphasizing the structure and meaning of different parts of your documents over focusing on formatting. For this reason, you'll see examples of SGML syntax throughout this book that are marked up like the following:

```
<! DOCTYPE HTML "-//W3C//DTD HTML 3.2 Final//EN" >
```

Because SGML lets you define the structure and organization of your documents before you've even written one, some examples of SGML syntax can look like programs in a weird computer language. Don't let this put you off! Most people won't have to worry about SGML syntax anyway, because most SGML applications hide that stuff from you. You don't have to know any programming to use SGML — all you have to know is how to think about the content of your documents in terms of their basic structure. "Books contain parts, parts contain chapters, chapters contain sections. Each of these has its own title . . ." and so on.

Throughout this book, you'll also see things in the text of the document that look like this. These are usually reserved for SGML keywords, addresses on the World Wide Web where you can find more information, and e-mail addresses.

On the CD

The CD in this book provides some sample SGML declarations, specifications, and software so that you can get started learning more about SGML and working with it right away. The CD includes:

- ✔ A 90-day demonstration version of Corel WordPerfect — other than the time-limit, this is a fully-functional version of all of the tools you'll need to work with SGML in WordPerfect, including WordPerfect itself, Corel's Logic Compiler, and Corel's Layout Designer.

- ✔ A demonstration version of Digitome Electronic Publishing's IDM Personal Edition and its associated documentation. IDM is a powerful software package for generating Windows Help, RTF, and Lotus Notes format files from SGML input files.

- ✔ Sample SGML applications from SGML Systems Engineering, including SGMLC-Lite, a Lite version of their core toolset, their Generic SGML Viewer, their SGML Normaliser, and their SGML Parser.

- ✔ The SP SGML Parser for Win95 and NT PCs.

- ✔ A 45-day demonstration version of HyTime's HyBrowse Browser, an SGML/HyTime-aware browser and educational development system.

- ✔ DTDs such as the TEI-Lite and DocBook DTDs.

For more information on the CD, including system requirements and installation, see Appendix C.

Where to Go from Here

Think of *SGML For Dummies* as a friendly tour guide on the road to SGML. I hope you have as much fun reading it as I've had writing it. Either the Beatles' "I hope you all enjoy the show" or the Grateful Dead's "What a long, strange trip it's been" might be appropriate send-offs. Let me know.

Other than that, Chapter 1 would be a good start.

Part I
Introduction to SGML

The 5th Wave   By Rich Tennant

"I FOUND THESE TWO IN THE COMPUTER LAB REUSING AND SHARING
INFORMATION IN THEIR DOCUMENTS."

In this part . . .

SGML stands for the Standard Generalized Markup Language and was designed to reduce the number of headache remedies purchased by documentation professionals. More specifically, SGML was designed to provide a flexible, open approach to documentation development and management.

This part introduces some basic concepts of documentation development and shows how common problems in documentation development and maintenance led people to develop a more general approach: SGML. I discuss some of the common documentation questions addressed by SGML and provide a short history of its development.

The final chapter provides some solid business incentives for adopting SGML and demonstrates how an SGML approach to documentation can reduce problems, increase efficiency, and increase productivity whether you're just one writer working alone or whether you're managing documentation development for a Fortune 500 company. Fortunately, these features of SGML scale nicely — the larger the group you're working with, the more you're likely to gain from adopting an SGML approach to documentation!

Chapter 1

Writing Documents on a Computer: Form(at) vs. Function

In This Chapter

▶ Figuring out what a markup language is

▶ To manually format or not to manually format, that is the question

▶ Aren't style sheets good enough?

▶ Introducing SGML

▶ Thinking about SGML's features and benefits

*T*ext formatting and word-processing programs were among the earliest programs written for interactive computer systems. I never found it much fun to write anything on a typewriter, even with erasable bond paper and a 55-gallon drum of White-out. Maybe I'm just not a very good typist or speller. It also can be hard to convince yourself to reorganize something after you've already typed 200 pages of copy.

Today's computer software for creative, business, and technical writing gives you the freedom to experiment, painlessly makes major changes in the tone and organization of your documents, and generally empowers writers. However, sometimes power can be a dangerous thing because you can spend more time worrying about the appearance of a document rather than its content. You can also create documents that are so thoroughly customized that they become nightmarish to work with if you want to do something as simple as changing the size of the paper they're printed on.

This chapter discusses how documents are written on a computer, shows different approaches to writing documents on a computer, and introduces the Standard Generalized Markup Language (SGML) as a solution to many of the problems that plague writers, writing groups, and documentation managers.

What Is a Markup Language?

In documentation circles, the set of formatting commands associated with any element of a document is typically called the *markup* for that element. A *markup language* is the set of commands that you use to tell your word-processing or publishing package how to format a specific part of your document. The term "markup" has its roots in the history of printing — editors used to "mark up" the copy for a newspaper or book, writing down formatting instructions for the person who was setting the type. When looking at a document in a text editor, word-processing, or publishing package, a good way to think of markup is "everything in your document that isn't the text of the document." The computer uses the markup commands to do special things for you, such as making text bold, centering it, and so on.

The following is an example of a markup language, showing some of the formatting commands used by the standard UNIX document formatter, troff:

```
.ce
.ps 24
\fBThis is the Title of Chapter One\fP
.ps 11
.ad l
```

The special codes used in troff are lines that begin with a period and three-character sequences starting with a backslash (\). Line-by-line, this sample troff code says

- Start centering the following text.
- Change the point size to 24 point.
- Switch to a bold font, display the text "This is the Title of Chapter One," and revert to the previous font.
- Change the point size to 11 point.
- Switch to a filled, left-justified environment.

That's a lot of work simply to format a single part of your document, and it would be incredibly tedious if you have a large document. To simplify things, most word-processing and publishing software lets you define *macros* or *styles* that allow you to apply the same formatting to different parts of a document. These are specific formatting attributes that are associated with different elements of your document. For example, you may create a style that defines the way that you want top-level headings to appear in your document — they should be numbered automatically, printed in 24-point bold Helvetica, and always left-flush on the page. Troff provides a macro package that lets you identify something as a title by simply saying

```
.TI "This is the Title of Chapter One"
```

Applying a style to a specific part of your document is frequently referred to as *tagging* that part of the document with that style.

When using older word-processing and publishing software like troff, you create your documents as text files, embed the appropriate markup commands, and then process them with troff to generate an output file that is formatted for your printer. You can create the text files for your document using whatever text editor you like. Today's graphical word-processing and publishing software frees you from having to use text files and embed cryptic commands in them, but internally they still do the same thing. Some software packages, such as Corel Word Perfect, allow you to examine what's going on under the covers. Figure 1-1 is a sample screen from WordPerfect showing its Reveal Codes feature.

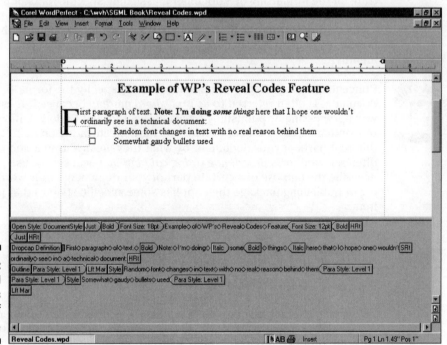

Figure 1-1: The Reveal Codes feature of WordPerfect.

I have used this example to show that markup languages aren't something old or archaic, though my troff example certainly is. Word-processing and publishing software always needs to associate different parts of your document with how they should be formatted. Markup languages are even somewhat coming back into vogue, thanks to HTML, the HyperText Markup Language that is used to create documents on the World Wide Web. However, like WordPerfect, which uses markup commands under the covers but doesn't show them to you unless you ask, many word-processing and publishing packages can produce HTML without your having to do anything special.

Since you've read this far, I'll let you into an ugly secret that few people know — HTML is actually just one specific instance of SGML. More about this later. . . .

Nightmare on Format Street

As mentioned in the previous section, there are two basic ways to write a document using a word-processing or publishing program. You can concentrate on the formatting of a document, assigning specific fonts, font sizes, and justification to each part of the document as you write it. Or you can focus on the logical organization of your document, making sure that it is composed of chapters that each have multiple sections that you can easily identify.

Concentrating on using markup commands to specify the formatting of a document is often referred to as *procedural markup* because it tells a specific word-processing or publishing package exactly what to do when displaying or printing certain parts of the document. Concentrating on identifying different parts of your document by what they mean within a document is often referred to as *descriptive* or *logical markup* because you use markup to describe the *purpose* of a certain part of your document. Your word-processing or publishing package then applies some specific style to that particular item.

Choosing your focus: disposable versus durable

People create two basic types of documents — *disposable* documents, like personal letters, and *durable* documents, like the documentation for a software product. It doesn't really matter how you organize a letter or whether you use a specific set of styles in it because you'll probably never use it again after you write and mail it. Durable documents, like technical and user manuals, are documents that you and others will update and reissue over the lifetime of a product. Not all products actually have a lifetime, but we should at least hope that they will!

Problems with durable documents

Focusing on how a document is formatted is fine for one-time documents because you simply want to write it once and make it look nice. However, for durable documents, you want to minimize the number of times that you manually tweak the formatting of different parts of the document. This is important for several reasons:

✔ Documents that contain a lot of manual formatting are more difficult to maintain. It's not always easy to tell that something has been changed manually. Even if you're writing in a program that lets you see the exact formatting codes for each piece of the document, it's often hard to spot small changes. Making small changes in manual formatting throughout a documentation set is time-consuming and painful!

✔ You often make small changes in response to the way a specific word or paragraph currently looks in your document. The next time you modify the document, a page break or relationship between two paragraphs may not matter anymore or may actually do the wrong thing.

✔ Similar to the preceding bullet, you often make small changes to a document to "fix" the way it prints on a specific printer or from a specific word-processing or publishing application. If you switch printers or word-processing programs, your document may format or print incorrectly.

That's a lot of work to do throughout a large document. For large documents or for sets of documents that are supposed to look the same, we'll probably all agree that it's better to work in a way that lets you uniformly apply the same formatting attributes to parts of your document that serve the same purpose throughout a document.

Aren't Style Sheets Good Enough?

Most word-processing and publishing software allows you to group the set of macros and styles that you want to use on a single project into *style sheets*, which all writers working on the same project use. Writers can either copy the style sheets onto their computers or share a single copy from a central source on a network. In theory, when everyone uses the same style sheet, finishes their work, and prints the final version of their piece of the document, you combine everyone's documents together, and they all look the same.

Unfortunately, that's rarely the case. Style sheets don't provide many of the consistency guarantees that you might like to see in your documents. Imagine a simple style sheet that contains these four elements:

- ✔ **Chapter heading** — the title of a chapter in your document. This uses a specific font, is automatically numbered, and so on.

- ✔ **Intro paragraph** — an introductory paragraph following a chapter heading that describes the contents of a chapter.

- ✔ **Text paragraph** — a normal paragraph of text in your document.

- ✔ **Section heading** — the title of a section in your document.

Most applications that use style sheets allow you to specify a default value for the next element in your document. In this example, you can specify that the paragraph that follows a chapter heading has the intro paragraph style. You and any writers using this style sheet agree that you'll all follow this convention, maybe even writing it down into a style guide, and off you go.

Unfortunately, style sheets don't prevent people from ignoring conventions. If a style guide isn't available and someone forgets to tell a new writer what conventions to use, she might use the text paragraph style everywhere, even where she should use the intro paragraph style. Unless the two styles look glaringly different, you might not catch this mistake until after you print the document.

Style sheets also can't ensure that everything that's supposed be in a document is actually there. Nothing prevents you from accidentally forgetting to include an introductory paragraph in a new chapter, even though it's present in all the other chapters in a book.

Finally, you should know that style sheets are usually specific to a particular word-processing or publishing package. If you decide or need to switch to a different word processor or publishing system, you may not be able to transfer the style sheets into that program. You may have to reenter all of that information in the new system.

Introducing SGML

The Standard Generalized Markup Language (SGML) was created to solve many of the potential problems raised in the previous sections. SGML is the result of years of working with documents on computers. Here are the basic principles of SGML:

- ✔ It provides you with a way to define the structure of your documents and to easily identify the different parts of that structure.

- ✔ It separates the structure and content of your documents from their appearance.

- ✔ It is an open approach to documentation that is not tied to a specific word-processing or publishing package. Many popular word-processing and publishing packages support SGML, either directly or through add-in software.

SGML rigorously enforces structure and consistency in your documentation, which is one of the reasons that it has become so popular. Because SGML documents conform to a specific structure, they are easier for computer programs to work with. For example, you can write programs that translate SGML documents into other common formats, such as the HyperText Markup Language (HTML), fairly easily because you can always predict the parts of a document that you can encounter next when translating it. Similarly, if you want to store an SGML document with many similar records (such as a catalog) in a database, you can set up and enforce the relationships between the different records that hold different parts of the document without too much trouble.

Writing documents in SGML is much like writing programs in a computer language because most SGML tools verify the structure of your document as you write it. They do this by enforcing syntax. Just like in the English language, SGML documents have a certain form that they have to follow. In English, sentences have to (or, at least, should) follow basic rules, like "subject verb object." In SGML, documents have to conform to some basic structure that says something like "documents consist of a title, followed by chapters and appendices." Enforcing the structure of a document prevents many common errors and also simplifies writing many types of documents. It's always clear what parts of a document can come next, and it's also impossible to forget to insert a mandatory part of a document. Although this can be constraining, it can help guarantee a structurally consistent and complete documentation set.

WARNING!

Acronym alert!

Anyone working in the computer field knows that it's impossible to pick up a computer-related text that isn't saturated with acronyms. Although they sometimes make text look like an explosion in an uppercase factory, acronyms do provide a way to quickly refer to concepts that would otherwise be a mouthful. BTW (By The Way), this book is no different.

SGML is an accepted standard defined by the International Standards Organization (ISO, a non-partisan group whose whole purpose is to promote standardization in the sciences) in ISO Standard # 8879. Because SGML is a standard, some industries require that documentation work be done in SGML. For example, any contractor or subcontractor doing work for the Department of Defense or many aerospace companies must submit any associated documentation in SGML form.

Basic concepts

The markup used in SGML documents consists of *elements,* which are the building blocks of an SGML document. Each element is surrounded by a pair of beginning and ending expressions called *tags.* A sample sentence in SGML looks like this:

```
<PARAGRAPH><KEYWORD>SGML</KEYWORD> is very cool.</PARAGRAPH>
```

In this sentence, `<PARAGRAPH>` and `<KEYWORD>` are beginning tags, and `</KEYWORD>` and `</PARAGRAPH>` are their corresponding ending tags. In most cases, the ending tag associated with any beginning tag is the name of the begining tag preceded by the slash character — there are some possible exceptions to this which are discussed in Chapter 3. Tags are usually referred to using the name of the opening tag, such as in the expression "the `<KEYWORD>` tag." SGML tags do not have to be in uppercase, but I'm using that convention to make them stand out more in the examples used throughout this book.

SGML elements identify the purpose of the text that they contain. In this example, "SGML is very cool" is identified as a paragraph, and the word "SGML" is identified as a keyword within that paragraph. SGML elements have to be correctly nested within each other. For example, you should not close the `<PARAGRAPH>` element before closing the `<KEYWORD>` element.

Most SGML software automatically prevents you from making such syntax errors. For example, incorrect markup of the preceding example would be the following.

```
<PARAGRAPH><KEYWORD>SGML</PARAGRAPH></KEYWORD> is very cool.
```

Elements are the fundamental building blocks of an SGML document. Tags identify the boundaries of an instance of an element, which is just a fancy way of saying "an element with some specific content."

The set of elements available to you when writing a document depends on the *Document Type Definition* (DTD) associated with that document. How you actually apply these elements and how they are displayed on the screen depends on the word-processing or publishing software you use. You can create your own DTD to define and enforce your own documentation requirements, or you can use one of many that are freely available on the Internet. Most word-processing and publishing software that supports SGML comes fully loaded with one or two of the most common DTDs. See Chapter 3 for more information on DTDs and how they are organized.

It's important to understand how SGML word-processing and publishing software provides support for different DTDs. An SGML document contains introductory markup that specifies the DTD used by that document. The SGML software then loads the files associated with that DTD, and away you go!

Because I haven't filled my quota of acronyms in this section, there's one more that's central to SGML's open approach to documentation. This is the *Formatting Output Specification Instance,* or FOSI. A FOSI is one common way of defining the formatting that is associated with each part of a DTD. You specify things like page size, margins, the fonts used by various elements, and so on, in the FOSI. You can create multiple FOSIs for a single DTD and then specify which one you want to use when you print your document. Just as with creating a DTD, the way you create a FOSI depends on which SGML word-processing or publishing package you use. See Chapter 9 for more information on FOSIs and other ways of specifying the formatting of an SGML document.

Different strokes for different folks

Different word-processing and publishing packages have different terms for central SGML concepts like the DTD and FOSI. Not all SGML software even uses a FOSI, but all SGML word-processing or publishing software has to have some way of defining how its SGML documents are formatted. If you use Adobe FrameMaker+SGML, you are probably on a first name basis with its Element Data Dictionary (EDD) files, which is its FOSI equivalent. If you use Corel WordPerfect, you are probably familiar with its Logic (LGC) files, which is a compiled form of its DTD, and its Layout Specification Instance (LSI) files, which is its FOSI equivalent. No matter what you call them, DTDs and FOSIs are critical pieces of the SGML puzzle because they define the structure of your documents and keep the content of your documents separate from their formatting.

Besides using different terminology, different SGML word-processing and publishing packages take very different approaches to how your document appears on the screen while you work on it. If you are used to What-You-See-Is-What-You-Get (WYSIWYG) word-processing and publishing software, you will be in for a surprise when you see various SGML tools. Some very popular and powerful SGML software packages, such as Arbortext Adept and Softquad's Author/Editor products, emphasize the structure of a document rather than try to display what it will look like when printed. I call packages like these "QUASIWYG" software packages because what you see on the screen is something like what you'll see when you print your document, but not really. These packages are also sometimes referred to as "WYSIWYN" (What-You-See-Is-What-You-Need), since their focus is on showing you the structure of a document plus some visual hints as to what parts of a document are different levels of headings, and so on. Figure 1-2 is a sample screen from a document in Arbortext Adept.

Other SGML software shows your documents in more or less the same way as they'll look when they're printed. Software such as Corel WordPerfect and Adobe's FrameMaker+SGML are good examples of this type of software. Figure 1-3 is a sample screen showing an SGML document in Corel WordPerfect. Figure 1-4 is a sample screen showing a document in Adobe FrameMaker+SGML.

The approach that different tools take to display your documents tends to show the roots of the company. Arbortext and Softquad have always produced SGML tools, so their emphasis has always been on structured documentation. Corel and Adobe produced word-processing and desktop publishing software long before becoming involved in SGML, so their SGML tools can't afford to alienate their existing customers.

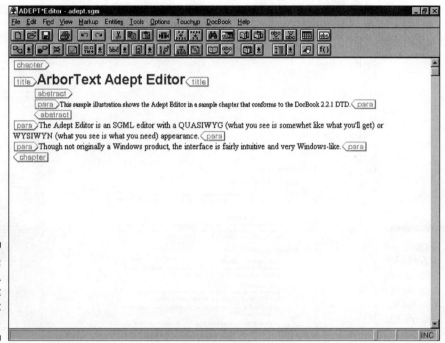

Figure 1-2:
An SGML
Document
in Arbortext
Adept.

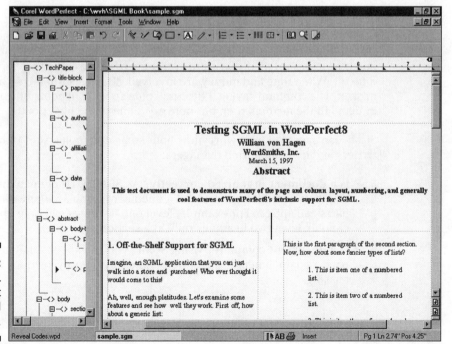

Figure 1-3:
An SGML
Document
in Corel
WordPerfect.

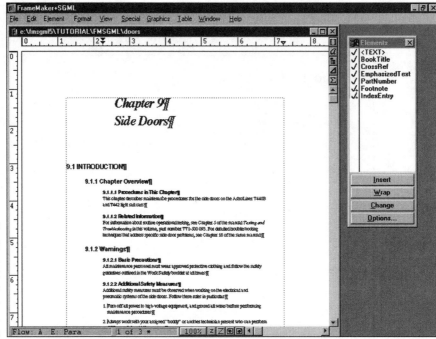

Figure 1-4:
An SGML
Document
in Adobe
Frame-
Maker+SGML.

Features and Benefits of SGML

Depending on how much documentation you already have, how large it is, and how it was originally written, switching to SGML can either be easy or difficult. When time and money are involved, "Don't fix it if it isn't already broken" is a common saying. I discuss some specific benefits of using SGML in detail in the next chapter, but here are some of the high points.

SGML can save you from worrying about some common issues that plague writers and documentation managers:

✔ **Is a document organized correctly?** An SGML DTD defines the relationship between different parts of a document, such as where certain parts can appear. For example, level one headings can only appear in a chapter, level two headings only in a section, and so on.

✔ **Is a document complete?** Using SGML, you can specify that certain parts of a document are required and easily identify sections that are missing.

✔ **Do similar parts of a document look the same when they are printed?** Parts of an SGML document with the same purpose (headings, paragraphs, lists, and so on) print exactly the same way.

✔ **Can I produce documents in different styles and formats from a single documentation set?** By separating the structure and appearance of your documents, SGML makes it easy to change output formats, page sizes, and printers.

✔ **What am I going to do if I ever switch word-processing or publishing packages?** SGML is a standard that is independent of specific software packages. You can edit and use SGML documents in any SGML tool that can use your DTD.

✔ **How can I reuse text in different documents?** SGML makes it easy to create documents out of many smaller pieces. These modular documents help you share *boilerplate* information between different documents, which is typically introductory or background information that you want to write once but use in many places.

I go into these topics in more detail later, but you should be able to see the benefits that just these few basic points can bring. If you've ever struggled to make two documents look exactly the same, anguished over why a certain part of a document is formatting the way that it is, or kicked yourself for not noticing a problem until after a document was printed, you should realize that SGML can help eliminate these sorts of problems. Hindsight is 20/20 — you can't fix the past, but you can learn from it and plan for a better future.

Because SGML separates the content of a document from how that document appears when it's printed, writers and documentation groups that use SGML can be more productive than others. In part, this is because they do not have to spend lots of time concentrating on formatting details. They also have the ability to make better use of the documents that they've already written, sharing information between documents, easily producing abstracts, extracts, or catalogs.

An interesting anecdote is that my copy of *The SGML Handbook* by Charles Goldfarb, the official bible of SGML, is bound upside down — if you open the front cover, you see the last page, upside down. Clearly, SGML is not the cure for every documentation problem! SGML may not even be right or cost-effective for you or the types of writing that you do. Like any other change to how you currently work, it costs more than just the purchase price of the software. You may have to learn to write documents in a structured fashion or learn a new set of styles and conventions. For many writers, focusing on the elements that make up a document requires some rethinking of how they work, simply because they may never have thought of documents in a structured fashion before. Also, you or someone you work with will have to become an expert in the SGML tools you use. There's a startup cost in every home improvement.

A short history of SGML

SGML is a descendent of two efforts for standardizing the documentation industry in the late 1960s, coming from different ends of the spectrum. One was an industry effort to standardize the control codes used internally by composition hardware, which sets the type used when printing a book. The other was an effort at IBM to develop a common set of standards for creating its internal and product documentation.

Prior to the late 1960s, the layout and formatting information for specific printers and typesetters was embedded in documents that were to be printed on those devices. If you wanted to get a different firm to print your documents on different hardware, you usually had to pay a conversion fee to convert everything to the codes used by the new hardware. You also had to factor the time required for the conversion into your schedule. To try to solve this problem, the Graphic Communications Association (GCA for you acronym buffs) created GenCode to standardize the formatting and layout codes used by different printing and typesetting hardware.

Starting in 1969, a group at IBM led by Charles Goldfarb, the father of SGML, developed the Generic Markup Language (GML) to build upon the ground laid by the GenCode initiative. GML added the notion of defining a document type that specified the relationships between all of the parts of a document.

In the late 1970s, the American National Standards Institute (ANSI), the people who brought you such popular standards as ASCII (American Standard Code for Information Interchange), established a committee to build on the ideas introduced by GML. ANSI wanted to develop a truly standard markup language. It brought together people who had worked on GML, such as Goldfarb, with people who had worked on the GenCode project. The first draft of the SGML standard was published in 1980. The final text of the SGML standard was published in 1986.

The U.S. government started using SGML in 1983, when the Internal Revenue Service (I think we all know their acronym!) and the Department of Defense adopted a draft of the SGML standard. In 1987, the U.S. government's Computer Aided Logistics and Support (CALS) program (designed to develop formal procedures for any facet of governmental purchasing or contracting) organized a committee to examine SGML as a standard for government work. This is one case when the phrase "good enough for government work" is a good thing. In 1988, this committee published a military standard for SGML, MIL-M-28001.

Chapter 2
Why Bother with SGML?

In This Chapter

▶ Understanding SGML's portability

▶ Increasing the lifespan of your documents

▶ Complying with government and industry requirements

▶ Ensuring consistency in large documentation sets

▶ Simplifying information sharing

▶ Integrating other applications with SGML tools

▶ Increasing productivity with SGML

*I*f you have existing documents that you want to convert from some other format into SGML, you have some work to do. Even if you've been meticulous in following style guidelines and verifying anyone else's work, you're going to hit some surprises and potholes along the way. You will also have to map the styles used in your current documents into the elements that are available in the SGML documents that you'll be converting to. The possible elements in an SGML document are defined in its Document Type Definition (DTD) — DTDs are discussed in more detail in Chapters 3 and 4.

If you're moving existing document sets into SGML, a cost that might not occur to you right away is the cost of analyzing your documents and selecting (or deciding to write) an appropriate DTD. At a high level, this consists of analyzing all your documents, identifying their current structure, determining what structure you want them to follow, and so on. Document analysis is discussed in Chapter 13, but it's a very real cost that you have to take into account when considering a move to SGML.

If you're lucky enough to be thinking about SGML before actually writing any documents, you have much less work to do. However, you still have to write all your documents, so you'll be busy too!

Whether you're moving existing documents into SGML or starting from scratch, you still have to select a DTD and verify that it works well with the SGML word-processing or publishing software that you select. You may also have to develop a FOSI (or its equivalent) that defines how your SGML documents will be formatted. For more information about FOSIs and other ways of specifying the formatting of an SGML document, see Chapter 9. This chapter expands on the features and benefits of SGML that I introduced in the previous chapter, giving you the ammunition and the determination to use SGML for any documents you write or are responsible for.

SGML: A Movable Feast

Most word-processing or publishing software stores the documents you create in their own special formats. This makes it easier for them to read and update the files that you create, but makes it harder for you to use any other software package than the one that you started with. Even if you are able to import a document written in one word-processing or publishing package into another, you know that it doesn't always work correctly, especially when you create and use complex style sheets in your documents. Recapturing all of this information in the new package you select can be very expensive in terms of both time and frustration!

SGML is an open system because it isn't tied to any specific word-processing or publishing system. SGML is not just a single software package; it's a general approach to documentation that is available from many different software vendors. Therefore, if you use a standard DTD that's provided with another SGML software package, you can instantly load existing SGML documents based on that DTD into that package and start working. If you use a custom DTD, most SGML word-processing or publishing systems allow you to read in your DTD. Some word-processing or publishing packages call this "loading" your DTD; others call it "compiling" your DTD. Whatever you call it, it means that it's relatively easy to move SGML documents from one SGML word-processing or publishing system to another.

What makes it portable?

Two basic features of SGML make SGML documents portable to other software packages:

> ✔ Both SGML files and the DTD files that define the structure of a document are usually stored as standard text files on your system. They aren't in any custom, binary format and provide all the information necessary to work with your SGML document. You provide the SGML

word-processing or publishing package with a description of the structure of your document (the DTD) and the content of your document (the SGML document itself), and voilà! It just works.

✔ Because SGML separates the formatting of your document from its structure and content, SGML makes it very easy for you to access and publish that information in other types of applications. You don't have to worry about software-specific formatting getting in your way.

A paradigm shift

This would hardly be a respectable book about the computer industry if it didn't use the word *paradigm* at least once! Now that we're covered in that respect, the use of SGML is actually one of those instances in which *paradigm* is the right word to use, because moving to an SGML approach to your documentation actually involves a change in the way you approach standardization.

The previous sections explained why SGML gives you an approach to documentation that is software independent. Typically, businesses standardize on a certain software package or application suite because this means they can easily exchange or share files between users without losing any information. Standardizing on a certain package has some up-front purchase and training costs, but it doesn't take long before the value of the information in that application or suite is much greater than the cost of the package itself. At that point, businesses often feel locked-in to that software package, because moving all of your corporate information to another package is very expensive — you either pay in lost information or in the cost and effort involved in preserving 100 percent of your data.

Selecting an SGML approach to documentation lets you standardize at an even lower level, because SGML lets you exchange data between different applications without losing any information. SGML gives you standardization at the data level, the actual information in your documents, rather than just at the application level. This is especially important in industries such as the aircraft industry, where you have to maintain technical manuals for the service life of an aircraft. Because many aircraft have service lives longer than the entire history of most software companies, you may want to consider whether adopting an SGML solution now may pay off for you in the future. If your documents have a chance of outliving your software vendors, SGML is for you!

No rose without a thorn . . .

There is one small cloud in this otherwise idyllic scene. If you plan to print your SGML document after moving it into another SGML word-processing or publishing package, you will probably have to redefine how your SGML documents are formatted by that software package. This is less of an issue if the focus of your documents is online delivery, but let's face it — many people still like paper documents.

At the moment, there is no single, standard way of defining how SGML documents are formatted by different SGML software packages; each SGML word-processing and publishing package provides its own way of defining and maintaining formatting information. One early approach was the Formatting Output Specification Instance (FOSI). FOSIs are discussed in Chapter 9. People are working hard to resolve this situation, but no solutions are ready for prime time today. One of the most promising solutions is the Document Style Semantics and Specification Language (DSSSL) that is being proposed by the International Standards Organization (ISO). DSSSL is designed as a general way of describing the formatting associated with a valid DTD. As it matures, DSSSL should allow you to describe software independent formatting, but this is still a ways off. Even if the DSSSL standard succeeds, it will still take some time before it's available in SGML tools. See Chapter 9 for more information about DSSSL.

Compliance with Government and Industry Requirements

Depending on the industry in which you work, you may not have a choice about whether or not to use SGML. Many government agencies and sectors of the aerospace industry require that the documentation for any internal or contracted project be submitted in SGML. There are several reasons why.

First, SGML can guarantee that documents are complete by identifying certain mandatory parts of the document in the DTD that defines the structure of those documents. Government projects are notoriously large and complex — using SGML can guarantee that their documentation contains certain types of information. For example, the documentation for software projects done for the government guarantees that complete syntax descriptions are provided for every function and command that is documented. (SGML can't guarantee that every function or command is actually documented, but that's a separate issue.) See the next section for a more detailed discussion of this feature of SGML.

Second, SGML documents aren't tied to any specific word-processing or publishing system. Therefore, SGML documents have a longer life span than documents that can be used only with a word-processing or publishing package that stores documents in a proprietary format that is used only by a single word processor or publishing system. This can be very important in long-lived government or industry projects, or in joint projects in which many different vendors have to interoperate.

Finally, using SGML can make it easy to extract selected pieces of information for use elsewhere. For example, suppose that the DTD used for research papers contains mandatory elements that provide the title, an abstract, and a catalog number for all research papers. It would then be relatively easy to extract these elements from any SGML document that uses this DTD and compile these elements into another document that can be used as a printed or online catalog. This makes it easy for a large corporation, such as the government, to publish summaries and reference texts that they share with the public.

Guaranteeing Consistency in Documentation Sets

The bane of any writer or documentation manager's existence is a huge documentation set in which each document looks subtly (sometimes even grotesquely!) different or is missing certain sections that violate your guidelines. Consistency is hard to enforce even in small documentation sets, and the chances of remaining consistent shrink as the number of writers and documents involved in a project increases.

Making it all look the same

SGML enforces consistency in documentation sets of any size, providing they use the same DTD and FOSI (or other way of defining the appearance of a formatted document). Separating structure from appearance and output format is one of the basic principles of SGML. Unlike word-processing or publishing packages that let you define your own styles and their appearance, SGML word-processing and publishing software forces you to adhere to the structure and types of content defined in the DTD when the document was created. Similarly, SGML software guarantees that your printed documents print the same way, with the same formatting, because the FOSI (or other formatting definition) specifies the appearance of the formatted document.

This is not to say that an enterprising writer who is intimately familiar with your SGML tools can't modify the DTD or FOSI to produce a document, but he or she almost has to want to break the SGML model in order to do it. Most companies that use SGML word-processing or publishing software store DTDs and FOSIs in a centralized location that only authorized individuals have access to. DTDs and FOSIs used for final document production can be stored on a shared disk drive or network file system, in which any writer can access them but only selected writers can modify them. At least you know where to point the finger if something changes in a DTD or FOSI!

Verifying the bits and pieces

As I mentioned in the preceding section, using an SGML word-processing or publishing package gives you the opportunity to guarantee that every document or section of every document contains certain information. The easiest way to do this is to verify that certain items are required in the DTD that you use so that you can't produce a document that doesn't contain those items. If you're writing a cookbook, you can at least guarantee that every recipe lists the ingredients it requires. If you're documenting the control panel of a jet airplane, you can ensure that your description of every dial and indicator is complete As you've probably guessed, you still have to verify that the information contained in mandatory parts of a document contain accurate information, but you can at least rest easy that these elements will be present in any document created with that DTD. It would take an SGML tool with artificial intelligence capabilities to do both for you, and I've never seen one. At some point you have to trust yourself and people who work with you to. Identifying required parts of a document makes it impossible for anyone to forget to include those elements in a document, which is probably the most common problem.

Simplifying Information Sharing

SGML places tremendous emphasis on producing documents that conform to the structure defined in the DTD. This gives you a good deal of power in how you or the company you're working for takes advantage of the information in your documents.

Suppose that you're writing a guide for using a specific piece of software. This type of document typically includes background material on the task that this piece of software does and why its approach is best. At the same time, 20 floors up, the marketing department needs that same information because it is producing a white paper or background piece on that same piece of software. Historically, you might have given the marketing department a copy of your guide, maybe even the word-processing files so that it could cut and paste the parts it needs. Need I say it? If the information is actually suitable for use in both documents, SGML can help you share that information directly.

Like anything that sounds too good to be true, information sharing isn't something that "just happens." Successful information sharing requires some planning up front if you know that multiple groups will share parts of a document. If you realize that you want to share information after you write it, you may have to do some rewriting to guarantee that the information works in both contexts.

Taking a modular approach to your documents

SGML word-processing and publishing packages simplify information sharing because SGML's structured approach makes it easy to identify the parts of a document that you want to share. This identification can happen at two different levels. First, the tagging of the elements in your document makes it easy to find a specific type of information. Secondly, SGML documents are not usually stored as one huge file, but are usually composed of many smaller files that reflect the structure of your document at some level. SGML documents are often stored as many smaller files that are included in larger files, such as sections and chapters, that are themselves combined to create an entire document. This approach is often referred to as a *modular* approach to documentation. A modular approach to documentation simplifies sharing portions of a document between different documents because smaller pieces of your documents are available for reuse.

Modular documentation can pay off even within the context of a single documentation set. As you may know, using the same DTD in multiple documents guarantees that they have the same structure. Most printed documents contain front matter with standard sections that describe things like the formatting conventions used in those documents, contact information, and so on. If SGML is going to ensure that the front matter always contains these sections, why not actually use the same sections by including them in every document?

Different FOSIs mean never having to say you've formatted incorrectly

SGML's separation of structure and formatting also simplifies information sharing. Guide documents and technical marketing literature, for example, are formatted and laid out in completely different ways. This isn't a problem if each group has its own FOSI (or other formatting description) that defines the look of their documents. When each group includes your introductory information in its document, that information will be formatted according to its FOSI and will look like it was written to be a part of its document.

Integrating SGML Tools with Other Applications

The structured approach that SGML provides naturally lends itself to integrating other types of applications with your SGML tools. Because you can always predict the elements that will be present at any point in an SGML document, it's easier to integrate your SGML documents with other structured applications.

Database applications are probably the most common type of application that is integrated with an SGML tool. Database systems are frequently used to store SGML documents, especially if those documents are highly modular, as discussed in the previous section. The next section discusses some common ways in which you can integrate SGML documentation systems and databases.

One from document A, one from document B

Previous sections discuss ways in which the modular approach to documentation that SGML provides can make it easier to share information between different documents. Modularity and wanting to share information also lends itself to developing a standard way of storing the shared pieces of your documents. Creating a centralized repository for these documents, such as a network disk drive or directory, is a quick solution, but why not simply store the shared pieces of a document in a database? When publishing a document, you can simply extract the documentation modules that comprise that document, and you're ready to print! If you're ambitious, you can even store the set of database entries that make up a document in the database and then assemble a document with a single database request.

SGML documents lend themselves well to being stored in almost any database system. Besides being modular, they are almost always stored as standard text files. Text files don't require any special types of fields in a database system because most of the information stored in database systems is composed of letters and numbers, just like your documents.

But why only go half way? You receive many more benefits than just an easier way to share information when you use a database to store your SGML documents. You can also use a database system to provide a layer of meta information about your documents, such as which documents a specific module is used in, when and by whom they were last modified, what their review status is, and so on.

Implementing a complex database system to manage your documentation can be a lot of work, especially if you don't have database experience and no one is available to help you. If you work in a corporate environment with an established Management of Information Science (MIS) group, it may be able to help you. You also can find help in many commercial products that support storing and managing SGML documents in database systems. See Chapter 18 for a more thorough discussion of integrating and using database systems with SGML tools. See Appendix B for a list of vendors who provide software designed for this purpose.

Source code and version control for documentation?

Since the day that documents began to be created online, writers and documentation managers have agonized over how to track the documents used for specific products and product releases. The most common approach to this problem is to save a copy of all of the files that were used in each release of a specific document, *archiving* the documents associated with each product release. Unfortunately, this process lends itself to human error — it's easy to overlook a document or to forget to include a module in a complex document. History also teaches that documents that aren't correctly archived are precisely the documents that you will need to recreate or reprint at some point in the future.

SGML documents lend themselves well to integration with version control systems. Unlike non-SGML word-processing and publishing systems, SGML applications usually store their files as standard text files. Version control systems typically track changes by recording information like "line 10 is different," and "5 additional lines have been added after line 25." Non-SGML word-processing and publishing systems usually store their files as binary files, which means they are a single, continuous stream of characters. At best, it's much harder to track specific changes in binary files!

If you work in a software development environment, your company probably already uses a source code control system. Well, hopefully! If so, you should be able to find experts at your workplace who can help you evaluate how (or whether) to use the local version control system.

Increasing Productivity with SGML

Getting more bang for your writing buck is attractive to anyone in the writing business, whether contracting to produce a manual within a specific period of time or managing the budget for a large documentation group. One way to do this is to streamline processes so that you and/or your team is more efficient. Another way is to charge less or pay less. I want you to consider some ways to increase productivity and streamline processes and ignore that second option.

Adopting an SGML solution to your documentation provides some immediate benefits to you and anyone you work with. Because SGML separates structure and content from formatting, you should train yourself not to agonize over formatting problems while writing a document. This can be a hard thing to do if that's the way you're used to working. SGML isn't a wonder cure for all documentation problems — you probably will still have to fix a few formatting problems when you prepare the final version of your document for production. Still, SGML word-processing and publishing packages should help remove the tedious task of fixing formatting problems from your daily routine, if you're willing to let go of them.

Optimizing the Production Cycle

Because SGML provides such a clean break between writing a document and producing a final version for production, you often can centralize the responsibility for final copy. Your "designated formatter" may see the same types of formatting problems in different documents, which may help you identify improvements that you can make in your FOSI. Formatting problems are easiest to spot in WYSIWYG (What-You-See-Is-What-You-Get) software. SGML tools that are not WYSIWYG provide a preview mode. Viewing your documents in preview mode lets you see how each page of the document will format when it's printed. This can help you identify formatting problems before you actually print a document.

As I discuss in a previous section, SGML word-processing and publishing packages can help standardize your documents, both in terms of appearance and completeness. Nothing is more irritating than printing the final version of a 300-page document and then noticing that you omitted a mandatory section on page 35. Not only does this waste your time, but you have to try to ignore the looks of outrage from any ecology buffs that you work with. If all of the mandatory parts of a document are marked as being required in your DTD, it's impossible to produce a document that doesn't contain all of those sections. Unless you use an SGML word-processing or publishing package, you have to verify manually that a document actually contains everything that it's supposed to. And, unfortunately, manual procedures are prone to human error.

Part II
Defining the Structure of a Document

The 5th Wave
By Rich Tennant

And this is Bud Mellnick who writes all of our SGML.

<PAR>Hello.</PAR>

In this part . . .

This part discusses one of the two basic parts of an SGML solution to documentation — the Document Type Definition (DTD). I first discuss the DTD in hazy, philosophical terms. . . . No, not really! I first discuss the DTD in general terms, but only because understanding what a DTD buys you is the best way to really plug yourself into the SGML approach to documentation.

After I show you how to view the structure of a document, I just add a few dashes of syntax — and we have a DTD! I then the syntax in which all SGML DTDs are written and look at how to transform your conceptual understanding of the elements of a document into a DTD for that document type.

Having developed a simple DTD, I examine how we can make it richer by using some of the more advanced concepts of SGML DTDs. Because this strategy means that the DTD will be getting somewhat more complex, I also look at some of the ways that you can provide shortcuts that let you work more efficiently and flexibly in an SGML environment.

To provide an even more familiar example of a DTD, I also talk about the HyperText Markup Language (HTML) and the HTML DTD. Yep, that's right — HTML is just one instance of an SGML DTD, and the tools you've been using to create HTML documents are really SGML tools that are wired to a specific DTD.

By the time you get to the end of this part of the document, you'll have a firm understanding of DTDs and will be raring to see a real DTD in captivity. I conclude by discussing some of the more common DTDs that are publicly available, and I provide sources from which you can obtain them.

Chapter 3

Introducing Document Type Definitions

In This Chapter

▶ Understanding how you can use DTDs

▶ Looking at a few examples

▶ Deciding whether to use one or two DTDs

*T*he previous two chapters have set the stage — now it's time to get down to the meat and potatoes of using SGML for your documentation work. What's involved? What do you need to have to start working with an SGML documentation tool?

In order to answer these two questions, you need to become one with the core concepts of SGML. This chapter discusses the Document Type Definition (DTD), the core concept that enables you to define the structure of a document in a portable fashion. (The other is how you actually format an SGML document for some output format, which I discuss in Chapter 9.) Remember that independence from any specific word-processing or publishing package is one of the basic principles of SGML. Any SGML tool is just an implementation of the basic SGML standard, packaged for your convenience by a software vendor. In order to produce documents that are truly software independent, you have to have a generic way of describing their structure. Enter the DTD.

Remember, the basic things that make up an SGML document are the following:

✔ An SGML declaration that defines the details of how an SGML application will process the DTD and your SGML document (discussed in Chapter 4).

✔ The DTD that defines the elements that can be used in your document, and their relationships (introduced in this chapter and discussed in more detail in the next few chapters).

✔ Your text (the *document instance*, in SGML-speak). This part is up to you!

This chapter provides a detailed introduction to DTDs — why they are so important, what they do, and how to start thinking about different types of documents and the DTDs that you can use to describe them. The chapter concludes by discussing some issues to consider when thinking about the DTDs that you use in the types of documents.

Before I actually dive in, I need to define some of the terms and symbols introduced in this chapter. A DTD is a very flexible thing and can contain many different types of elements. That's the first term — *element*. In SGML, an element is any component of a document's structure, typically identified by a beginning and ending tag. Actually, the proper name for an element is a *generic identifier* because there is no one set of predefined element names; the names of the elements that make up a DTD are defined in that DTD. In pure SGML terms, each occurrence of an element in your document is referred to as an *instance* of that element. For example, the phrase `<TITLE>This is the Title</TITLE>` is an instance of the `<TITLE>` element whose content is `This is the Title`.

Why a DTD?

As mentioned before, the Standard Generalized Markup Language (SGML) was created to provide a flexible, general approach to working with documents. However, the focus of SGML is more than just working with documents — it's really about working with information. SGML separates the structure and content of your documents from the formatting required to provide the final "look" of a document. After you accept this basic idea, you can view the documentation you write as more than just the raw material or source code for the manuals for your company. The information you capture in the documents that you write is a corporate resource, and it's your responsibility to make that resource as usable as possible. Arise documents, and cast off your formatting!

In order to separate the structure and content of your documents from the specific formatting necessary to produce those documents in different formats, you must have a specific way to define each aspect of a document:

✔ One way to describe the structure of your documents

✔ Another way to describe the appearance of the content associated with each part of that structure

You use a Document Type Definition (DTD) to define the structure of an SGML document. You describe this structure by defining each possible component of any part of the type of document you're creating the DTD for and where each of those parts can appear. To use the actual SGML terminology, a DTD describes each *element* of a document and the contexts in which that element is valid.

As mentioned in Chapter 1, you enclose each part of an SGML document that corresponds to an element defined in a DTD within tags that identify it as being that type of element. The set of tags available to you when writing a document, therefore, depends on the DTD associated with that document when it was written.

The examples in this book use longer names than are permitted in the default SGML declaration. I did this intentionally to make it easier to visualize how elements map to structural parts of your document. However, SGML parsers that strictly adhere to the SGML standard will generate error messages if you try to parse this DTD. To resolve this, modify your SGML declaration to use a higher value for NAMELEN, such as for 44. For more information, see the section on SGML Declarations in Chapter 4.

For example, consider the following SGML fragment:

```
<BODY>
<CHAPTER>
<CHAPTER-TITLE>How Do You Write an SGML Document?
</CHAPTER-TITLE>
<PAR>This chapter explains:</PAR>
   .
   .
   .
</CHAPTER>
</BODY>
```

In this example, <BODY>, <CHAPTER>, <CHAPTER-TITLE>, and <PAR> are the available tags. The text between the opening <CHAPTER-TITLE> and closing </CHAPTER-TITLE> tags is an instance of the <CHAPTER-TITLE> element. You will probably have more than one <CHAPTER-TITLE> element in a long document, but you can have only one within each set of <CHAPTER> tags. (The opening and closing tags for a specific element are often referred to as a set of tags of that type.) Similarly, the text This chapter explains:, inside <PAR> tags, is an instance of a <PAR> (paragraph) element.

DTD looking for FOSI, non-smoker, must love PostScript, A4 paper....

Besides a DTD, the other part of any SGML tool that produces formatted output is the way that you describe the appearance of the content associated with each part of a document. A current standard for describing the formatting of an SGML document is the Formatted Output Specification Instance (FOSI), which is a fancy way of saying that each FOSI defines one of the many possible ways that you can produce formatted output from an SGML document that conforms to a specific DTD. Formatted output actually means output in any format — it doesn't mean just a specific printed output. See Part III of this book for details on FOSIs and other ways of formatting SGML documents.

The context in which a specific element is valid is nothing more than a list of the other elements inside which that element can appear. In the previous example, the <CHAPTER-TITLE> element is certainly valid inside a set of <CHAPTER> tags. But it probably would not be valid inside the set of <PAR> tags, even though <PAR> tags themselves are clearly valid within a chapter. This works both ways — the <CHAPTER-TITLE> element is probably not valid outside the set of <CHAPTER> tags, even though the <CHAPTER> tags themselves are clearly valid inside the <BODY> tags. The DTD defines where different types of elements are valid and therefore prevents these sorts of silly errors. Of course, meaningful names for the elements in a DTD help too!

Aren't DTDs complex?

Just because a DTD is one of the core concepts of SGML and is the thing that actually makes your SGML documents work doesn't mean that you have to be a rocket scientist to understand or write one. (You can certainly still write one if you are a rocket scientist, so don't worry.) In SGML, as in nature, some of the most elegant things are created from the simplest elements! A DTD is a text document that can actually be very simple to read and understand once you know the basic structure. Because it's a text document, you don't even need SGML software in order to create a DTD. You do need SGML software in order to test it, as well as SGML software to verify that documents that are supposed to conform to that DTD actually conform to the DTD.

This is not to say that DTDs can't be written so that they are hard to read — many are, especially the more complex DTDs that tend to be developed by SGML wizards, for SGML wizards. As Charles Goldfarb says in *The SGML Handbook* (p.349): "Obfuscatory is one of those wonderful words that describes itself."

If you write a DTD, remember that other people have to be able to read and understand it. Elegance in DTD design walks a fine line between using every possible feature and using the right number of features in the right way.

The chapters in Part IV of this book can help you decide whether you even need to create your own DTD. If you work in an industry that requires documentation in SGML format, like many parts of the government and the aerospace industry, you probably have to use a specific, predetermined DTD. It's still a good idea to become familiar with the way in which a DTD encapsulates the structure of a specific type of documents. You or the people you work with need to understand the DTD in order to apply it correctly to the documents you develop.

What else does a DTD tell me?

SGML documents that are written using a specific DTD are often said to conform to that DTD. A DTD not only tells you the elements that an SGML document that conforms to a specific DTD *can* contain, it also tells you the elements that the SGML document *must* contain. As discussed in Chapter 2, this aspect of SGML can provide consistency guarantees throughout a large set of documents, which is something that every documentation manager certainly prays for at one time or another.

DTDs also tell you what characters are valid inside specific elements. This feature is very valuable in technical documents in which you may have large blocks of text that are supposed to be displayed in verbatim fashion (in other words, exactly as shown, without being processed by the SGML word-processing or publishing package). For example, it would be very difficult to write a book about SGML in SGML without this capability because the SGML software would try to interpret every example of a tag as an actual tag, not an example.

Verifying the structure of your documents

Though I discuss the details later in this chapter, you should know now that a DTD enforces things like structure and content. All true SGML tools contain a piece of software called a *parser*. A parser is a piece of software that knows how to analyze the structure of (in this case) your documents. SGML tools use *validating parsers,* so called because they take two pieces of input — your document and a description of a specific structure to compare it against (you guessed it — that's your DTD).

Exactly when an SGML tool runs its validating parser depends on the authors of the SGML tool. An SGML word-processing or publishing package must always run its parser before it actually begins formatting your document. Some SGML word-processing or publishing packages run the parser all the time, so the software constantly checks to make sure that your document always adheres to the structure of the DTD it uses. This is often known as consistency checking.

Different types of elements in a DTD

DTDs are made up of three basic types of elements:

- ✔ Structural elements
- ✔ Elements that identify document content
- ✔ Elements that indicate special formatting

Hey, how'd formatting make it into the list? The sad truth is that most documents are still printed, and you sometimes need to include special formatting information in your documents. You rarely should create and use SGML elements of this sort, but you should never deny the fact that you may occasionally have to do so in order to produce nice-looking printed output.

You'd expect to find the first two types of elements in an SGML DTD. Ninety-nine percent of your DTD should be composed of these two types of elements. Structural elements identify general parts of the structure of your document, such as chapters, chapter headings, paragraphs, sections, section headings, and so on. Structural elements are likely to be the same in different DTDs, even if they are separately defined in each DTD, because the structure of most documents is similar at some level. Elements that identify the content of your document are the types of elements that you will most likely need to create yourself because they may be specific to your products, document types, or goals.

Help Stamp Out TAS! (Tag Abuse Syndrome)

Tag Abuse Syndrome, where you use the wrong elements in specific cases because they "just happen to work" and because "you'll remember why you did that," is one of the great killers of structured documents today. Every year, thousands of hours of possibly productive labor are lost to this silent killer. If you're tempted to "do the wrong thing," consider its impact on future generations who may actually try to use the information you've written.

TAS — just say no!

If you don't want to create or expand a DTD or are required to use a certain DTD because of the industry you work in, you can always overload the meaning of some other element that already exists in the DTD you use. *Overloading* an existing element means to select an element in your DTD that is valid in the right contexts and which you would otherwise not use. You then use this element to represent the content-oriented element that you otherwise would have created. This is generally a bad idea because it would be easy to forget exactly what you meant by the overloaded element and because you may someday want to import a document that actually uses the overloaded element. Oops!

The Only Good DTD Is a Complete DTD

As a more concrete example of what goes into a DTD, consider the general structure of a book. "Books just consist of chapters," you might say — generally true, but not exactly. How usable a DTD is depends on how accurately it describes all of the possible elements of the type of document that it defines. You could just as easily say that "Books just consist of characters" — you'd be right, but it would be tough to format and publish a book like that in any meaningful fashion.

A DTD has to be accurate at two different levels. It has to contain an accurate list of all of the elements that a specific type of document can contain and the contexts in which those elements can appear, and it also must provide enough elements that you can distinguish between things that really are different. Consider the implications of the statement "Books just consist of characters." There's no question that this statement is true. But if you use it as your DTD, you couldn't tell one chapter from another. You couldn't produce a table of contents because you couldn't tell the title of a chapter from the text of the chapter itself. You couldn't start each chapter on a new page since you couldn't tell where one chapter ends and another begins.

Maybe that was overkill, but it's important to make the point that the primary responsibility of a DTD is to define the structure of a document. In other words, the DTD must identify all of the things in your document that you want to be able to tell apart. This is important for various reasons, most of all these:

- You probably will want to produce the document in some format, at some point. If you don't provide enough structural information that the formatter can use to differentiate between different things, you won't be able to format them differently.

- If specific parts of your documents get special treatment in your current formatter, try to determine why they get that treatment. A separate element or an additional attribute might be justified.

- One of the key features of SGML, as discussed in Chapter 2, is that it allows you to share information with other applications and documents. You may not think you need to share information with other applications and documents right now, but you will have a difficult time retrofitting changes to the elements in your documentation set, especially as it gets larger, if you later want to share information.

Another way to think about the importance of information sharing as related to using the right elements in the right ways is by looking at something as simple as producing a table of contents for a book. This is essentially "internal information sharing" because in the process of producing the final version of your book you must extract different types of headers, identify the level at which they appear, and combine them into the table of contents for the book. If you haven't separately identified the different levels of headers that you want to appear in your table of contents, you won't be able to extract them when you're trying to produce your final copy.

Example 1: a software user's guide

Consider a software user's manual; you probably have seen your share of those. Glancing through one that's handy, I see the following possible elements that each have some structure that is specific to them (this isn't a complete list — I'm just identifying some examples):

- Title page
- Warranties, liabilities, and copyright page
- Table of contents
- Introduction

- Chapters
- Appendixes
- Index

Each of these, of course, contains its own special set of elements. For example, the title page contains the following:

- Title
- Author's name
- Information about the publisher

That should be pretty standard across all books. The same with the warranties, liabilities and copyright page, the table of contents, and the index — pretty standard stuff. Consider a chapter that contains the following:

- Chapter title
- Paragraphs of text, figures, and lists
- Multiple sections, each with its own section title, composed of paragraphs, lists, and figures
- Multiple subsections, each with a subsection title, composed of paragraphs, lists, and figures

Appendixes are organized in the same way as chapters, except that they are numbered differently, and the index is composed of index entries. At this point, it sounds like you could define a book using just these tags. Before congratulating yourself, look at two other types of books.

Example 2: a software reference manual

Luckily, I have a reference manual for the same software package handy. Examining its contents, I find the following elements:

- Title page
- Warranties, liabilities, and copyright page
- Table of contents
- Introduction
- Chapters
- Appendixes
- Index

On the surface, it appears to be much the same. A chapter contains

- Chapter title
- Paragraphs of text
- Multiple sections, each with its own section title, composed of paragraphs of text

Examining a section, however, I see that the section is actually composed of a large number of specialized subsections, each of which is a page or two that provides reference information about a specific command. These reference pages are formatted differently than the other pages and contain many small topics. Each topic consists of a heading followed by pairs of options and arguments to those option. Options and arguments to those options are formatted differently, though the same formatting rules seem to apply to each option/argument pair. Starting to get a headache?

Example 3: a software catalog

As a final example, I still have the catalog from the place where I bought that software package. Examining its structure, I find the following elements:

- Ordering information
- Table of contents
- Chapters
- Index

That's pretty different! Looking at it, even calling the different sections of the catalog "chapters" is being pretty kind because they're so short. Looking at one of these chapters, it contains

- Chapter title
- Product descriptions, each of which contains
  - A paragraph describing the product
  - A picture of the product packaging
  - A stock number
  - The price of the product

It's easy to see that you need a very different set of tags to describe the structure and content of the catalog than you need to describe the structure and content of the user's guide or the reference manual.

Some conclusions

From just examining three different books related to a single product, you can see that the documents are very similar at a high level but differ widely when examined in detail. When creating a DTD that has to handle both of these documents, you can see that the most general rules of a DTD are the following:

- ✔ You can use the same elements only for things that always serve the same structural purpose.

- ✔ You can use the same elements only for things if you do not need to differentiate between them. (This is true based on what I've told you so far — in Chapter 5, I discuss attributes, which provide you with a way to identify differences between elements of the same basic type.)

For example, the title page, warranties and liabilities page, table of contents, and chapters serve the same purpose in the first two types of documents, so it would be reasonable to use the same elements at those levels. Each of those consists of their own set of elements, but I want to keep the discussion at a fairly high level for now. After all, I am discussing how to understand the structure of a DTD rather than actually designing one. You may never make it out of this chapter alive if I probed all the way to the bottom at this point! (In the next chapter, I actually begin designing a small DTD — I think we can safely agree that designing a complete DTD for all software documentation is probably outside the scope of this book. Anyone for a homework assignment?)

When deciding how to tag a document, you may want to consider the things that you may want to extract or uniquely identify, as though you were formatting a document by applying logic rather than font changes or page breaks. Conceptually, the information that different elements provide to a formatter (via a specific FOSI) is much the same as the ability that different elements provide you with in terms of extracting or simply identifying those elements. Elements have to be uniquely identified in order to be handled differently. Frankly, the tagging required by a formatter is much more superficial than the tagging you may want to apply to prepare for extracting or reusing information in the future. Suppose that you need to print a manual that contains tags identifying keywords and function names in running text. The formatter may simply display these both in bold-face type, but you want to extract the meaning of these tags in order to identify the parts of a document that contain keywords or the location of the first reference to a function name.

Two DTDs or Not Two DTDs? Good Question!

From the examples in the previous section, it's easy to see that documents that appear to be composed of the same top-level elements can actually be very different at lower levels. This begs the question of whether each type of document should have its own DTD, or whether you should create different DTDs for each type of document. Of course, this dilemma is only really meaningful if you plan to create your own DTD — if you are moving to SGML because you must use a specific DTD, you clearly won't have to create one. The remainder of this chapter is oriented toward people who are considering developing their own DTDs.

How similar are the different documents?

Before you do very much, you should determine how much structure the different types of documents actually share. For example, though the guide and reference manuals discussed in the previous sections only differ at the subsection level, they are very different at that level. If you were to develop a FOSI for both of these types of documents, you could use much of the same formatting information. Some of the formatting information that you created for subsections of the reference document would simply not be used when processing the guide documents.

Is there any information to share?

One of the primary benefits of moving to SGML is the ability to share information between different documents. Using a single DTD makes it easy to share information between documents that conform to that DTD because they all use some subset of the tags that are available in that DTD.

When deciding whether to try to use a single DTD, you should ask yourself whether you'll want to share any information between these different documents. The short answer is that it's always best to try to use a single DTD. In the next few chapters, I look at the actual syntax of a DTD and also explore ways to create different DTDs that you can still use as one DTD by including one DTD within another. Actually, a family of DTDs with a modular design that lets you share sets of elements is a good solution to many SGML documentation needs, since this gives you specialized DTDs for particular classes of documents as well as compatibility between those DTDs at certain levels.

What costs are associated with single and multiple DTDs?

You also should examine the costs associated with maintaining and using a single large DTD to handle every type of document you produce. Large DTDs require more resources in your computing environment, can be difficult to learn, and can provide so many different types of elements that they're difficult to use. Another factor has to do with how your SGML software uses the DTD. If your SGML software constantly validates your document against the DTD, you need a fair amount of computing resources to work with your document — especially as they get larger! On the other hand, if you use just a text editor to create your SGML documents and plan to validate them against a DTD later, you need the same amount of computing resources, regardless of the size of the DTD.

Using a single large DTD that you're maintaining yourself has a hidden maintenance cost, which is complexity. If you create a single large DTD that spans different types of documents, you'll probably find that the interaction between low-level items in those documents will be more complex (which you'd expect!). The next chapter shows how to start writing a DTD. For now, just note that DTDs have to determine the context in which any element of the DTD is valid. When writing a DTD, you typically use shorthand for the locations in which parts of the DTD can appear. As you get more and more elements, the interaction between these becomes much more complex.

On the other hand, life isn't perfect just because you choose to use several smaller DTDs. Although smaller DTDs can be easier to learn and work with, using multiple DTDs means that you have to provide different training for anyone else who uses the DTDs. They have to understand when to use each and become familiar with using different sets of tags in different types of documents. Also, if your release schedules have different types of documents coming due at the same time, the chance exists that you'll have problems with both at exactly the same time.

Where Do You Go after This Chapter?

This chapter introduced you to the concepts behind the things you must do when moving your documents into SGML: selecting a DTD, analyzing the structure of your documents, and summarizing the different types of documents you're responsible for. I discuss each of these topics in more detail in subsequent chapters, but I present them here to plant some seeds.

Moving document sets from one tool into another is always a challenging task. It can be even more challenging if you're moving from a non-structured tool into one that enforces a structured approach to information management like SGML. It is not impossible! You also have to consider whether the benefits you'll reap from switching to SGML (discussed in Chapter 2) will far outweigh any short-term hassles you may have to put up with.

Chapter 4

I Want My DTD!

A complete and accurate Document Type Definition (DTD) is a thing of beauty. As discussed in Chapter 3, a good DTD is one of the two keys in an SGML document's declaration of software independence — the other is how you describe the formatting of your SGML documents, which I discuss in Part III of this book.

The syntax descriptions of the various portions of a DTD in this chapter use the same symbols (shown in Table 4-1) that are used to describe the contents of various elements if you are actually writing a DTD. Reading these syntax descriptions will help you learn to read DTDs, which is one of the goals of this book! I follow each of these syntax descriptions with some actual examples that show instances of these syntax descriptions.

A DTD is the definition of the structure of your document, the elements that it contains, and the order and context in which each can appear. For the most part, the SGML software that you use enforces the rules that are expressed in your DTD. That's fine if you and all the writers you work with plan to work exclusively in your authoring tool. I know many writers who prefer to write their SGML documents in a text editor, only importing their documents into the authoring tool as a sanity check at various points. After all, if one of the primary features of SGML is software independence, why not take advantage of it? When writing a DTD, completeness is mandatory, but readability is a big consideration. If your DTD is well-designed, cleanly implemented, and well-documented, you and any writers using that DTD can learn to write documents that conform to it without having to rely on your SGML authoring software to enforce its rules. This isn't to say that you'll be perfect at it, but with a little practice (and a few mistakes!), you'll be comfortable enough to write your documents using the software that you're most comfortable with.

In this chapter, I use the term *SGML authoring software* to refer to the part of your SGML software which is designed to help you write your documents. The previous chapter introduces the concept of a parser, which validates the structure of your documents against a specific DTD as you write them. The parser is typically integrated into your authoring software, which then uses the parser to help you identify the SGML tags that are valid at any point in your document.

This highlights something that you should keep in mind if you create your own DTD. Please document it! After all, as a writer or information specialist, you should be good at documenting things — why not take your own mission to heart and serve as your own missionary. A well-documented DTD makes it easy for others to read the DTD and know exactly when to use the different tags that it contains and, hopefully, why those tags were created in the first place. A well-documented DTD is also much more maintainable than one that just looks like an explosion in a cryptic symbol factory. Everyone changes jobs nowadays; a well-written, well-documented DTD is a permanent legacy that you can hand over to someone else with a clean conscience.

Some Basic SGML Terms and Symbols

In Chapter 3, I introduced some basic SGML terms such as elements, beginning and ending tags, and instances. In discussing DTDs up to this point, I've stressed that a DTD specifies that some elements are mandatory in a specific document, some are only mandatory if other elements are present, some must appear in a certain order, some are optional — I think you get the picture! SGML provides some standard ways of indicating these sorts of things. Throughout the rest of this book, I use the symbols shown in Table 4-1 to group elements and define how and whether they must appear in a document.

As you read this book, you'll probably want to refer to this table to help interpret various SGML examples. Why not put a Post-It note on this page now or fold the corner over — anything that will help you find it later!

Table 4-1	Special Symbols Used in SGML Definitions		
Symbol	*Description*	*Example*	*Explanation*
SGML Connectors			
I	One element or the other	paragraph I list	Either a paragraph or a list is valid at this point.

Symbol	Description	Example	Explanation
,	Elements must be present in the specified order.	paragraph, list	A paragraph must be present, followed by a list.
&	Both elements must be present, in any order.	paragraph & list	Either a paragraph followed by a list, or a list followed by a paragraph, must be present.
SGML Occurrence Indicators			
?	Element is optional.	paragraph?	A single paragraph appear at this point.
*	Any number (including zero) of this element can be present.	paragraph*	Any number of paragraphs (including zero) can be present.
+	One or more of this element must be present.	paragraph+	At least one paragraph must appear at this point.
SGML Grouping Indicators			
( )	Used to group associated elements	((paragraph | list), paragraph+)	A paragraph or a list, followed by any number of paragraphs, must appear at this point.

This may look alien at first, but you'll quickly see how this notation makes it easy to understand which elements are valid in any part of a document or DTD. The names of elements, marked up with these symbols, plus different types of data define the *content model* of any element in a DTD. This is just a fancy way of saying "the elements that are valid within any other element in an SGML document," but speaking the jargon can help you get past the door at a party thrown by your local SGML motorcycle gang.

The Document Type Declaration

The first part of a complete definition of an SGML document is the SGML declaration, which is discussed at the end of this chapter. You don't need to worry about it for now because you rarely need to modify an SGML declaration. Let's jump right into the fun stuff!

Remember, the basic things that made up an SGML document are the following:

- ✔ An SGML declaration that defines the details of how an SGML application will process the DTD and your SGML document
- ✔ The DTD that defines the elements that can be used in your document, and their relationships
- ✔ Your text (the *document instance*, in SGML-speak)

The first line in a DTD uses the `<!DOCTYPE` keyword to identify itself as the beginning of a DTD and specifies the name of the document type that you're defining. The name of the document type you're defining is just like any other element in your document, but it must be the same as the top-level element in that document type.

The `<!DOCTYPE` keyword has a slightly different meaning when it appears as the first line of an SGML document instance. In this case, the `<!DOCTYPE` keyword identifies the DTD used when the document was written and specifies the location of that DTD, either directly through a SYSTEM identifier, or indirectly through a PUBLIC identifier.

Whether you're writing a DTD or using a DTD in a document that conforms to a certain DTD, you use this syntax for the `<!DOCTYPE` keyword:

```
<!DOCTYPE generic-identifier ((SYSTEM ("system-loc")?) |
  ((PUBLIC, "public-id")("system-loc")?))?
  ([ declarations* ])?>
```

Yow — what a mouthful! What's it mean in English? "A document type declaration consists of the `<!DOCTYPE` keyword, followed by the name of the document type, optionally followed by one of the SYSTEM or PUBLIC keywords and related text, followed by some optional declarations. If the SYSTEM keyword is present, it may be followed by something enclosed in double-quotation marks that gives the location of some or all of the declarations for that DTD on your computer system. If the PUBLIC keyword is present, it must be followed by a public identifier in double-quotation marks that your SGML software can then look up to get information about, and then can optionally be followed by information about where to find additional markup declarations on your system." I think that you can see why the shorthand used above can come in handy! The hardest part of reading the SGML shorthand is matching associated pairs of parentheses, but this skill comes with practice.

Information, please? I'm looking for a PUBLIC identifier

The PUBLIC keyword simply means that this is an item that is freely available for use in multiple SGML documents or DTDs on your system. The definitions of PUBLIC identifiers are typically stored in a *catalog,* which is a specially formatted text file that identifies the location of the items that correspond to each public identifier. The SYSTEM keyword means that the system (your SGML software) knows how to find the specified item. For this reason, SYSTEM entities frequently give the actual path to a related DTD. More about this in Chapter 6.

If you were actually defining a DTD, the SYSTEM and PUBLIC keywords and their associated identifiers would be absent, and the declarations section would be full of all of the element definitions and related items that actually make up the DTD. The declarations section actually has two purposes — to enable you to define either a complete DTD or a set of declarations that extend a specific DTD by providing some special declarations that apply only to the current document. Chapter 15 discusses the concepts and details behind extending an existing DTD.

The following real examples should help clarify how a DOCTYPE statement identifies the DTD that a specific document conforms to:

```
<!DOCTYPE Book PUBLIC "-//Davenport//DTD DocBook V2.4//EN">
```

This is the standard entry that you see at the top of any SGML document that conforms to the DocBook DTD, one of my favorite DTDs. This statement says that "This document conforms to the Book DTD, whose location you can find out by looking up the PUBLIC identifier //Davenport//DTD DocBook V2.4//EN, and no special declarations are to be used in this document." From the name of the public identifier, you can infer that this document conforms to version 2.4 of the DocBook DTD, but that's only an assumption. It would be silly if that were not the case, but it could happen.

```
<!DOCTYPE HTML PUBLIC "-//W3C//DTD HTML 3.2 Final//EN">
```

This is a standard entry that you see at the top of any well-groomed HTML documentation on the World Wide Web. This statement says that "This document conforms to the HTML DTD, whose location we can find out by looking up the PUBLIC entity -//W3C//DTD HTML 3.2 Final//EN." From the name of the entity, you can infer that this document conforms to the HTML 3.2 specification, but again, that's only an assumption. Although you hope that the authors give some semantic meaning to the name of a public entity, nothing forces them to do so, except the reasonable person principle.

Elementary, My Dear Watson!

The previous section shows how a DOCTYPE declaration either specifies the DTD used in a document and where to find it, or introduces a DTD. In the remainder of this chapter, I focus on using the DOCTYPE declaration to create a sample DTD that defines a technical paper. This example is designed to show how to create and organize a DTD, not to serve as a DOCTYPE declaration to end all DOCTYPE declarations.

As mentioned in the previous section, the name of the document type that you define in a DOCTYPE statement is actually the highest-level element in a DTD. The sample DTD defines a technical paper, so I call this element "TechPaper." So far, the sample DTD consists of the following:

```
<!DOCTYPE TechPaper [
]>
```

Throughout this chapter, I evolve a DOCTYPE declaration. As such, remember that the DOCTYPE declaration for the TechPaper DTD isn't complete until the end of the chapter.

In order to start defining the elements that make up a technical paper, you have to analyze the structure of that type of document. When you analyze the structure of a document, you ordinarily must extract all of the structural and content components of your document. For this example, since it is just an example, you just need to perform a cursory analysis of the major structural elements in a sample technical paper. Chapter 13 provides a more complete discussion of analyzing document structure and content.

At a high level, assume that a technical paper consists of the following general elements:

- ✔ A title-block, composed of the title of the paper, the author's name, the company he works for or the university where he studies, and the date.
- ✔ An abstract, giving a short summary of the subject and goals of the paper. This consists of blocks of text.
- ✔ At least one section, composed of a section title, some blocks of text, and zero or more subsections. Each subsection consists of a subsection title followed by one or more blocks of text.

I fill in other sections as I go along, but that should be a good starting point. The goal now is to expand each of these into elements and the elements that these should contain.

Because an SGML DTD focuses on defining the structure of at least one type of document, now's a good time to point out that SGML documents are *hierarchical* in nature. The DTD defines the highest-level element in a document (usually the document itself), and then proceeds to break that high-level element into its components, those components into their components, and so on. In computerese, this is often referred to as a *tree structure*, because trees have one trunk, some number of branches, each of which has its own branches, and so on. Throughout this book, I refer to elements as high-level, low-level, and so on. This usage is just a convenient shorthand that generally identifies the position of these elements in the hierarchy of a document.

Portions of an element declaration

Here is the generic form of an element declaration:

```
<!ELEMENT element-name omitted-tag-info? content-model
exceptions?>
```

The <!ELEMENT keyword identifies that what follows it is an element declaration. The *element-name* is the name of one or more elements that this element declaration defines. If a single element declaration defines multiple elements, those elements must appear within parentheses, separated by one of the symbols shown in Table 4-1. When defining multiple elements in a single element declaration, I typically use the "or" symbol (|) to make a multiple element definition more readable. In general, DTDs with separate declarations for each element are more readable, but those declarations can get very long for complex document types. The readability vs. length issue doesn't really apply in the example DTD discussed in this chapter because it's a fairly simple DTD.

The *omitted-tag-information* portion of an element declaration is actually two fields in the declaration. These two fields (which must be separated by at least one space) define whether the beginning tag (first field) or the ending tag (second field) can be omitted in a document that conforms to this DTD. Each of these fields can either consist of a dash (|) or the letter O (or o). The dash indicates that the tag must be present. The letter O indicates that the tag can be omitted. The entire omitted-tag-information section is optional if the OMITTAG feature in your SGML declaration is set to NO. See "The SGML Declaration" at the end of this chapter for information on the OMITTAG feature. For now, assume that it is set to YES, so that this part of an element declaration is necessary. In this example, assume that both the starting and ending tags must be present for every element. For more information on the why's and wherefore's of omitting tags and on other shortcuts in your SGML documents (often referred to as *markup minimization*), see the section "What's the point of omitting tags?," later in this chapter.

The most important part of an element declaration is the description of its content. This content description uses the symbols introduced earlier in the "Some Basic SGML Terms and Symbols" section to separate different elements that can appear within this element. The next section provides examples of element content, based on the description of the content and structure of a technical paper.

The content of an element can also be defined using special SGML keywords, such as EMPTY, CDATA, #PCDATA, RCDATA, or ANY. See "What's the point of omitting tags?" later in this chapter for details on the EMPTY tag. The ANY tag means that a specified element can contain any tag in the DTD or any type of character data; you usually used it only as a placeholder when developing a DTD. CDATA, #PCDATA, and RCDATA are just different types of basic character data (the *C* in each of these stands for *C*haracter, and the *DATA* stands for, well, *data*). The examples in the next section use CDATA, which means simple character data — in other words, any sequence of characters that cannot contain any lower-level elements. Any element whose content is defined as CDATA terminates when the closing tag for any element is encountered. (If it isn't the closing tag for the proper closing tag for an element, the parser will report an error!) For information about the differences between CDATA, #PCDATA, and RCDATA, see the section later in this chapter called "How many types of characters are there, really?"

The final part of an element declaration is a list of exceptions to the content you've just defined. This is a fairly advanced concept that's outside the scope of this simple document type definition. After all, I think you'd like to see some examples of elements before you drown in SGML syntax! For more information about advanced SGML concepts like exceptions, see *Developing SGML DTDs*, by Eve Maler and Jeanne el Andaloussi. This is an excellent guide to developing DTDs and also contains reference information on every possible SGML bell and whistle.

Element declarations in a sample DTD

Returning to the quick analysis of the structure of the technical paper, let's look at how you can define the identified elements. Remember that this technical paper consists of three basic structural elements (one title block with various information about the document, one abstract, and some number of sections), all of which are mandatory and must appear in a certain order. Defining these first gives you:

```
<!DOCTYPE TechPaper [
  <!ELEMENT TechPaper - - (title-block, abstract, section+) >
]>
```

This statement specifies the content of the highest-level element in the DTD and states that these items must occur in this order (because I used the , [comma] separator). The declaration (or *content model*, in SGML-speak) for the TechPaper element is an example of *element content* because the element is defined as consisting only of other elements. This element declaration also says that the technical paper can have multiple sections but that it must have at least one (because I used the + symbol). After all, it would be hard to get approval for a technical paper with no content. (Though after having read some of the ones that I've seen, you might start to wonder!)

The first of these structural elements, the title-block, is composed of the title of the paper, the author's name, the company he works for or the university where he studies (I call that his "affiliation"), and the date. Again, assume for now that all of these are mandatory. You can represent these items in the sample DTD with the following:

```
<!DOCTYPE TechPaper [
<!ELEMENT TechPaper - - (title-block, abstract, section+) >
<!ELEMENT title-block - - (paper-title, author, affiliation,
date)>
]>
```

I also need to specify the content of each of these elements. Since I am creating just a simple DTD, assume that the content of each of these is just some sequence of characters:

```
<!DOCTYPE TechPaper [
   <!ELEMENT TechPaper - - (title-block, abstract, section+) >
   <!ELEMENT title-block - - (paper-title, author, affiliation,
   date)>
   <!ELEMENT    paper-title - - CDATA>
   <!ELEMENT author        - - CDATA>
   <!ELEMENT affiliation - - CDATA>
   <!ELEMENT date          - - CDATA>
]>
```

To get a bit fancier, remember that I said that you can group different elements with the same content model together in an element declaration. I use this feature only in large DTDs because I think that it sometimes makes it harder to locate specific element declarations, but it's fine in such a simple example:

```
<!DOCTYPE TechPaper [
   <!ELEMENT TechPaper - - (title-block, abstract, section+) >
   <!ELEMENT title-block - - (paper-title, author,
   affiliation, date)>
   <!ELEMENT(paper-title | author | affiliation |date) - -
   CDATA>
]>
```

Now, I need to add a definition for the second portion of the technical paper, the abstract, which consists of blocks of text. I call these paragraphs. Now the sample DTD looks like this:

```
<!DOCTYPE TechPaper [
   <!ELEMENT TechPaper - - (title-block, abstract, section+) >
   <!ELEMENT title-block - - (paper-title, author,
   affiliation, date)>
   <!ELEMENT abstract - - (paragraph)+>
   <!ELEMENT paragraph - - (#PCDATA)>
   <!ELEMENT(paper-title | author | affiliation |date) - -
   CDATA>
]>
```

Now to add the final element, the section. Earlier in this section, I defined a section as being composed of a section title, some blocks of text (now called paragraphs), and optional subsections. If subsections are present, they consist of a subsection title followed by one or more paragraphs. Now the sample DTD gets slightly more interesting:

```
<!DOCTYPE TechPaper [
   <!ELEMENT TechPaper - - (title-block, abstract, section+) >
   <!ELEMENT title-block - - (paper-title, author,
   affiliation, date)>
   <!ELEMENT abstract - - (paragraph)+>
   <!ELEMENT section - - (section-title, paragraph+,
   subsection*)>
   <!ELEMENT subsection - - (subsection-title, paragraph+)>
   <!ELEMENT (section-title | subsection-title) - - CDATA>
   <!ELEMENT paragraph - - (#PCDATA)>
   <!ELEMENT(paper-title | author | affiliation |date) - -
   CDATA>
]>
```

That's all there is to a very simple DTD! Admittedly, I designed this DTD purely as an example, and therefore, I ignore many of the structural elements, such as lists, figures, and so on, that you expect to find in a well-designed DTD. However, even in such a trivial example, you can see that marking up a technical paper using this DTD makes it possible to extract summary information, such as the author, title, date, and abstract for reuse in some other type of document, such as a catalog of technical papers.

What's the point of omitting tags?

In documents that conform to complex DTDs, it may become difficult to read the SGML text for a document due to the large number of tags that it can contain. Omitting some of these tags helps make your SGML document more readable. Also, let's face it — depending on the software you're using, it can be tedious to type in all of those tags, especially when the elements that follow a closing tag explicitly indicate a new environment. An example of this is the closing tag of a paragraph that appears immediately before the opening tag for a new section of a document — from the fact that a new section has begun, you can infer that the previous paragraph is closed.

Tags can only be omitted under two circumstances:

✔ When the definition of that element permits it (as discussed in a previous section, "Portions of an element declaration")

✔ When you can unambiguously determine that the current element has closed (as in the previous example) or that you have begun a new element (such as, for example, when a TITLE element must immediately follow the opening tag for a SECTION element)

Here are some general rules for omitting tags:

✔ Unless you need to, don't. This is my particular preference, since omitting tags requires that the reader of an SGML document have a much better knowledge of the DTD. Explicitly forcing each beginning tag to be closed later makes a document more readable because it always shows the structure of your documents.

✔ You should rarely allow beginning tags to be omitted. Allowing beginning tags to be omitted means that the reader must understand, for example, that the first thing in a `<CHAPTER>` is always a mandatory `<TITLE>`. Like the previous bullet, omitting beginning tags makes SGML documents less readable and harder to work with as far as I'm concerned.

Omitting tags is only one of several ways that SGML lets you save characters when creating an SGML document. Omitting tags is related to the more general SGML concept of *tag minimization*, which allows you to eliminate or abbreviate opening and closing tags under certain circumstances. I think that all of these types of minimization are generally more historical than they are necessary today. Before the advent of specialized SGML editors and authoring tools, writers generally had to enter all of the tags in an SGML document by hand, which could be time-consuming, so anything that saved a few characters was potentially a good thing.

Here are some other types of tag minimization:

✔ You can always close the most recently used tag with the symbol `</>`. (I don't particularly hate this one, because it's pretty clear what's going on when you see this in an SGML document.)

✔ If two tags appear together, you can eliminate the closing delimiter for the first one, as in `<CHAPTER<TITLE>context</TITLE</CHAPTER>`. Yeech!

✔ You can abbreviate the opening and closing tags for a simple element as `<ELEMENT/content/`. Yeech!

Most of today's SGML tools make much of this minimization unnecessary because they let you tag selected text by pulling down a menu and selecting the appropriate tags, as well as hide or minimize tags in your documents. Also, not all SGML software supports all of these forms of minimization — if you plan to use these features, test your software's support for them before writing 10,000 pages of tag-minimized SGML!

Some people are tremendous fans of tag and markup minimization. At best, I'm from Missouri on this issue: "Show me why this is the right thing to do!" In general, I think that all of these forms of minimization make your documents less readable, and therefore, you should avoid them whenever possible.

Entities — SGML Shortcuts

You use entities to define variables and their values in a DTD or SGML document. As a variable, they can represent any portion of a document from a single special character to paragraphs, chapters, or even entire documents! Entities can save lots of time when writing an SGML or DTD document, but they also can make your document more difficult to read because readers have to ferret out their definitions. If you've ever seen an SGML document that contains a string of characters beginning with an ampersand or percent sign and ending with a semicolon, then you've seen an entity. This section introduces the basic notion of an entity, introduces different types of entities, and provides some simple examples. Entities are discussed in all their glory in Chapter 6.

SGML documents use two different types of entities, *general* and *parameter* entities. General entities begin with the & symbol and can be used in a document itself or as part of the SGML markup for that document. Parameter entities begin with the % symbol and can be used only in DTDs. Of the two, you are far more likely to encounter general entities because they are used commonly in SGML documents to represent characters that can't usually be typed from the keyboard or which might be interpreted as markup.

The less-than symbol (<) is the most common example of an entity that represents a character that might otherwise be interpreted as markup (it might be interpreted as the opening character for an SGML tag if explicitly typed in your SGML documents). You may already be familiar with this entity if you've done a lot of work in HTML!

Common examples of entities used to display symbols that aren't present on most keyboards are the entities that represent the copyright symbol (©) and registered trademark symbol (™). Entities such as © whose second character is a pound sign (#) tell your SGML software that the remainder of the entity (up through the ; symbol that ends the entity) is the character code for the character that is to be displayed. This sort of entity is less portable than named entities, since the numeric portion of this sort of entity refers to a specific character position in a specific character set.

Most existing DTDs include publicly available sets of entities that contain standard sets of entity declarations. Many of these standard sets of entities, defined by the International Standards Organization (ISO) are publicly available at many locations on the Internet. For example, the ISOnum set of entity declarations contains all of the entities mentioned in the previous paragraph. These general entities are typically defined as a parameter entity, which is then included in your DTD, as in the following example:

```
<!ENTITY % ISOnum PUBLIC "ISO 8879:1986//ENTITIES Numeric
and Special Graphic//EN">
%ISOnum;
```

In this example of a parameter entity, the first line declares this entity as pointing to whatever the PUBLIC identifier ISO 8879:1986//ENTITIES Numeric and Special Graphic//EN resolves to. The second line actually includes this data in your DTD.

For a more complete discussion of entities, see Chapter 6.

Declaring your own general entities

Declaring your own entities makes it easy for you to centralize information across all your SGML documents. For example, you can declare an entity that represents the code name of a product that is currently under development. You can then use this entity throughout any documentation that you are developing in parallel with the creation of the product. After your marketing group selects a "real" name, you can simply change the declaration of that entity in your DTD, and any documents that you subsequently formatted pick up the new name.

The syntax for this type of general entity declaration is

```
<!ENTITY entity-name "entity-value">
```

As an example, consider the following entity declaration for the working name for a new type of workstation:

```
<!ENTITY otter "new development workstation">
```

Marketers would never allow "new development workstation" to be a product name, so when the machine is actually finally released, you can update all of your documents by updating the entity declaration to be something like this:

```
<!ENTITY otter "DN3000">
```

How many types of characters are there, really?

The "Portions of an element declaration" section introduces some special SGML keywords to describe the characters that are valid inside different types of elements: CDATA, RCDATA, and #PCDATA. Most alphabets and number sets contain a limited number of characters, so what's the difference between these three magic keywords?

The difference between these types of basic character data lies in how an SGML parser interprets them. As mentioned previously, CDATA stands for Character Data — in other words, any sequence of characters that cannot contain anything that requires further interpretation, such as other elements or entities. Any element whose content is defined as CDATA terminates when any closing tag is encountered, not just a specific closing tag.

The nerdy way to think of CDATA is that it is character data that is uninterpreted by an SGML parser — it passes straight through the parser until any closing tag is encountered. No further interpretation is required in an element whose content is CDATA, so CDATA is often referred to as defining the *declared content* of such elements. No further interaction with the DTD is required because data just doesn't get much simpler than characters.

RCDATA (Replaceable Character Data) is slightly more sophisticated than plain old CDATA. RCDATA is CDATA that can contain entities but not any elements from the DTD. The nerdy way to think of RCDATA is that it is character data that is only slightly interpreted by an SGML parser, which makes any replacements for entities that are encountered in an element whose contents are defined as RCDATA. Otherwise, elements whose contents are defined by RCDATA pass straight through the parser until the closing tag for that element is encountered. Like CDATA, RCDATA is often referred to as defining the *declared content* of elements whose content is defined as RCDATA because no further interaction with the DTD is required to analyze the content of such elements.

CDATA and RDATA elements are often used in element declarations that are used to hold verbatim blocks of text, such as program code. Because many programming languages use the < and > symbols, you can identify blocks of sample code as

- ✔ Elements whose declared content is CDATA if you never want to make any entity substitutions in the block of sample code.

- ✔ Elements whose declared content is RCDATA if you want to use special symbols like Copyright, Trademark, and Registered Trademark in them. In many cases, any SGML authoring software automatically makes these types of substitutions for your elements whose content is defined as RCDATA.

#PCDATA (Parsed Character Data) is the fanciest type of character data. Elements whose content is defined as #PCDATA can contain characters, entities, and any other element that is valid in the context of that element. Elements whose definition includes #PCDATA are commonly referred to as *mixed content* elements because they can contain both other elements and standard character data. As an example of using #PCDATA, consider the definition of the <PARAGRAPH> element from the sample DTD used earlier in this chapter:

```
<!ELEMENT paragraph - - CDATA>
```

I noted earlier that this definition of a paragraph omits standard items that you might expect to see (and want to mark up) in an SGML document. You can use #PCDATA to add lists to the sample DTD fairly easily:

```
<!ELEMENT paragraph - - (#PCDATA | list)+>
<!ELEMENT list       - - (list-item)+>
<!ELEMENT list-item - -  RCDATA>
```

This section of the DTD now says that a paragraph is defined as one or more occurrences of parsed character or a list, in any order, and that lists consist of at least one list item, which is defined as RCDATA.

Mixing and matching content models

This section discusses some common problems that you may encounter when defining the lower-level elements in your DTDs. If you're not writing a DTD, you can skip this section for now, and refer to it when (if) you ever do. If you are writing a DTD and never encounter the sorts of problems discussed in this section, "Mister, you're a better man than I!"

A common problem that many people encounter when writing an SGML DTD is an *ambiguous content model*. Ambiguous content models occur when an instance of an element can satisfy more than one token in its content model without the SGML parser that is validating your document using look-ahead. Now there's a mouthful! In English, this means that you have a potential problem when you define elements whose content can match more than one of the possible types of content for that element (as defined in the DTD) without the SGML parser's peeking at the next token — in other words, when the content is ambiguous because it could match more than one of the possible forms of the element as defined in the DTD.

There are several types of ambiguous content model problems that you may encounter when writing DTDs. Some ambiguous content models can be eliminated by disallowing tag omission, or by ensuring that elements with mandatory and optional elements list the mandatory elements first in the content model. The latter guarantees that the parser will test for the presence of the mandatory elements first, and then (if other characters are available) will check to see if they fit the optional element.

The most common type of ambiguous content model problem is known as a *mixed content model* problem. This problem arises when elements in your DTD can contain both elements and #PCDATA.

For example, assume that you had the following element declarations in a DTD:

```
<!ELEMENT subsection - - (subsection-title, #PCDATA)>
<!ELEMENT subsection-title - - (#PCDATA)>
```

On the surface, this seems reasonable, because you might think of a subsection as simply being a <SUBSECTION-TITLE> followed by some random characters until you encounter another tag. However, let's look at a small example:

```
<SUBSECTION>
<SUBSECTION-TITLE>Getting Started</SUBSECTION-TITLE>
This is some random text.
</SUBSECTION>
```

When an SGML parser attempts to validate this example, it generates an error upon encountering the opening tag for the <SUBSECTION-TITLE> element, because the newline after the opening tag for the <SUBSECTION> element is treated as data. Since the first element in a <SUBSECTION> must be a <SUBSECTION-TITLE>, the parser assumed that this newline represented the contents of the element and then generated an error when the <SUBSECTION-TITLE> element was actually encountered. In order to eliminate the mixed content model problem, a better way to write the element declarations for these elements would be:

```
<!ELEMENT subsection - - (subsection-title, (par)+)>
<!ELEMENT subsection-title - - (#PCDATA)>
<!ELEMENT par - - (#PCDATA)>
```

To avoid mixed content model problems, the SGML standard recommends that you only use #PCDATA as a content model for elements where it is the only content model for that element, or where the '|' or connector is the only SGML connector used in the content model for that element.

The SGML Declaration

Many DTDs have an SGML declaration associated with them. An SGML declaration sets basic parameters for your SGML authoring software. These are low-level items like how much storage your authoring software should allocate for different parts of your DTD, the character sets that your DTD uses, and so on. The SGML declaration is a simple way to keep your DTD software independent. If you ever look at the source code for a computer program, you may notice that the SGML declaration is much the same type of thing as all of the variables that a program declares. Because your goal in this chapter is to be able to read a DTD, the following code shows a sample SGML declaration section from version 2.4.1 of the DocBook DTD.

In most cases, you never have to modify the values in an SGML declaration; if you don't specify them, your authoring software sets them to default values that only it knows. If you're not interested in the gory syntax of an SGML declaration, you can just skip this section — it's always here if you need it for reference someday.

```
<!SGML  "ISO 8879:1986"
    -- DocBook SGML declaration V2.4.1 --
CHARSET
BASESET "ISO 646:1983//CHARSET
   International Reference Version (IRV)//ESC 2/5 4/0"
DESCSET
         0    9    UNUSED
         9    2     9
        11    2    UNUSED
        13    1    13
        14   18    UNUSED
        32   95    32
       127    1    UNUSED
BASESET "ISO Registration Number 100//CHARSET
    ECMA-94 Right Part of Latin Alphabet Nr. 1//ESC 2/13 4/1"
DESCSET
       128   32    UNUSED
       160   96    32
CAPACITY SGMLREF
      TOTALCAP 99000000
      ATTCAP    1000000
      ATTCHCAP  1000000
      AVGRPCAP  1000000
      ELEMCAP   1000000
      ENTCAP    1000000
      ENTCHCAP  1000000
      GRPCAP    1000000
      IDCAP    32000000
      IDREFCAP 32000000
SCOPE DOCUMENT
SYNTAX
```

```
SHUNCHAR  CONTROLS
     0    1    2    3    4    5    6    7    8    9
    10   11   12   13   14   15   16   17   18   19
    20   21   22   23   24   25   26   27   28   29
    30   31  127  128  129
   130  131  132  133  134  135  136  137  138  139
   140  141  142  143  144  145  146  147  148  149
   150  151  152  153  154  155  156  157  158  159
BASESET
  "ISO 646:1983//CHARSET
   International Reference Version (IRV)//ESC 2/5 4/0"
DESCSET
     0   128    0
FUNCTION
     RE           13
     RS           10
     SPACE        32
     TAB SEPCHAR  9
NAMING
     LCNMSTRT ""
     UCNMSTRT ""
     LCNMCHAR ".-"
     UCNMCHAR ".-"
NAMECASE
     GENERAL YES
     ENTITY  NO
DELIM
     GENERAL  SGMLREF
     SHORTREF SGMLREF
     NAMES    SGMLREF
QUANTITY SGMLREF
     ATTCNT    256
     GRPCNT    253
     GRPGTCNT  253
     LITLEN    8092
     NAMELEN   44
     TAGLVL    100
FEATURES
     MINIMIZE
         DATATAG  NO
         OMITTAG  NO
         RANK     NO
         SHORTTAG YES
```

(continued)

(continued)

```
    LINK
        SIMPLE    NO
        IMPLICIT  NO
        EXPLICIT  NO
    OTHER
        CONCUR    NO
        SUBDOC    NO
        FORMAL    YES
>
```

Yikes! I think you can see why you'd prefer to never modify that! However, even in all of that text, there are some things you should know.

The first line of this SGML declaration identifies it as being an SGML declaration that conforms to ISO 8879:1986, which is a specific version of the SGML standard. (See "A Quick History of SGML" in Chapter 1 for a short discussion of the SGML specification.) The next line, CHARSET, defines this as the start of the definition of the set of characters used in the DocBook DTD. Each pair of BASESET and DESCSET keywords define a set of characters used in the document. The BASESET keyword defines the name of a specific character set, and the associated DESCSET keyword defines characters in that character set that are either UNUSED or map to some other characters in that character set. For example, lines like 9 2 9 in a DESCSET area tell you that "if you encounter the next two characters starting with character 9 in the current character set, use the next two characters of that character set." In other words, lines such as this map ranges of characters from one character set to another.

I warned you that vivisecting an SGML declaration was not for the weak of heart, so I want to skip to some of the more interesting parts of the SGML declaration, the CAPACITY, QUANTITY, and FEATURES sections. In the following sections of this chapter, I highlight some of the more commonly used SGML declarations in each of these sections. For a complete discussion of all of the possible portions of an SGML declaration and a complete list of all possible values found in each of these portions, see *Developing SGML DTDs*, by Eve Maler and Jeanne el Andaloussi.

CAPACITY *declarations*

You use capacity declarations to help identify the amount of storage that an SGML application should reserve to store DTDs and documents that conform to those DTDs. Today's computer systems don't impose the same limitations on working memory and machine allocation that the systems of a few years ago did, so capacity declarations are not as important today as they once were. However, many SGML applications sometimes use capacity declarations to limit the amount of resources that they pre-allocate when loading a DTD or document. Some of the more common capacity declarations that you may want to change are shown in Table 4-2.

Table 4-2 Some CAPACITY Values That You May Need to Change

CAPACITY *Entry*	*Purpose*
TOTALCAP	Represents the total amount of memory that can be allocated by the SGML software to process any document that conforms to that DTD. You may need to increase this value if you are processing extremely large documents that conform to a large and complex DTD.
IDCAP	Represents the total amount of memory that is reserved for defining cross-reference Ids, which are the targets of the cross-references in a document. Large document sets that contain many cross-references sometimes require that you increase the CAPACITY value for this entry in your SGML declaration. For more information on ID attributes, see "Different types of attribute values" in Chapter 5.
IDREFCAP	Represents the total amount of memory that is reserved for defining the locations from which cross-references to cross-reference targets are being made. Large document sets that contain many cross-references sometimes require that you increase the CAPACITY value for this entry in your SGML declaration.

Whether your software requires that you change capacity values depends on how much attention your SGML software actually pays to the CAPACITY values given in an SGML declaration. If you use an existing DTD with a commercial SGML software package, you may be able either to use the SGML declaration that accompanied the DTD (if there was one) or to contact the customer support personnel for your SGML application for information on any required CAPACITY changes. If your software simply allocates more memory as it is required to store your DTD and parse documents against it, and the operating system on which you are running your SGML software provides support for virtual memory, you may never have to change the value of any CAPACITY statements for your DTDs.

QUANTITY *declarations*

You use QUANTITY declarations to define the maximum length of various things in your DTDs and documents, and the number of different types of things that can exist. If you use an existing DTD that requires changes to the default values for different QUANTITY declarations, you should have received an SGML declaration with the DTD that contains these changes.

If you are creating your own DTD, Table 4-3 shows some of the QUANTITY values that you may want to consider changing.

Table 4-3	Quantities in an SGML Declaration That You May Want to Change	
QUANTITY *Entry*	*Default Value*	*Purpose*
LITLEN	240	The maximum length of a literal string of characters used in a parameter entity declaration or attribute value.
NAMELEN	8	The maximum length of an attribute, element, or entity name.
PILEN	240	The maximum length of a processing instruction. (See Chapter 10.)

You may want to change some of these values to increase the readability of your SGML documents or the DTD itself. For example, you may prefer element and entity names that are longer than the default value of eight characters. I typically increase the default value to at least 16 because doing so lets you use element names that more clearly communicate their function in your documents. For example, using the default NAMELEN of 8 characters would have forced me to use some odd names in the sample DTD developed earlier in this chapter. To me, an element name like "affiliation" is always clearer than a fragment like "affil." Being able to use realistic element and attribute names also lets you spend time fine-tuning your DTD, rather than spending time coming up with clever short names for your tags.

For general information on attributes, see Chapter 5.

FEATURES *declarations*

The FEATURES section in an SGML declaration lets you enable or disable certain of the capabilities that an SGML application can use when parsing a DTD or SGML document that conforms to that DTD. Like the other parts of an SGML declaration, you disable these features to try to limit the memory requirements of an SGML application; or you enable them when the application should probably prepare to allocate more memory. Features are enabled by following them with the word "YES" and are disabled by following them with the word "NO."

Table 4-4 shows some of the more common features that you may want to enable or disable, depending on your preferences. This is not a complete list — the FEATURE statements that are listed in Table 4-4 all involve tag minimization, which is the most common feature that I enable or disable. For more information about markup or tag minimization, see the section "What's the point of omitting tags?," earlier in this chapter.

Table 4-4	SGML Minimization Features That You May Want to Enable or Disable
Feature	**Purpose**
FORMAL	If enabled, means that the public identifiers in your DTD must conform to the rules for formal public identifiers. These rules are discussed in Chapter 6.
OMITTAG	If enabled, lets you omit the closing tags in elements whose definition allows this. If enabled, the definition of every element in your DTD must include tag-minimization information. (See "Portions of an element declaration," earlier in this chapter, for more information.)
SHORTTAG	If enabled, lets you use empty and unclosed tags to minimize the tagging in your SGML documents. (See "What's the point of omitting tags?," earlier in this chapter, for more information.)
SHORTREF	If enabled, lets you use the position of text within a structural element and the presence of certain characters to indicate markup even when no tags are explicitly used. For more information, see Chapter 13.

Chapter 5

Elements and Attributes — What, Which, and Why?

This chapter introduces you to attributes. You use attributes to get more power out of the elements you declare in a DTD, including the primary element for your document itself. Attributes are the spices that make elements more palatable and powerful, providing more than simple structural information. Attributes allow you to reduce the number of elements that a DTD contains by enabling you to extract the similarities between different elements that you think you might need. This leaves you with a few different flavors of your basic elements, providing you with a way to distinguish between different instances of the same element. I can't resist saying this — attributes are an important part of the recipe for a simple yet robust DTD!

What's an Attribute?

In the sample DTD I began in the previous chapter, I created simple structural elements, like paragraphs and lists. As you may know, documents are somewhat more complex than that; there are many types of paragraphs, such as hanging paragraphs, indented paragraphs, and outdented paragraphs, just as there are many types of lists, such as bulleted lists, numbered lists, alphabetical lists, and so on.

As I mention many times in this book, one of the basic tenets of SGML is to separate the structure and content of your documents from their formatting. SGML allows you to encapsulate structural items and their content, thereby "isolating" them as much as possible from the way that they look if you ever print or otherwise publish your documents. At the same time that SGML provides you with these lofty philosophical goals, it doesn't totally ignore the actual needs of the documentation industry, one of which is certainly the ability to print a book. This is exactly the situation that arises when you're faced with issues such as how to create SGML elements that correspond to elements with the same structural purpose but that need to be represented somewhat differently.

When creating the elements that make up a DTD, your first inclination is probably to represent all of these "separate but similar" concepts as different types of elements. There's actually nothing wrong with that, but taking this approach tends to bloat your DTD because you end up with many elements that are essentially the same thing. It also introduces a certain amount of confusion in people that have to work with your DTD. If you use different elements for every "separate but similar" concept, you always have to be conscious of every type of paragraph and list that's available and which one you want to use in every situation when writing your documents.

Attributes provide you with a much simpler way of associating additional information with the elements in a DTD. They provide you with an easy way of specifying this information and also provide convenient shortcuts by allowing you to provide default values for this additional information.

An example of an attribute

The declaration of a list in the sample DTD looks like the following:

```
<!ELEMENT list       -- (list-item)+>
<!ELEMENT list-item --  RCDATA>
```

In my DTD, I thought of lists as a structural element that is a set of individual entries (<LIST-ITEM>s) that are subsets of a larger structural item (the <LIST>). So what's the best way to differentiate between plain lists, which are just a set of related items, bulleted lists, which are a nicer way of displaying a plain list, and numbered lists, which are often a series of items that you have to perform in a specific order? The "bloat my DTD" approach says that you should create separate elements for each of these:

```
<!ELEMENT list        -- (list-item)+>
<!ELEMENT bullet-list -- (list-item)+>
<!ELEMENT number-list -- (list-item)+>
<!ELEMENT list-item --  RCDATA>
```

When the formatting part of your SGML software encounters each of these different elements, it can represent each <LIST-ITEM> differently, applying the appropriate formatting. In your document, these would look like the following:

```
<LIST>
<LIST-ITEM>This is item one of a generic list.</LIST-ITEM>
<LIST-ITEM>This is item two of a generic list.</LIST-ITEM>
</LIST>
<BULLET-LIST>
<LIST-ITEM>This is item one of a bulleted list.</LIST-ITEM>
<LIST-ITEM>This is item two of a bulleted list.</LIST-ITEM>
</BULLET-LIST>
<NUMBER-LIST>
<LIST-ITEM>This is item one of a numbered list.</LIST-ITEM>
<LIST-ITEM>This is item two of a numbered list.</LIST-ITEM>
</NUMBER-LIST>
```

However, as an SGML wizard in training, you should strive to do this task more elegantly with attributes. First, the declaration from the DTD can look like this:

```
<!ELEMENT list     -- (list-item)+>
<!ATTLIST list type
           (alpha | bullet | none | number) "none" >
<!ELEMENT list-item --  RCDATA>
```

Using this approach, the example lists would look like the following:

```
<LIST>
<LIST-ITEM>This is item one of a generic list.</LIST-ITEM>
<LIST-ITEM>This is item two of a generic list.</LIST-ITEM>
</LIST>
<LIST TYPE="bullet">
<LIST-ITEM>This is item one of a bulleted list.</LIST-ITEM>
<LIST-ITEM>This is item two of a bulleted list.</LIST-ITEM>
</LIST>
<LIST TYPE="number">
<LIST-ITEM>This is item one of a numbered list.</LIST-ITEM>
<LIST-ITEM>This is item two of a numbered list.</LIST-ITEM>
</LIST>
```

I'd say that this is a win on two levels — it's simpler to use and is also more elegant, SGML-wise. The alternative, declaring many different types of lists, makes a DTD larger, though it can make it easier to exchange SGML documents with other applications that don't understand or handle SGML syntax very well.

What's in an attribute declaration?

Here is the basic structure of an attribute declaration in a DTD:

```
<!ATTLIST element (name contents/values default-value)+ >
```

Each of the fields in an attribute definition has the following meaning:

- ✔ *Element* is the name of the element that the attribute is associated with.

- ✔ *Name* is the name of the attribute.

- ✔ *Contents/values* is either an SGML description of the content of the element or a list of possible values for that attribute.

- ✔ *Default-value* is the default value for the attribute. This is either a special SGML keyword or an SGML *string literal* providing a default value.

An SGML string literal is a series of characters enclosed in quotation marks. String literals can contain entities (explained in Chapter 6) or quotation marks.

In SGML values, you must quote any values that contain characters that are illegal in SGML names. For example, if you want to create an attribute with a value of "foo bar," you must quote this value because the space character is otherwise illegal in an SGML name — if you do not quote this value, an SGML parser will interpret the space as meaning that you've encountered the end of the token "foo," and will interpret the following token, "bar," as the next token. Depending on where this occurred in an SGML element declaration or document, this will usually generate an error. When in doubt, enclose things in quotation marks — this is never wrong.

Quoting things in SGML

In SGML, you must quote any values that contain characters that are illegal in SGML names, or values that actually require a list of values. It doesn't matter whether you use single or double quotation marks when you're quoting something, unless the thing that you're quoting itself contains quotation marks. If so, you must use the other type of quotation marks. For example:

```
<!ENTITY alexbell 'He said "Watson, Please come here".'>
```

In this case, you need to use single quotation marks because the value of the entity value contains double quotation marks. If the string you're quoting contains both types of quotation marks, you'll have to use entities to represent one or both types of quotation marks. Here's an example:

```
<!ENTITY foo "When inventing the 'telephone', he said &lq;Watson, please come here&rq;.">
```

Here is an example of the *type* attribute of a list:

```
<!ATTLIST list type
               (alpha | bullet | none | number) "none" >
```

Each of the fields in an attribute definition has the following meaning:

- ✔ *List* is the element that the attribute is associated with.

- ✔ *Type* is the name of the attribute.

- ✔ *(alpha | bullet | none | number)* is a list of the possible values of the attribute, in standard SGML syntax, saying that the value of the "list" attribute "type" can be any one of these four possible values.

- ✔ *"None"* is the default value for the *list* attribute type. Any <LIST> tag in a document that doesn't provide an explicit value for the *type* attribute is assumed to have a type value of "none."

In this example, I provided a specific set of values because I know the specific types of lists that I'm interested in telling apart. Trying to provide any other value than one of the ones I listed generates an error when an SGML document that uses this DTD is parsed.

Defining multiple attributes for an element

Like most other aspects of SGML, the syntax of attribute declarations was designed to be as flexible as possible. The attribute declaration provided earlier in this chapter declares a single attribute. However, you've now seen that you may want to associate several different attributes with an element in order to provide different kinds of information about those elements. The sample attribute declaration provided earlier looks like this:

```
<!ATTLIST list type
          (alpha | bullet | none | number) "none" >
```

Suppose that you also want to be able to re-use your lists in different types of documents. It may be useful to be able to identify the type of information that a list contains, to make sure that you can extract only lists of certain types. The easiest way to do this would be to add an additional attribute to your list element:

```
<!ATTLIST list type
          (alpha | bullet | none | number) "none"
          content NAMES #IMPLIED >
```

Each element in your DTD can have only one list of associated attributes, so the ATTLIST lets you declare multiple attributes in a single statement. To put this in SGML syntax, you might think of this as

```
<!ATTLIST element (attribute)+>
```

Where each attribute expands to

```
name contents/values default-value
```

In this example, the new content attribute is defined as having the possible value of NAMES, which means that it can be one or more valid SGML names. I selected NAMES in this case for two reasons:

✔ At the moment, I don't want to try to predict all the different values that this attribute can have. Right now, "parts" and "procedure" are the only types of lists that occur to me, but other types may occur to writers as they develop documents using the DTD that contains the <LIST> element.

✔ It's equally possible that certain lists may fall into multiple categories in the future. Using the plural form of the NAME attribute value lets writers say that a specific list has different types of content. As an example, consider a list of steps for installing a piece of software. This is certainly a "procedure," but you may also want to mark this list as having "installation" content so that you can re-use it in a general installation manual. You can then define a content attribute of "procedure installation," and you're covered.

TIP

What's in a NAME?

Using the NAME or NAMES values for an attribute is a two-edged sword. On the one hand, they provide a flexible set of values for an attribute. They can be very useful when developing and refining a DTD because they let writers develop a set of possible values as they write your documents. On the other hand, since they do not define a specific set of values to use, this flexibility can be a noose that can hang you in the future or may at least require some reworking of your documents. Continuing with our example from the previous section, nothing prevents one writer from assigning a content value of "procedure install" and another assigning it "process installation."

I generally only use NAME or NAMES values when people need to use a DTD as it's being developed. After documents are written using this flexible approach, it's fairly easy to use (or write) a small script or program that extracts the set of NAME values that have been used in a document, examine that list, and either verify the set that's in use or decide on a specific set of values to use. You can then represent this as an explicit set of values, perhaps with something like this:

```
<!ATTLIST list type
            (alpha | bullet | none | number) "none"
            content (install | parts | procedure) #IMPLIED >
```

This helps guarantee that none of your lists slip through the cracks due to naming permutations. Using the NAMES construct lets you put your DTD in the field as quickly as possible. It's hard to cover every possibility when planning your DTD — the only real sin is not planning for the possibility that you haven't thought of everything!

Different types of attribute values

This section and the next provide detailed information about the possible values you can specify when defining an attribute and about how to specify default values for your attributes. If you're just reading this chapter to come up to speed on SGML attributes, you can skip the next two sections and come back to them for reference at any time.

SGML, of course, provides a powerful and flexible approach to defining the possible values for an attribute. Table 5-1 shows all of the possible values of an attribute.

Table 5-1	Possible Values of an Attribute
Value	*Meaning*
CDATA	String of characters that will not be parsed or evaluated by an SGML parser, enclosed in quotation marks if it contains characters that are illegal in SGML names. No entity or element substitutions will be made.
	Example: Sample attribute value
ENTITY	Any general entity available in the document. When providing the entity's name, do not include the standard entity delimiters (& and ;)
	Example: lt
ENTITIES	A list of one or more of any general entities available in the document, enclosed in quotation marks. When providing the entity names, do not include the standard entity delimiters (& and ;).
	Example: lt gt
ID	A symbolic name that will be associated with the element. ID attributes are most commonly used to mark the targets of different types of cross-references in a document. The value of each ID attribute must be unique in the SGML document.
	Example: chap1
IDREF	A reference to the symbolic name associated with an element in the current SGML document.
	Example: chap1

Value	Meaning
IDREFS	A reference to one or more symbolic names associated with an element in the current SGML document. Example: chap1 figure1
NAME	A valid *SGML name*. An SGML name is a series of characters beginning with an alphabetic character, containing digits, hyphens, periods, or other alphabetic characters, whose length is less than or equal to the NAMELEN value specified in your SGML declaration. The SGML declaration is discussed in Chapter 4. Using NAME as the type for your attributes lets you specify the type of content that this attribute can contain without limiting it to a set of specific values. See the sidebar earlier in this chapter for information on the NAME and NAMES values. Your SGML application should subsequently interpret the specific value for this attribute and use it in some way. Example: SYNTAX
NAMES	One or more valid SGML names. (See the NAME attribute value for more information.) Example: SYNTAX C-PROG
NMTOKEN	A valid SGML name, with the difference that the first character of the name need not be alphabetic. Example: 1stChap
NMTOKENS	One or more valid SGML names, with the difference that the first character of each name need not be alphabetic. (See the NMTOKEN attribute value for more information.) Example: 1stChap 1stList

(continued)

Table 5-1 *(continued)*

Value	Meaning
NOTATION	One or more notation names that are valid in the current document. You use NOTATION names to identify different types of non-SGML data in an SGML document, most commonly different types of graphics files. NOTATION names generally tell an SGML application to invoke some external application to process this type of element. If you specify more than one NOTATION name as an attribute value, you must enclose the names within parentheses and separate them by one of the SGML symbols shown in Table 4-1. The vertical bar (I) is typically used to separate different NOTATION names. Example 1: EPS Example 2: (EPS | PCX | GIF | JPEG)
NUMBER	A string composed entirely of numbers. Example: 196463818
NUMBERS	One or more strings composed entirely of numbers. Example1: 196463818 Example2: 196463818 174443215
NUTOKEN	A NUMBER string that can contain other valid SGML characters after the initial number. Example: 196-46-3818
NUTOKENS	One or more NUMBER strings that can contain other valid SGML characters after the initial number. Example1: 196-46-3818 Example2: 196-46-3818 174-44-3215

You should consider these general rules for attribute values:

✔ You need to use quotation marks only when the attribute value contains one or more characters that are not valid characters in SGML names.

✔ The values of attributes are not case-sensitive — foo and FOO are the same thing, unless the type of the attribute is declared to be CDATA.

✔ The maximum length for an attribute value (or each item in a list of attribute values) is the NAMELEN value specified in your SGML declaration (or the LITLEN value for attributes whose value is declared as CDATA). The maximum number of attributes that you can associate with an element in your DTD is the ATTCNT value specified in the SGML declaration. See the last section of Chapter 4 for more information about SGML declarations.

✔ With the exception of NOTATION, if an attribute value can contain more than one item, you must enclose the entire list in quotation marks and separate each item from the next with a space. The NOTATION attribute value only appears to be an exception — an attribute can have only one NOTATION value. A list of possible notation values is just the set of possible NOTATION values, from which you can select only one for a given element.

✔ You should use the plural form of an attribute value (IDREFS, NAMES, NUMBERS, NUTOKENS) rather than the singular form if the attribute must have at least one value.

✔ With the exception of the attribute values CDATA, NMTOKEN, NMTOKENS, NUMBER, NUMBERS, NUTOKEN, and NUTOKENS, the first character of an attribute value must be alphabetic. The remainder of the attribute value can consist of any alphabetic or numeric characters, as well as periods (.) or hyphens (-).

Specifying default values for an attribute

Specifying the default value associated with an attribute is a mandatory part of an attribute declaration. The default value ensures that the SGML parser knows how to handle each type of attribute that is associated with an element. Table 5-2 shows the different types of default values that you can specify for an attribute, and explains when and why you might use which value.

Table 5-2	Possible Default Values for Attributes
Default Value	*Meaning*
value	One of the possible values for an attribute that was declared to have one of a specific set of values.
	Example value: (alpha | bullet | none | number)
	Default value: "none"

(continued)

Table 5-2 *(continued)*

Default Value	Meaning
#CONREF	The attribute either has content or is EMPTY. If a CONREF attribute is specified, that instance of the element is treated as though it had an EMPTY content model. If the attribute is not specified, the element has whatever content model was specified in the DTD. Yow! You typically use elements with attributes that take this value in cross-references. Example attribute: `<!ATTLIST CHAPREF xref IDREF #CONREF>` Example1: See `<CHAPREF>Chapter 1</CHAPREF>` for... `Example1: See <CHAPREF xref="chap1"> for...`
#CURRENT	The attribute has the same value as the last attribute of this type on the same sort of element. Using the *list* element's *type* attribute as an example, if the default value was #CURRENT and the previous list in the document was of type *alpha,* the next list in the document would have a default value of *alpha.*
#FIXED "value"	The attribute can only have one value, which is specified as *value.*
#IMPLIED	The attribute value is optional. If specified, it can be anything that is valid for the declared value of the attribute. You use attributes of this type to hold information that is used by other applications to identify specific elements in a document for extraction or special handling.
#REQUIRED	The attribute value is mandatory and must be supplied each time you use an element of the associated type. You usually use this type of attribute to ensure that writers associate IDs with the different structural levels of a document.

Put your DTD on a diet?

The sample *type* attribute associated with <LIST> elements earlier in this chapter shows how you can use attributes to help reduce the number of elements in a DTD by allowing you to provide extra information about those elements. Although this is a very common way to use attributes, some people see this as shaky ground for using attributes because using attributes in this way is specifically oriented toward formatting and presentation, which are two of the bogey-men of SGML.

One of the key elements of designing an SGML solution for your documentation needs is to design a solution that works for you. There are certainly aspects of SGML that you can't violate, such as its syntax. But if you have to design a DTD, much of your solution is up to you. The remainder of this chapter discusses some ways to think about whether to use elements or attributes and discusses some types of information that are well suited to being represented as attributes of the elements in your documents, including the document itself. If you're already committed to using an existing DTD that has a set of attribute declarations that you can't modify, the remainder of this chapter should help you understand why someone created these things as attributes in the first place.

When to Use Which

So how do you decide when to use an attribute rather than a new type of element? Good question!

You typically use elements either to represent structural portions of a document or to identify specific types of content in your documents. Attributes usually provide additional information about an element, such as special instructions for its appearance or some special characteristic of the element in question. Attributes are like adjectives or other qualifiers for the elements in your documents.

This section discusses various ways to think about the conceptual differences between elements and attributes and how to identify when one is more "reasonable" to use than the other. In many cases, you can flip a coin — more than one SGML-induced brawl has broken out in smoky conference rooms over this particular topic. I have my opinions, and you'll have yours. The most basic rule I can give is "do what you think is right." Hopefully, the next few sections will help you make the "right" decision.

If it walks like an element and talks like an element . . .

Perhaps the best way to approach the issue of "when is an element not an element" is to examine some of the things for which you use attributes. As used in the examples given so far in this chapter, attributes identify slight differences between structurally similar elements, typically for the purpose of subsequent formatting or presentation. However, a look at Table 5-2 shows that you can use attributes for many other purposes — such as attributes of the ID type, which associate a specific label with an instance of an element. If SGML didn't support attributes of this type, you would still want to represent this type of information, and might be tempted to do something like this:

```
<SECTION>
<LABEL>chap1</LABEL>
<SECTION-TITLE>...
```

An SGML parser can certainly validate this sort of construction, assuming that you correctly declare the `<LABEL>` element, but any SGML application that processes this type of document still needs to associate a label with a specific chapter. When referring to label elements elsewhere in a document, your SGML application has to determine the appropriate level for numeric cross-references, in which you want to generate a string like `Section 2.4`. This construction also makes it slightly more complex for your SGML parser to guarantee that all labels within a document are unique, though it wouldn't be impossible.

In this case, you don't have to use a separate element to hold this information because things like labels are information about specific elements and don't really have their own existence within the structure of your documents. Therefore, I give you this general rule: *When an item is always associated with an element and has no structural purpose of its own, you may as well make it an attribute of that element.*

In the sample DTD introduced in Chapter 4, I provide the following syntax for the `<TITLE-BLOCK>` element:

```
<!ELEMENT title-block -- (paper-title, author,
affiliation, date)>
```

Can't you represent these as attributes of the `<TITLE-BLOCK>` element? The quick answer is "yes, they certainly can be." I chose to make them separate elements because I always want to publish them as part of my technical paper, in any format. First, making them all attributes of the `<TITLE-BLOCK>` element makes that element somewhat cumbersome to work with; I think it is easier for a writer to work with a document in which these are elements rather than attributes. Second, in most of the SGML software I've seen, it's easier to associate formatting and presentation with elements than it is with attributes. Finally, I chose to make them elements because I consider them to be part of the actual structure of the document. They're not just information about the purely structural `<TITLE-BLOCK>` element; they are instead actual information that should be present in the document itself.

Yet another kind of data — meta-data!

As introduced in the previous section, you commonly use attributes to provide information that is always associated with the elements in your documents and that has no life of its own. In the same way that you use attributes to provide specific information about parts of your documents that are structurally similar, you can easily use attributes to provide information that you use for internal purposes. This information is known as *meta-data* about the different elements in your documents. Meta-data is just a cool term for "information about information."

If you think about it, you always need to preserve a certain amount of information about your documents. If you've ever been responsible for documents that have a long lifetime and have therefore gone through many revisions, you or any writer who works with you may need to answer questions like "who modified it last," "when," and "why." On the surface, you can answer these questions by keeping a log of all of the parts of all of your documents, maintaining a written list of who's responsible for them, who's modified them, when, and why. Unfortunately, this type of paper trail can quickly become unmanageable, depending on the size of your documents, the number of different pieces of those documents that you need to track, and the frequency with which your documents are updated. A nicer solution to this potential mess is to see whether you can encapsulate this information inside the documents themselves. In combination with a revision control system and, perhaps, a database, you have a powerful way of having this information at your fingertips!

An example of document meta-data

This section provides a few examples to help get you started thinking about ways that you can use attributes to provide additional information about the elements in your documents.

As introduced earlier in this section, one important way to use elements is to provide meta-data about your documents. In the sample DTD introduced in Chapter 4 and used as an example throughout this chapter, I use the ⟨TITLE-BLOCK⟩ element to contain mandatory information that I want to be a part of the document itself, such as the author and the date on which it was written. However, in real life, technical papers often pass through many hands other than their authors' and are revised multiple times before they actually hit paper or the web. You might want to associate some of this information with the ⟨TECHPAPER⟩ element itself, as in the following example:

```
<!ELEMENT TechPaper -- (title-block, abstract, section+) >
<!ATTLIST TechPaper
          updated   CDATA #REQUIRED
          editor    CDATA #REQUIRED>
```

Using these attributes, I can easily identify the last person to edit the document and the date on which it occurred.

Just from this simple example, you may already be thinking of ways that you can use attributes in a DTD to capture some of the information that you now maintain by hand, if at all. That's really what SGML is all about: making it easier for you to manage and work with the information you're responsible for. This isn't to say that SGML makes difficult tasks easy, but it does provide a way to automate many tasks that were done manually at one time. It also provides hooks for you to move your documents into the future as an information resource, not just a stack of papers or a few floppies full of text and format codes.

Chapter 6

Reusing and Sharing Information in Your Documents

• •

In This Chapter

▶ Using PUBLIC and SYSTEM entities in DTDs and documents

▶ Centralized sources of entity information

▶ A modular approach to SGML documentation

▶ Creating a boilerplate for your documentation set

▶ Producing different versions of your documents from the same source

• •

*T*his chapter discusses ways of sharing information between different documents. This kind of information sharing takes place at two different levels: when you're creating or using a DTD, and when you're designing a document or documentation set.

SGML makes it easy for you to create new types of documents by defining and enforcing their structure. The definition of an SGML document extends all the way from the top-level structural element down to the types of characters used in different parts of your document. As you move down through the structure of a DTD, you reach lower levels at which there is no real reason for things to be associated with just one document type. These things are so low-level that they really apply to all of the documents you're writing. For example, if everyone who ever designs a DTD has to define each of the characters that are valid in each element of that DTD, I think we'd still be writing the third or fourth DTD ever — I certainly wouldn't have written this book!

SGML provides the concept of entities as a way of sharing low-level items across different documents and DTDs. Entities are introduced in Chapter 4 as ways of providing shortcuts in your documents and DTDs, by using entities as a sort of "SGML variables" when writing a document or DTD. Entities are more than just shortcuts for single characters or commonly used expressions — they provide ways for declaring common sets of characters for use throughout your documents.

This chapter provides more detail about entities from the perspective of how they make it easy to share and re-use information throughout your documents, and how your SGML software locates different kinds of entities. This chapter ends by showing how related SGML constructs provide you with other ways to create documents that are designed to share information.

While entities are fundamental to SGML and will become your friends, some of the later sections of this chapter explore the syntax of fairly low-level SGML constructs. Each of these sections is identified by a technical stuff icon and may provide more detail than you'll ever care about. You don't have to read all of these sections now in order to become comfortable with SGML. I did not write them to show off or to scare you; in fact, you may rarely use many of these low-level items. I present the information here because these are things that I've had a hard time finding in the past. I want this book to be a useful reference for you, not just a "Highlights of SGML" film.

Using Entities in Documents and DTDs

As discussed in Chapter 4, SGML documents use two different types of entities, *general* and *parameter*. General entities begin with the & symbol and can be used in a document itself or as part of the SGML markup for that document. Parameter entities begin with the % symbol and can be used only in a DTD or in local declarations in a DOCTYPE statement. Because you'll probably spend more time writing documents than writing or extending DTDs (hopefully!), you are far more likely to encounter general entities, because they are commonly used in SGML documents as shortcuts for frequently used strings of text, or to represent characters that can't usually be typed from the keyboard or which might be interpreted as markup. General entities that are designed to make it easy for you to type specific characters are often referred to as *character entities*.

When writing a DTD, you typically include publicly available sets of entities that define standard sets of characters and general entity declarations. Many of these are defined by the International Standards Organization (ISO) and are publicly available at locations on the Internet. These sets of characters and general entities are typically defined as parameter entities that are included in the DTD you're using.

Syntax of a general entity declaration

This section provides a detailed description of the syntax you use to declare a general entity. You stand a good chance of wanting to define a general entity at some point in your use of SGML, but this might not be that time. If you're reading this chapter to get a general feel for different types of entities and how you use them in SGML documents, you may want to skip this section for now. You can always return to it for reference at any time.

The general syntax of a general entity declaration is the following:

```
<!ENTITY name value >
```

Well, that looks pretty simple! You can use this type of declaration for most general entity declarations, such as the example given in Chapter 4 in which I define a general entity to use as the name of a product that is under development:

```
<!ENTITY otter "new development workstation">
```

When using this in your documents, you could write something along the following lines:

The &otter; comes in a number of standard configurations:

When the product under development is actually finally released, you can update all of your documents by updating the entity declaration to be something like this:

```
<!ENTITY otter "DN3000">
```

This seems pretty straightforward, but do not forget that SGML is designed to provide you with a standard, flexible way of defining the structure and content of your documents. So you expect its syntax for declaring variables such as entities to be fairly robust, and it is! Table 6-1 shows all of the possible ways of specifying the value of a general entity.

Many of the possible ways of defining the value of a general entity seem designed to help you win an "obfuscated SGML" contest, but there are situations in which each of these is useful. Well, I assume so — I've used many only as experiments, and I confess that I've never used some of them.

Table 6-1	Ways of Expressing the Value of a General Entity
Value	*Meaning*
`"value"`	The string of characters enclosed in double quotation marks.
`CDATA "value"`	A string of uninterpreted character data. You can use this notation to define general entities that contain other general entities or SGML tags that you don't want your SGML application to process.
`ENDTAG "value"`	A string of characters that should be interpreted as being enclosed within the delimiters used for an ending tag in SGML. By default, these are the opening delimiter </ and the closing delimiter >. Defining an ending tag in this way ensures that it works correctly even if someone redefines the characters used to identify ending tags. (Maybe on April Fools day?)
`MD "value"`	A string of characters that should be interpreted as being surrounded by the characters used to identify markup declarations. By default, these are the opening delimiter <! and the closing delimiter >.
`MS "value"`	A string of characters that should be interpreted as being surrounded by the delimiters used to define a marked section, which is a way of conditionally including or excluding certain portions of the text in an SGML document. By default, these are the opening delimiter <![and the closing delimiter]]>. See the discussion of marked sections later in this chapter for more information.
`NDATA "value"`	A string of non-SGML data. You can use this notation to include graphics or any other type of information that is produced by an application external to your SGML application.
`PI "value"`	A string of characters that will be interpreted as a processing instruction, which is an output-format-specific instruction used to pass commands to a specific output formatter. Processing instructions are discussed in Chapter 10.

Value	Meaning
PUBLIC "public-id" ("system-loc")	A string of characters that should be interpreted as a public identifier that your SGML software can then look up to get information about. The *public-id* can optionally be followed by a *system-loc*, which tells your SGML software where to find this PUBLIC entity on your system. The *system-loc* is typically either a filename or an additional entity that your SGML software can look up to locate the specified *public-id*. Like the SYSTEM declaration later in this table, the PUBLIC declaration identifies something external to your document that your SGML application needs to be able to locate.
PUBLIC SUBDOC	The entity should be looked up through a means that is already known to the SGML software, so that no location need be specified. Once located, the contents of the entity are considered a separate SGML document with its own DOCTYPE declaration. This need not be the same as the current DOCTYPE.
SDATA "value"	The value of this general entity is the string of "system-dependant data" enclosed within double quotation marks. You typically use SDATA to identify special characters that are available on a specific computer system and, therefore, may not be portable to other systems.
STARTTAG "value"	A string of characters that should be interpreted as being enclosed within the delimiters used for an opening tag in SGML. By default, these are the opening delimiter < and the closing delimiter >. Defining an opening tag in this way ensures that it will work correctly even if someone redefines the characters used to identify beginning tags. (Maybe on Guy Fawkes Day?)
SYSTEM "system-loc"	A string of characters that should be interpreted as a system location where your SGML software can find this entity on your system. The *system-loc* is typically either a filename or an additional entity that your SGML software can look up to locate the specified entity. Like the PUBLIC declaration later in this table, the SYSTEM declaration identifies something external to your document that your SGML application needs to be able to locate.
SYSTEM SUBDOC	The entity should be looked up through a means known to the SGML software. Once located, the contents of the entity are considered a separate SGML document with its own DOCTYPE declaration. This need not be the same as the current DOCTYPE.

Using data produced by other applications

The previous section described NDATA (non-SGML data) as one possible value for the contents of an entity. This raises an interesting point — how do you integrate data produced by other applications into SGML applications? You certainly don't want an SGML application to attempt to parse things like graphics files in PostScript files! However, declaring every external object as an entity whose type is NDATA seems a bit extreme. There must be some easier way to do this . . . .

SGML provides the NOTATION declaration to identify external data. The NOTATION declaration must appear in a DTD and has the following form:

```
<! NOTATION name ((SYSTEM "system-id")|(PUBLIC "public-id"
   ("system-id")?)))>
```

An example of a NOTATION description for PostScript graphics is the following:

```
<! NOTATION ps SYSTEM>
```

Once declared, a NOTATION is attached to any elements that contain it, as in the following example:

```
<! NOTATION ps SYSTEM>
<!ELEMENT figure - - (graphic, caption)>
<!ELEMENT caption - - (#PCDATA)>
<!ELEMENT graphic - - CDATA >
<!ATTLIST graphic type NOTATION ps ps>
```

You could then use this in your documents in the following way:

```
<FIGURE>
<GRAPHIC TYPE="ps">/usr/wvh/perq.ps</GRAPHIC>
<CAPTION>A PERQ T2 Workstation</CAPTION>
</FIGURE>
```

Besides naming specific entities that you create, you want to define one specific general entity while you're writing a DTD. This is a special general entity whose name is #DEFAULT. The value that you assign to this general entity is used if you ever accidentally reference an entity that hasn't been declared yet. Suppose you declare this entity in the following way:

```
<!ENTITY #DEFAULT "OOPS! Bogus entity!">
```

If you mistype the name of an existing entity, such as &lt, in one of your documents and your typo doesn't happen to be the name of another entity, you see the string OOPS! Bogus entity! in any formatted version of your document. This message provides a visual clue that there's a problem without prohibiting your document from being successfully processed by parts of your SGML application, such as the parser and formatter.

Syntax of a public identifier name

Danger, Will Robinson! The most important aspect of the name of a public identifier is that your SGML software knows how to locate it. However, you must follow a well-defined syntax for these names in certain cases. This section explains that formal syntax in all its gory detail.

Public identifier names come in two flavors: formal and informal. You need to use a formal identifier if the FORMAL feature in your SGML declaration is set to YES. (See the last section of Chapter 4 for detailed information about an SGML declaration.)

Here is the formal syntax of a public identifier name:

```
"owner//class description//language//version"
```

The meaning of each of these is shown in Table 6-2. You may never have to translate one of these, but knowing how to interpret them makes them look a little less like they were written using a shotgun loaded with random characters.

Table 6-2	Components of a Formal Public Identifier Name
Name Component	**Meaning**
owner	The owner of the public identifier who is responsible for its creation and maintenance. If the public identifier is an official identifier from the International Standards Organization (ISO), the owner gives the ISO publication number of the standard. If the owner is not the ISO but has registered this identifier with them, the owner begins with the string +//. If the owner is not the ISO and has not registered this identifier with it, the owner begins with the string -//.

(continued)

Table 6-2 *(continued)*

Name Component	Meaning
class	An SGML value that identifies the content of the item associated with the public identifier. Common values for *class* are `CHARSET`, `DTD`, `ELEMENTS`, `ENTITIES`, and `NOTATION`.
description	An arbitrary description of the entity and when it's intended to be used.
language	The language used in the text of the item associated with the public identifier. In the United States, the most common one is `EN`, which stands for "English."
version	(Optional!) Used to identify a specific version of the item associated with the public identifier. If the version is not specified, you can omit the double slash marks in front of this part of the public identifier name.

A few examples of general entity declarations

You use general entities to provide shortcuts when writing documents or to let you enter characters that either aren't on a standard keyboard or might be misinterpreted by an SGML parser. Here is an example:

```
<!ENTITY bride "The Bride Stripped Bare By Her Bachelors">
"One of Marcel Duchamp's most famous paintings is
&bride;...
```

In this example, the general entity `bride` has been defined to stand for a string that is probably going to be repeated many times but that could quickly grow cumbersome to type.

```
"The tag used to define the beginning of an unordered list
in HTML is &lt;UL>."
```

In this example, the general entity `lt` is an entity that represents the character `<`, which could otherwise be misinterpreted by a parser as being the beginning of the name of a tag. (I chose not to show this entity declaration because it is found in the `ISOnum` entity set that comes with many SGML software packages.)

Syntax of a parameter entity declaration

This section provides a detailed description of the syntax used to declare a parameter entity. Unless you're writing or extending a DTD, you may never need to declare a parameter entry. If you're reading this chapter to get a general feel for different types of entities and how you use them in SGML documents, you may want to skip this section for now. You can always return to it for reference at any time.

The "general" syntax of a parameter entity declaration is the following:

```
<!ENTITY % name value >
```

The percent symbol identifies this as a parameter entity, which therefore can only be used in markup declarations in a DTD or in the additional declarations portion of a DOCTYPE declaration. The % symbol must be separated from the entity name by a space!

Because you use parameter entities in more limited circumstances than general entities, you have fewer ways of expressing the value of the entity. These are shown in Table 6-3.

Table 6-3   Ways of Expressing the Value of a Parameter Entity

Value	Meaning
`"value"`	The string of characters enclosed in double quotation marks. You use it to supply a specific value for the parameter entity.
`PUBLIC "public-id" ("system-loc")?`	A string of characters that should be interpreted as a public identifier which the SGML must locate using its entity manager. You can optionally provide a system identifier after the public identifier. If the software can't locate the system identifier, it will fall back to looking up the public identifier.
`SYSTEM "system-loc"`	A string of characters that should be interpreted as a system location where your SGML software can find this entity on your system. The *system-loc* is typically either a filename or an additional entity that your SGML software can look up to locate the specified parameter entity.

A few examples of parameter entity declarations

You commonly use parameter entities to provide shortcuts when writing or extending a DTD. If you don't have to do either of these, you may never need to use parameter entities. Just in case, here is an example:

```
<!ENTITY % ISOnum PUBLIC "ISO 8879:1986//ENTITIES Numeric
and Special Graphic//EN">
%ISOnum;
```

The first line of this example defines ISOnum as a parameter entry (because of the % sign), states that it is a PUBLIC entity, and associates a name with that entity. The name of this entity isn't a valid SGML token, so it's enclosed in double quotation marks. The second line actually includes this entity in your DTD. Refer to the section of this chapter titled "Syntax of a public identifier name" for the secret decoder ring necessary to interpret the name of this PUBLIC identifier.

If you're writing a DTD, you may just cut and paste your favorite ISO character and general entity declarations from other DTDs that you've written and used. However, you may find that you want to declare your own parameter entities to provide shortcuts when you have many different entities that share certain types of content. Here is an example:

```
<!ENTITY % generic "paragraph | list" >
<!ELEMENT body - - (%generic;)+ >
<!ELEMENT footnote - - (%generic;)+>
```

You can use this type of parameter entity to simplify your DTDs by centralizing basic concepts in a parameter entity. This also makes it easier to modify the definition of low-level elements if you find that you want to expand them at some point. However, as mentioned in the introduction to entities in Chapter 4, you don't want to use this feature frivolously. You should use this feature only if you have a reason to because abusing this feature can make it more difficult and frustrating to read a DTD. Elegance is a by-product of a well-written and well-thought-out DTD, not of an attempt to use every SGML construct known to person-kind.

How SGML Software Finds Entities

PUBLIC and SYSTEM identifiers tell an SGML application where to locate specific information, such as entities. A PUBLIC identifier tells the application that it has to look up this information in whatever centralized repository it uses to catalog this information. Since this is PUBLIC information, it can be used in any DTD or document (as appropriate). Different applications use different repositories for the location of PUBLIC entities.

Using a SYSTEM identifier means that the SGML application knows where to find this information. Typically, a system identifier contains the full pathname (or URL, nowadays) of the file where the information is located. If the SGML application was written to look in a specific location for files containing entities, DTDs, or anything else named by a SYSTEM identifier, the system identifier may only be followed by the name of the file containing that information.

SGML software uses an *entity manager* to identify and locate the items associated with `PUBLIC` or `SYSTEM` entities that are referenced in your documents. The phase entity manager describes what an entity manager does, not how it does it; each SGML software package has its own concept of how an entity manager should locate and retrieve entities that are referenced in your documents. For example, SGML software packages that are tightly integrated with database systems may store sets of entities as records associated with a specific key that is the `PUBLIC` identifier associated with that entity.

An entity manager that is elegant in its simplicity is the *catalog* style entity manager used by Arbortext Adept. The catalog is nothing more than a text file in which each entry contains three fields — the type of entity (usually `PUBLIC`), the identifier for that entity, and the location of the file that contains that entity declaration in the filesystem on your computer. The catalog approach provides a centralized repository for entity information that is not dependent on any external software package. The fact that this information is centralized and stored in a text file makes it easy to look things up in the catalog. The fact that this is a standard text file that doesn't require a special package to modify makes it easy to update this file.

Creating your own sets of entities

If you are writing or extending an existing DTD, you probably will want to create your own centralized collection of entities at some point. I find it most useful to put things like the official names of all of the books and products in a company-specific entity collection. Nothing is more frustrating than seeing two documents from your own company that refer to the same document by different names, or trying to update an entire document set when the names of all of your documents are hard-coded in the documents. This type of thing only increases inertia and frustration when you're trying to do something creative like reorganize or otherwise modernize a documentation set.

Creating your own set of entities that everyone can benefit from requires only three quick steps:

1. **Create the file containing the entity declarations.**

2. **Create a public identifier for that file.**

3. **Add the new set of entity declarations to your entity manager.**

After you complete these three steps, no one has an excuse for using a reference to an outdated document or product name!

An example

For example, your file of entity declarations might look like the following:

```
<!ENTITY SFS "Structured File Service">
<!ENTITY AFS "Andrew File System">
```

You could then create an entry in your entity manager that gives the public identifier for the file containing these entities, such as (in an ArborText catalog file):

```
PUBLIC "-//transarc//ENTITIES Product Names//EN" "/usr/doc
entities/prodnames.ent"
```

In your SGML documents, you could then include this by putting the following entries in the local declarations section of your documents, as in the following example:

```
<!DOCTYPE Book PUBLIC "-//Davenport//DTD Docbook 2.4//EN" [
<!ENTITY % Products "-//transarc//ENTITIES Product Names/
EN">
%products;
]>
```

You could then use the entities &SFS; and &AFS; in your SGML documents, updating them in the entities file if the product names ever change.

Using entities to standardize your documents

Another way that you can benefit from declaring your own sets of entities is by associating entity names with portions of your documents that you want to share between different departments or documents. I introduce this idea in Chapter 1, but you should pay closer attention to it now that you understand how to declare entities in your documents.

Most companies have standard chunks of information that they re-use in different documents. These information chunks can be anything from high-level product overviews that may be shared between marketing and product documentation, to warranties, liabilities, and copyright information that is included in every document they produce, to graphic elements that appear in every book for a software product, such as a keyboard layout diagram showing special key mappings used by their products. In all of these cases, separating these items into separate files and associating a general entity name with them provides an easy way to include them in different documents. Doing this also provides the added benefit that the companies only need to update this text or graphic in one place if their products change or they decide to rework the text. Everyone who references these chunks through entity references automatically inherits the enhancements the next time they process the documents. (Of course, you should tell all of the parties involved that you're updating the document; no one likes a surprise, especially if you're adding more material, which could change the page count that is often critical in marketing or other glossy documents.)

I've found that using entities in the front matter for technical documents frequently pays off. The front matter for this type of document usually follows certain general rules and contains lots of boilerplate text that shouldn't change much over time. Table 6-4 shows some common sections of front matter and whether they are common to multiple documents in a document set. This is just an example — your documentation may have more or fewer sections, depending on your style, DTD, and the type of product you're documenting.

Table 6-4	Common Sections of Front Matter in Technical Documents		
Section	*Common to All*	*Multiple Docs*	*Specific*
Audience			X
Organization			X
Related Documents		X	

(continued)

Table 6-4 *(continued)*			
Section	**Common to All**	**Multiple Docs**	**Specific**
Documentation Conventions	X		
Ordering and Customer Support Information	X		

In this example, you can declare entities that contained the text for your "Documentation Conventions" and "Ordering and Customer Support Information" sections, sharing these across all of the documents in your documentation set. With a little research, you can probably also derive one or two versions of your "Related Documents" section for use with certain groups of documents, such as administrative and programming documentation for a software product.

I don't want to give you the impression that other documentation tools don't have similar capabilities to support sharing files; I just want to point out that SGML intrinsically provides support for reusing existing information in multiple documents.

A Document for All Seasons

Similar to enabling you to share chunks of information between different documents, you may want to produce different versions of the same document by selectively formatting or hiding certain portions of the document. You may need to do this when preparing public and confidential versions of a single document, or when producing documentation for computer software that runs on multiple platforms. In each case, the majority of the content of the document remains the same, but certain sections should contain different information based on the audience.

SGML provides *marked sections* that allow you to selectively enable or disable certain portions of an SGML document. Marked sections identify sections of your document that should either be included, specially processed, or ignored when your document is formatted. These marked sections are frequently referred to as *conditional text* because they are included in your documents only when certain conditions are met. Not all SGML software supports marked sections, though they are part of the SGML standard. You may want to make this one of the questions you plan to ask when we go shopping for SGML software in Chapter 19.

The syntax of a marked section declaration looks like this:

```
<![ status [ content ]]>
```

The possible values for *status* are shown in Table 6-5. The value for *content* is the text that you want to enclose in the marked section. The *status* value determines how (or if) it is included and processed in your document.

You can use marked sections at any place in a DTD or document. You usually can include other marked sections within a marked section, unless the *status* of those marked sections is CDATA or RCDATA. In these cases, the first closing element for a marked section that's encountered (the]]> token) is interpreted as closing the original marked section declaration. Because the SGML parser performs little or no interpretation, it has no way to recognize whether a single marked section or a set of nested marked sections are present. Using marked sections with CDATA or RDATA is a very different animal than using IGNORE and INCLUDE *status* values. The latter is my favorite way of using marked sections.

Table 6-5	Possible Values for Marked Section *status*
Status	**Meaning**
CDATA	The contents of the marked section are included in the document as uninterpreted character data. No entities are expanded and no elements are formatted.
IGNORE	The contents of the marked section are excluded from the document. The SGML parser strips them as it processes the document.
INCLUDE	The contents of the marked section are included in the document. The SGML parser correctly processes any entities or elements in the marked section and the other parts of an SGML application.
RCDATA	The contents of the marked section are included in the document as replaceable character data in which entities are expanded but no elements are formatted.
TEMP	A synonym for INCLUDE that identifies parts of a document that may subsequently be removed. The contents of the marked section are included in the document. The SGML parser correctly process any entities or elements in the marked section and the other parts of an SGML application.

Because I usually write about computer software, I use conditionalized documentation most commonly when documenting a software package that runs on different platforms and therefore has slightly different installation requirements. For example, consider the following introductory sentence for the "Installation and Configuration" section of a software manual. The name inside the parentheses is the name of the computer system to which these instructions apply:

(Hewlett-Packard) Insert the distribution media and run **sam**, the system administration manager, to begin installing your software . . .

(IBM) Insert the distribution media and run **smit**, the system management interface tool, to begin installing your software . . .

(Sun) Insert the distribution media and run **pkgadd** to add the specific software package to your system . . .

(Windows 95) Insert the distribution media and click the Control Panel's **Add/Remove Software** icon to begin installing your software . . .

All of these entries do the same things, but in different ways. It would be a shame to have to maintain four different documents to support these minor differences.

You can use marked sections to simplify this situation, as in the following example that shows the inclusion of the IBM installation instructions and the exclusion of the others:

```
<!-- Instructions for HP systems -->
<![ IGNORE [
Insert the distribution media and run sam, the system
administration manager, to begin installing your
software... ]]>
<!-- Instructions for IBM systems -->
<![ INCLUDE [
Insert the distribution media and run smit, the system
management interface tool, to begin installing your
software... ]]>
<!-- Instructions for Sun systems -->
<![ IGNORE [
Insert the distribution media and run pkgadd to add the
specific software package to your system... ]]>
<!-- Instructions for Windows 95 Systems -->
<![ IGNORE [
Insert the distribution media and click the Control Panel's
Add/Remove Software icon to begin installing your
software... ]]>
```

This approach is manageable only if you have a relatively small number of sections that are system specific. Localizing the sections of your documents that are system dependent can reduce the size of your documentation set and simplify its maintenance by allowing you to share the majority of the document, the larger system-independent sections.

On the other hand, if you have a large number of system-specific information throughout your documents, changing this everywhere in your documents would be a pain in the anatomy. One way to simplify this is to use parameter entities for the IGNORE/INCLUDE portions of your marked section. To do this, assume that the local declarations section of your DOCTYPE declaration contains the following entity declarations:

```
<!ENTITY % hp "IGNORE">
<!ENTITY % ibm "INCLUDE">
<!ENTITY % sun "IGNORE">
<!ENTITY % win95 "IGNORE">
```

You could then replace the conditional text above with the following:

```
<![ %hp; [
Insert the distribution media and run sam, the system
administration manager, to begin installing your
software... ]]>
<![ %ibm; [
Insert the distribution media and run smit, the system
management interface tool, to begin installing your
software... ]]>
<![ %sun; [
Insert the distribution media and run pkgadd to add the
specific software package to your system... ]]>
<![ %win95; [
Insert the distribution media and click the Control Panel's
Add/Remove Software icon to begin installing your
software... ]]>
```

Using this approach, you don't need the comments (since the entity names are fairly intuitive), but more important, you only need to change the value of the entity on one place to activate all of the appropriate portions of text throughout your document.

Chapter 7
How Does HTML Fit into All of This?

In This Chapter

▶ How SGML and HTML are related

▶ Some HTML success stories

▶ Reasons why HTML won't replace SGML

▶ The structure of an HTML 3.2 document

▶ Glimpses of the future for HTML

I've hinted at times earlier in this book that SGML is the forbidden secret in HTML's closet, and I guess it's time to finally face the music and talk about it! Yes, HTML (the HyperText Markup Language) is actually just an SGML DTD (Document Type Definition). This chapter shows how HTML has already demonstrated many of the advantages of SGML that I've been preaching throughout this book — and in the world's biggest forum, the World Wide Web!

In this chapter, I first provide some background on the World Wide Web and then discuss why the success of HTML demonstrates many of the benefits you can reap from using SGML, and then I go on to discuss some of the basics of HTML. Without trying to steal the thunder from any book dedicated to HTML, I discuss some of the various HTML DTDs that are available, the basic elements and differences between them, and conclude with some of the upcoming trends in HTML and on the Web.

I Surf, Therefore I Am

As everyone who's ever created a Web page or Web site knows, the World Wide Web (usually simply referred to as "the Web" by its friends) is both the biggest source of information and the biggest time sink ever developed in the computer industry. Doom and Quake can hardly compete with the Web, in which anyone with some basic curiosity and an Internet connection can spend endless hours searching for information or just browsing Web sites. This "activity" is usually referred to as *surfing,* probably because the Web is like an ocean of information in which you can cruise forever looking for that last big wave or Web site — the one that either answers all of your questions about life or just takes 10 minutes to download so that you can see a high-resolution picture of someone's dog catching a Frisbee.

The Web has something for you, whether you're researching a paper, looking for product information, contacting friends in remote parts of the world, or searching for free risqué pictures of the opposite sex. You might say that the key to the success of the Web is that everyone has access to it. From my point of view, however, the real key is the way in which any two people who follow the rules of HTML can share information. I can write an HTML document in Whistlestop, Texas, using whatever software I want, from my favorite text editor to a dedicated bell-and-whistles HTML editor, put it on my Web site, and people in Vladivostok can instantly view it using their favorite HTML viewer. And what makes this possible, I hear you cry? The fact that I've written my Web page using HTML, that your Web browser understands the structure of HTML, and that the browser knows how to display that document. Let's see — HTML gives us highly portable documents with a common structure, which can easily be shared between many different applications that each have their own set of rules for displaying these documents. Sounds just like SGML to me!

Why SGML and therefore HTML?

SGML was selected as the basis of the information exchanged using HTTP because it provides several distinct advantages over any other generic way of representing information:

- ✔ SGML is independent of any specific hardware or software platform. This makes it easier to provide a general specification of the language that anyone who wanted to write a browser can implement.

- ✔ SGML provides an open and expandable environment that makes it easy to extend the HTML DTD as the need or demand for new features arises.

- ✔ SGML's emphasis on structure over specific formatting makes it suitable for exchanging information other than simple text, such as binary graphics information. The emphasis on structure is necessary because the author of a Web document can't make any assumptions about an end-user's display environment — much better to send a valid, structured document, and let each possible display environment handle the document appropriately.

Ye quicke history of the World-Wide Web & ye Web jargon

There are many excellent books about the World Wide Web and HTML, and this book isn't designed to be one of them. However, if you are new to the Web, here is some quick history and a few bits of actual Web jargon so that I won't surprise you by using new terms at random.

In 1989, what has become the World Wide Web first entered the world in the mind of Tim Berners-Lee at CERN, the European Laboratory for Particle Physics near Geneva, Switzerland. The term World Wide Web wasn't actually coined until 1990, when Tim Berners-Lee and Robert Cailliau submitted an official project proposal for developing the World Wide Web. They suggested a new way of sharing information between researchers at CERN who used different types of terminals and workstations by using a client/server model. In a client/server model, servers are computers running programs that wait to be contacted by clients. The clients are other computers that can request specific information using a "language" that both the client and server understand. This special language is referred to as a *protocol* that the client and server use to communicate. In the case of the World Wide Web, this protocol is known as HTTP, which stands for the HyperText Transfer Protocol. *HyperText* is just text with embedded links to other text in it. The most common example of hypertext outside of the World Wide Web is a Microsoft Windows help file, where you navigate from one help topic to another by clicking on keywords or other highlighted text.

On the World Wide Web, the servers are Web servers and the clients are the browsers, such as Netscape, Microsoft Internet Explorer, Spyglass Mosaic, and many others, running on your machine. To connect to a Web server, you enter its address as a Uniform Resource Locator (URL) in your browser by either typing it in or clicking on a link that contains a reference to that URL. Your browser contacts the server at that URL; the server responds by sending you a page of hypertext information that your browser displays appropriately, and you're off and running!

Today, browsers can understand many other protocols such as FTP (File Transfer Protocol, used to send and receive files), POP (Post Office Protocol, used to send and receive electronic mail) and NNTP (Network News Transfer Protocol, used to send and receive Usenet News postings). A URL specifies three basic things:

```
protocol://computer-host/
pathname
```

The *protocol* is one of FTP, HTTP, NNTP, or others and specifies how to contact the server running on *computer-host*. The *pathname* is an optional part of the URL that identifies a location used by the server to locate or generate information to return to you.

Web pages consist of a primary HTML document that can contain embedded graphics in either GIF (Graphics Interchange Format) or JPEG (Joint Photographers Experts Group). Both these graphics and the HTML text itself can contain links, which jump you to other files or URLs when you click on them.

It's certainly possible to argue that the Web's use of HTML is similar to sharing documents in any markup language between applications that understand it. In this sense, HTML is just a generic markup language that caught on in a big way. For example, I can share documents in TeX or troff (introduced in Chapter 1) between any two applications that have the appropriate macro packages and understand how to produce output for some printer or screen format. Does that make an HTML document and a Web browser superior to a generic TeX document and a formatter that can display a TeX document on my screen? I'd argue yes (big surprise!).

As with documents that conform to any SGML DTD, the elements used in Web pages written in HTML stress the structure of your documents. That structure can be validated using any SGML parser. This is what enables you to use different HTML editors to create your documents. Like any SGML editing environment, the HTML editors understand the structure of your documents and enforce it. Because you have a basic adherence to a well-defined structure, Web browsers can also easily generate output in multiple formats. For example, although the primary function of Web browsers is to display a Web page on a computer screen, all browsers let you print a Web document to your local printer.

Some HTML success stories

To some extent, some of the more specific successes of HTML illustrate the impact of the Web and HTML better than any amount of theory:

- Probably the most auspicious of these is Microsoft's announcement, in 1996, that future releases of the online help system for its Windows products would migrate towards HTML, away from the more format-oriented RTF (Rich Text Format) language that was previously used to create these online help systems.
- Many large companies, such as Novell and IBM, now primarily deliver their documentation online, in HTML and other SGML formats.

The point that many companies have elected to move their documentation to HTML is interesting for several reasons. First, by using HTML to deliver documents, these companies relieve themselves of the need to ship specific software for reading their online documentation. Almost everyone has access to a Web browser, many of which are free. Previously, software companies that wanted to deliver their documentation online had to ship software that was specifically designed to display whatever internal format they used for their online documentation. Because the cost of this software was inevitably passed on to the customer, the online documentation was more expensive than it had to be.

Secondly, since HTML is truly independent of a specific computer system or software package, documents in HTML can be viewed on any computer system for which a Web browser is available. Today, this pretty much means any modern computer system.

Finally, people who want to view online documentation in HTML can use a Web browser that they're already familiar with to view the documents. Therefore, they don't need to learn how to use a new software package each time they want to view online help from another company.

Other advantages of HTML for online documentation

Using HTML provides many advantages for delivering online documentation beyond those listed in the preceding section. Pretty high up among these is that delivering online documents in HTML automatically makes the documents suitable for use from anywhere on the Web. For marketers and sales folks, this is some sort of nirvana — if your online documentation is available on a Web site, any potential customer who is curious about your software or hardware package can view its documentation from anywhere on the Web. Assuming you've done a good job in creating it, this is the motherlode of free advertising!

HTML is also a standard that is still expanding. New capabilities that provide companies with enhanced ways of presenting online information are added or proposed in each new release of the HTML DTD. Companies such as Netscape and Microsoft that have created popular Web browsers can't afford to fall behind each other in supporting new features, which means that new features are usually made available to users as quickly as possible. The speed with which HTML is growing makes it easy for companies that provide their documentation in HTML to add new features to subsequent releases of their online documentation, and everyone benefits. Later in this chapter, I summarize the basics of the most recently proposed HTML DTD and discuss some other directions that HTML may be going in the future. (See "Some Glimpses of the Future for HTML and the World Wide Web" later in this chapter.)

Why not just write documents in HTML?

If reading this chapter has gotten you excited about the possibility of delivering your documentation online using HTML, you should be. However, remember that HTML is just one specific flavor of SGML that is uniquely suited to online presentation. HTML is just one SGML DTD. It provides many advantages because it is tied to the Web, but it does not provide all of the things that you will probably want to see in your documentation. HTML was designed to be easy to use by almost everyone. Even the latest versions of the HTML DTD provide a fairly limited number of elements. Although HTML documents can be well structured, the small number of elements that they provide limits them in terms of how they share information between different groups in your company, certainly more so than documents that are written in many other SGML DTDs.

A key aspect of HTML is that it is relatively easy to create HTML documents from documents that are written using other SGML DTDs. I discuss this process in Chapters 12 and 21, but now is a good time to plant the seed of this notion. If you write your documents in a more complex DTD that provides you with the power to manage and identify the types of information that your company uses, you can always map the elements used in your more complex SGML documents to the simpler set provided by HTML. For example, suppose you have different types of sections in your SGML documents that identify these sections as procedural, background, or reference information. You need this distinction to display the documents differently on the printed page or to allow you to reuse this information in different documents. However, this distinction is probably not important to you if you are simply interested in making this information available on the Web. In HTML, different levels of sections are identified by using a specific heading level — you can simply map all of these different sections in your documents to the same HTML heading level.

The dark side of HTML applications

HTML applications such as popular Web browsers, including Cello, Lynx, Microsoft's Internet Explorer, Mosaic, and Netscape, provide a Charles Dickens perspective on SGML — "*It was the best of times, it was the worst of times. . . .*" On the positive side, writing documents in HTML helps get people used to the idea of writing documents that conform to a specific structure, even if it is fairly simple. On the other hand, HTML applications have to be more forgiving than you would expect or want to see in SGML applications designed to be used by documentation or information professionals.

HTML applications enforce the general rules of the version of HTML that they support, but they are usually pretty forgiving regarding many violations of its SGML syntax, HTML structure. After all, the primary goal of the Web and HTML is to make it easy to share information. Making it easy to share information implies that writing an HTML document should be easy. For this reason, HTML applications are usually pretty forgiving about minor violations of HTML syntax, striking a comfortable balance between enforcing rules that have to be enforced and forgiving violations that aren't really fatal. The Web wouldn't be as popular as it has become if everyone had to be an HTML wizard before starting.

For example, HTML browsers simply ignore elements that they don't recognize — this was a part of the early HTML specification. On the other hand, a true SGML application with a strict validating parser would certainly complain and probably wouldn't allow you to use these elements in the first place. The forgiving nature of most HTML browsers pays off when people actually begin using HTML. Although many HTML editors make it easy for you to create HTML, many people simply create their HTML documents using a text editor and verify them by looking at them in a Web browser to "see what happens." What would you prefer to see the first time you try to display an HTML document in a Web browser — something on the screen that indicates where something went wrong, or a pop-up message that says "Syntax error in line 17"? The former? I thought so.

Another reason that HTML applications such as browsers are more forgiving than pure SGML applications is that they actually contain the DTD that they expect to receive documents in — they don't load different DTDs. SGML applications need to be more flexible because they are designed to enable you to work with documents that use many different DTDs. However, on the Web, HTML is the *lingua franca*. HTML is hard-wired into the browser, so it makes sense for authors who use HTML to be more forgiving about new features that are provided by a later version of HTML.

HTML also provides a certain set of basic formatting elements that you probably wouldn't see in SGML DTDs, whose goal is to strictly identify the structure and content of your documents. HTML contains many elements for specific font changes, such as bold, italic, and typewriter fonts. These elements are specifically oriented toward the presentation of your HTML documents and don't really tell you anything about the kind of information that is contained in these elements. Why? Probably because most HTML users are not documentation professionals; they are just people who want to get some information out on the Web.

One last point is that the different companies that provide commercial browsers want to make their browsers more powerful than the other guys', so they frequently create new elements that aren't actually present in the HTML specification. These let people do more interesting things in HTML documents that are designed for their specific browser, but basically breaks the SGML model, because these features are proprietary and are not present in the official HTML DTD. Proprietary features that are implemented and supported in a particular browser break both the DTD-centric and software-independent promises of SGML.

Your browser wears army boots

Many people are very polarized about the browsers they use and the features they provide. However, outside the Netscape and Internet Explorer browser enclaves lurks another camp of highly polarized browser aficionados — these are the people who love Lynx, the only text-oriented browser that I've ever seen. Netscape and Internet Explorer are highly graphical browsers that require that a window system of some sort (such as MacOS, Microsoft Windows, or the X Window System) be running. Netscape and Internet Explorer are largely oriented toward displaying graphics, animations, movies, virtual reality, sounds, and so on. They each support other applications, produced by third parties, that are designed to extend their capabilities and which integrate themselves tightly with the browser. Lynx ignores all these aspects of the Web because it is designed to operate on a terminal, in text mode — no graphics, no plug-ins, nothing but a pure stream of ASCII data slicing in hot off the Web.

Depending on how you look at it, Lynx is either a lean, mean browsing machine or a throwback designed for use by apes who have just learned to walk upright. If you want fast Web access, Lynx is a fine browser because you never have to wait for huge images to download or put up with silly rotating GIFs. That makes perfect sense to me, especially after waiting a few minutes for a truly trashy Web page to download all its useless bells and whistles. On the other hand, some people use Lynx to show their disdain for the whizzy features of modern computers, such as graphics, sound, and the other things that have moved the realm of the computer from the macho machine room into the family room. I find this somewhat sad and wish that someone would develop a browser for these folks that uses punched cards or paper tape.

The Structure of an HTML 3.2 Document

For those of you who are already Web wizards, this section may not give you anything more than a convenient reference for HTML DTDs. Unlike many HTML spiels, this section focuses on those aspects of an HTML document that are related to providing information about the document itself, not on the elements used in the body of a document. Many excellent books (such as *HTML For Dummies,* from IDG Books Worldwide, Inc.) provide this sort of information.

This section focuses on HTML 3.2, which is the latest and greatest standard proposed by the World Wide Web Consortium (W3C) at the time that I write this.

The basic structure of an HTML 3.2 document is the following:

```
1  <!DOCTYPE HTML PUBLIC "-//W3C//DTD HTML 3.2 Final//EN">
2  <HTML>
3  <HEAD>
4  <TITLE>Document Title</TITLE>
5  optional-document-meta-information
6  </HEAD>
7  <BODY>
8  document-content
9  </BODY>
10 </HTML>
```

Note: I've added the numbers at the left of this example to make it easy to refer to specific lines — they should not actually appear in your HTML documents!

Line 1 of this HTML 3.2 document template should tip you off that this is actually an SGML document because it's the same DOCTYPE statement that I discuss in Chapter 4. In this case, this statement indicates that this document conforms to the HTML document type whose location you can find using the PUBLIC document identifier "-//W3C//DTD HTML 3.2 Final// EN". The document identifier also tells you that

✔ This document type is an informal document identifier (-//) owned by W3C. An informal identifier is one that isn't owned by the International Standards Organization (ISO).

✔ It is actually a DTD.

✔ The document conforms to the final HTML 3.2 specification (HTML 3.2 Final).

✔ The terminology used in the DTD is in English (EN), regardless of the language used in this HTML document.

Line 2 is the opening tag for the <HTML> element, which is closed by the ending </HTML> tag in line 10. This element tells servers and browsers that this is an HTML document.

The next two sections discuss the content of the HEAD (lines 3–6) and BODY (lines 7–9) of this HTML 3.2 document template.

Web crawlers, spiders, and things that go search in the night

One of the things that makes the Web interesting and usable are the number of sites that provide information about the contents of the Web itself. Well-known sites such as Yahoo! (http://www.yahoo.com), Lycos (http://www.lycos.com), and AltaVista (http://www.altavista.digital.com) specialize in providing information about other sites on the net. You can connect to these sites and search their databases to find Web sites that contain the information you're looking for. These sites all do this by providing you with a *search engine*, which is just an application that accepts keywords that you enter and finds sites that it can match with those keywords.

To collect information about the content of other sites on the Web, Web sites that provide search engines typically use programs that automatically surf the Web, collecting information about sites that they find and sending that information back to the Web site from which they started. Because these applications traverse the Web step by step, following links from one site to another, they are often referred to as *Web crawlers*, *Web spiders*, or *Web robots*.

Why talk about this here? Because the text that you put in the <HEAD> element in your HTML documents is the information that these applications use to categorize and index your web pages. By understanding the elements that you can put in the <HEAD> element in your HTML documents, you can make it easier for others to find your web pages, as explained in the following section.

The <HEAD> *of an HTML 3.2 document*

The elements between the <HEAD> (line 3) and </HEAD> (line 6) tags in an HTML document provide various types of meta-data about your document. As explained earlier in this book, meta-data is information about information — in this case, information about your document. The browser in which this document is displayed and Web applications such as Web crawlers use this information to obtain information about your Web pages and associated HTML documents. The idea of providing meta-information about your documents is pure SGML. It works very well on the Web because it gives you the opportunity to share some information about the intent of your document with people or applications that view your document.

The information between the <TITLE> and </TITLE> tags is typically displayed by a browser as a heading for the window (most browsers) or screen (Lynx) in which the Web page appears.

Although the ⟨TITLE⟩ element is fairly vanilla, several optional elements in the ⟨HEAD⟩ portion of your HTML documents can provide various types of meta-information about your Web documents. Though there are others, I'll just focus on some of my favorites, since information about information is one of my (and SGML's) favorite things. For complete information about all of the elements that can appear in the ⟨HEAD⟩ element of an HTML 3.2 document, see your favorite book about HTML, or see the DTD itself (http://www.w3.org/pub/WWW/MarkUp/Wilbur/HTML32.dtd). Keep in mind the only element that's guaranteed to be used from the ⟨HEAD⟩ of an HTML document is ⟨TITLE⟩ — however, you can't lose by providing meta-information that can and will be used by some browsers and Web applications.

One thing to remember about the meta-data that you can provide within the ⟨HEAD⟩ element of an HTML document is that the attribute values that you specify for many of these elements are SGML CDATA. They are simply character data with certain recommended values, around which certain conventions have been adopted on the Web.

Here are my favorite elements used to provide meta-information in the ⟨HEAD⟩ element of an HTML document:

⟨BASE⟩

You use the ⟨BASE⟩ element to identify the actual location of the document. Your browser always knows the location from which it retrieved the document, but this may not be the actual home location of the document (such as when a Web page is *mirrored on* — or copied to — multiple Web servers). When you use the ⟨BASE⟩ element, you ensure that a browser can always follow relative links in your Web page to find the most recent relative documents (which may not have been mirrored as recently as a primary page). The syntax of the ⟨BASE⟩ element is always

```
<BASE HREF="primary-URL">
```

Note that the ⟨BASE⟩ element is an EMPTY SGML element (as discussed in Chapter 4), which means that there is no corresponding closing tag for the initial ⟨BASE⟩ tag.

⟨LINK⟩

⟨LINK⟩ is another very useful element that lets you specify relationships between this document and other documents. Like the ⟨BASE⟩ element, the ⟨LINK⟩ element is an EMPTY SGML element (as discussed in Chapter 4).

```
<LINK REL="string" TYPE="string" HREF="string">
<LINK REV="string" HREF="string">
```

The REL attribute specifies some relationship between the current document and another document. The REV attribute specifies a reverse relationship between the current document and another. As mentioned before, the values for the attributes are SGML CDATA (character data), so you're actually relying on a set of conventions that define how browsers handle specific words in the <LINK> element's REV and REL attributes. Sound confusing? Here are a few examples.

```
<LINK REV="made" HREF="mailto:wvh@dev-null.com">
```

Many browsers use this keyword/value pair to provide a quick way for you to send mail to the author of the Web page.

```
<LINK REL="previous" HREF="parent.html">
```

This use of the REL attribute identifies the HTML file "parent.html" as the "previous" document in a browsable sequence of HTML documents.

```
<LINK REL="next" HREF="child.html">
```

This use of the REL attribute identifies HTML file "child.html" as the "next" document in a browsable sequence of HTML documents.

The keywords specified in the <LINK> tag's REL attribute are often used to construct toolbars that help you navigate through a set of related Web pages. The keywords home, next, previous, and up provide navigational relationships between various Web pages, helping you establish a sequence between these Web pages and identifying the main page for the set (home) as well as the parent of a current series of Web pages (up). Other established keywords for the REL attribute, such as copyright, help, glossary, and index are used to give the URL for different types of centralized information about the set of pages.

```
<LINK REL="stylesheet" TYPE=text/css" HREF="http://www.dev-
null.com/whizzystyle.html">
```

This use of the REL attribute identifies an HTML file at the URL www.dev-null.com/whizzystyle.html as a style sheet of the MIME (Multi-Media Internet Mail Extensions) type "text/css". MIME is a set of formats used by Internet applications to identify different types of files and how to handle them. (For more information on style sheets and CSS in particular, see "Glimpses of the Future for HTML and the World Wide Web" later in this chapter.)

‹META›

‹META› is an extremely cool element that can be very useful in your documents. The ‹META› element is usually used to declare sets of variable and value pairs. Like the ‹BASE› and ‹LINK› elements, the ‹META› element is an EMPTY SGML element (as discussed in Chapter 4).The values for the attributes of the ‹META› element are SGML CDATA (character data), so you're actually relying on a set of conventions that define how browsers handle specific words in the ‹META› element's, HTTP-EQUIV, NAME, and CONTENT attributes. Sounds confusing? Here are a few examples:

```
<META HTTP-EQUIV="expires" CONTENT="17 May 1997">
```

If a browser loads this Web page after May 17, 1997 (in this case) and happens to have a copy of the page in its cache, the browser discards the cached copy of the page and retrieves a new copy of the page from the Web server. People often use this pair on pages that they update frequently to ensure that browsers will retrieve a new copy whenever the page has been updated.

```
<META HTTP-EQUIV="refresh" CONTENT="15,http://
www.dev-null.com">
```

The browser reloads the document from http://www.dev-null.com every 15 seconds. Developers often use this pair in Web pages that are frequently updated, such as Web pages that continually display updated statistical or graphical information. This feature may not be supported by all browsers.

```
<META NAME="author" CONTENT="Bill von Hagen">
```

This gives the name of the author of the Web document.

```
<META NAME="description" CONTENT="A cool page for the
amateur computer collector">
```

Search engines display a description of your Web page when referring to your page. By default, search engines display the first few lines of the body of your Web page as their description of your page. If a search engine encounters a ‹META› element whose NAME attribute has the value "description," the value of the CONTENT attribute will be displayed as the description for your web page. This lets you be clever in what they display as a summary of your page. Again, this is just a widely used convention — there are no guarantees that every search engine will "do the right thing."

```
<META NAME="keywords" CONTENT="PERQ, Xerox Alto">
```

This provides keywords that some search engines add to the list of keywords that Web crawlers automatically extract from your Web pages. If a search engine encounters a ⟨META⟩ element whose NAME attribute has the value "description," the value of the CONTENT attribute will be added to the list of keywords that will match your site. Use this pair if you know specific keywords that you want to associate with your Web page but that may not actually appear in the text of your Web page.

⟨STYLE⟩

⟨STYLE⟩, unlike the other elements that specify meta-information in the ⟨HEAD⟩ of an HTML document, requires both a starting tag (⟨STYLE⟩) and an ending tag (⟨/STYLE⟩). You provide different style specifications as sets of selectors (which define the element that this style information is associated with) and any number of property/value pairs, separated by semicolon and enclosed in curly brackets. In addition, you can identify external style sheets by their URLs using the @import statement. In general, a ⟨STYLE⟩ element looks something like this:

```
<STYLE TYPE="text/css">
<!-
@import url(http://gethip.com/styles/generic.css);
H3 {font-weight: bold ; font-size: large}
P  {color:red}
->
   </STYLE>
```

This produces third-level headings that use a large, bold font, and paragraphs displayed in red. Note that, in this example, the style declarations are embedded in SGML comments — this is because some older browsers don't handle the ⟨STYLE⟩ element well and may therefore display its contents if they are not enclosed in SGML comment delimiters. Luckily, this doesn't prevent style-conscious browsers from using the contents of a ⟨STYLE⟩ element. At some point, it shouldn't be necessary to use the SGML comments, because the idea of software that reads something which is enclosed within comments is a uniquely bad idea!

The ⟨STYLE⟩ element isn't widely used at the moment, but it will be soon. See "Cascading Style Sheets" later in this chapter for more information on the ⟨STYLE⟩ element.

The <BODY> of an HTML 3.2 document

Many books explain how to create exciting, dynamic, and visually attractive Web pages. Any of these can tell you more about the content of the body of an HTML document than you'd probably be willing to read through here. From an SGML perspective, I find the body of an HTML document to be less interesting than the meta-information about the document that you can supply in the <HEAD> portion of the document.

HTML 3.2 is designed to actually codify many of the HTML elements that have already been in common use for quite a while. Previous official versions of HTML were HTML 2.0 and the legendary but nonexistent HTML 3.0. HTML 3.0 never actually became official because various browser vendors were too busy extending HTML to bother to agree on what HTML 3.0 consisted of. These are the most important things that HTML 3.2 makes official regarding the content of the body of an HTML document:

- ✔ Improved support for nicely formatted tables.

- ✔ Official support for Java applications using the <APPLET> element. This has been around for a while, but now it's official.

- ✔ Official support for logical divisions within an HTML document using the <DIV> element.

As always, the ultimate reference for HTML 3.2 is the HTML 3.2 DTD, available at http://www.w3.org, though only SGML-literate folks such as ourselves can probably easily use the information from this site. For an example that uses HTML 3.2 constructs in the body of actual HTML documents, see your favorite off-the-shelf HTML 3.2 reference. I certainly own several, as examples always help clarify things for me. Once again, this book isn't intended to cut into any HTML author's turf.

Some Glimpses of the Future for HTML and the World Wide Web

The World Wide Web is unique in the history of computing, not only as a global information pool that much of the Web has access to, but also because it provides a unique fusion of fun and functionality. Creating attractive and usable Web pages has become a business for many people because it provides a unique way to combine artistic ability with information presentation. In this sense, the Web and the creation of Web documents are like today's version of concepts such as printed books (Gutenberg) or desktop publishing.

One aspect of HTML and its use on the Web that limits this creativity to some extent is the fact that HTML applications currently have to contain an intrinsic knowledge of how to format the various elements in a certain HTML DTD. In other words, HTML applications such as browsers have to have built-in information about how to format and display a specific set of HTML elements. This is somewhat constraining for people that create Web pages, because they have to limit themselves to a "lowest-common-denominator" set of HTML elements that they can be sure will be understood by all Web browsers, or they have to face the fact that people using certain browsers won't be able to see their Web pages in all their true glory.

Most of the work that is currently going on in HTML-land is related to these basic subjects:

- ✔ Providing better ways of specifying the formatting and presentation of HTML documents

- ✔ Providing ways for HTML applications to explicitly contain or link to formatting information

- ✔ Providing ways for HTML applications to dynamically load different DTDs and associated formatting information (at which point your HTML application actually becomes an SGML application, and now provides support for other DTDs than the HTML DTD!)

If you look at most nicely formatted (or simply complex) Web pages today, you'll see that they're composed of either one or more image maps or some fairly hairy tables. You use image maps to move graphics onto the Web and then define the links and jumps associated with clicking on different parts of these images. Because image maps are pure graphics, they aren't constrained by the fairly simple layout capabilities provided by HTML. On the other hand, images can be very slow to download over the Internet, which might mean that people will punt a Web site before they ever see just how nice it is. You can also use tables to create a layout on a Web page. You define a table in your HTML documents and then populate some cells with images, others with text, and you can achieve a nice-looking page without too much effort.

The previous list identifies two different approaches to this problem. The first, providing better ways of specifying the formatting of existing HTML elements, is a fine solution for improving the appearance of existing Web sites — it provides a way for graphics artists and other artistic Web-site designers to improve the appearance of things as they stand today. The second is a better long-term solution, providing a way to free HTML applications such as browsers from the shackles of a specific HTML DTD or even from any HTML DTD. This is a step toward pure SGML on the Web!

Softquad's Panorama browser already supports SGML — hopefully, the tip of a trend iceberg! The current and previous generations of HTML browsers support a DTD with a small number of elements to increase performance. I can see that SGML is the way to go in the documentation industry, but I can't predict the classes of software enhancements that may emerge to eliminate performance problems such as this. But someone will. . . .

This section summarizes some of the ongoing projects that will provide better-looking HTML documents in the future. As all of these efforts are currently in progress, it's hard to say how any of them will turn out or which (if any) will emerge as the "one true solution" for formatting and presentation on the Web. Several of these projects may succeed because these projects are not incompatible. The next generation of browsers will just have to be a bit smarter in order to deal with multiple approaches to improved formatting.

Cascading Style Sheets (CSS)

Cascading Style Sheets are a generic way of specifying colors, fonts, spacing, and other aspects of page layout for HTML documents. The W3C recommended the first standard version of CSS, called CSS1, in December of 1996.

CSS contain sets of *selectors* (which identify the element that the style information is associated with) and any number of semicolons that separate property/value pairs, enclosed in parentheses. Here is an example of a trivial CSS:

```
H3 {font-weight: bold ; font-size: large}
P  {color:red}
```

This produces third-level headings that use a large, bold font, and paragraphs displayed in red. (This example was selected to be illustrative, not aesthetic!)

You can link CSS into HTML documents using the <LINK> element, embed them into HTML documents using the <STYLE> element, or import them into HTML documents using the <STYLE> element's @import statement. Both of these elements are found in the <HEAD> portion of an HTML document (see "The <HEAD> of an HTML 3.2 document," earlier in this chapter).

Some HTML browsers and authoring tools (see the next section) already support CSS, but they are somewhat limited in that they can define only style attributes of elements that are already known to an HTML application. This fact makes CSS a great solution for upcoming releases of the current generation of HTML applications. Presumably, HTML applications that support dynamically loaded DTDs also can take advantage of CSS definitions for the elements used in those DTDs.

Tools that support CSS

Netscape 4.0 (only available as a pre-release as I write this) supports CSS1, and Microsoft's Internet Explorer 3.0 supports a subset of CSS1. Various non-commercial and research browsers, such as the Arena browser available from the W3C, also provide support for different subsets of CSS1.

Several HTML authoring tools, such as Adobe's HoTaMaLe (an add-in for FrameMaker) and SoftQuad's HoTMetaL have announced support for CSS. The W3C's Amaya Web client supports CSS and HTML 3.2.

Document Style Semantics and Specification Language (DSSSL)

DSSSL is a language, based on the Scheme programming language, that enables you to associate specific formatting and processing instructions with the elements in any SGML DTD. Because it is not tied to any specific SGML DTD, DSSSL provides a rich and easily extended mechanism for defining how documents that conform to different SGML DTDs are formatted. One of the more common applications for DSSSL at the moment is transforming SGML documents into HTML.

DSSSL actually consists of three basic components:

- ✔ A transformation language that defines how to convert SGML documents that conform to one DTD into SGML documents that conform to another DTD

- ✔ A query language, the Standard Document Query Language (SDQL), that lets you extract or identify specific portions of an SGML document

- ✔ A style language that enables you to associate style information with the elements in a document associated with any SGML DTD

DSSSL applications that perform transformation, queries, and style mapping are usually referred to as DSSSL processors.

Several public-domain DSSSL processors are already available. Probably the best-known freely available DSSSL processor is Jade, by James Clark, who has authored many excellent SGML tools and was a major contributor to the DSSSL standard. Jade lets you transform SGML documents into output formats such as HTML, RTF, and TeX, and is available at http://www.jclark.com.

Because DSSSL provides a DTD-independent method of transforming SGML documents into various output formats, DSSSL is planned as a replacement for other generic ways of describing SGML document formatting, not just as a way of transforming SGML documents into HTML. For a comparison of the DSSSL and FOSI approaches to describing the formatting of an SGML document, see Chapter 9. You can obtain the current DSSSL standard in Postscript, SGML, or Adobe PDF formats from `ftp://ftp.ornl.gov/pub/sgml/WG8/DSSSL`.

Extensible Markup Language (XML)

The Extensible Markup Language is a simple dialect of SGML (a "profile" or "restricted form" of SGML, in SGML terms) that is designed for use over the Internet. XML is designed to free Web documents from the limitations imposed by HTML by providing Web documents with a way of including, or linking to, information about their structure. XML omits some potentially troublesome aspects of SGML, such as tag minimization and omission, to guarantee that XML documents are easily interpreted by applications and by humans. XML itself does not provide information about how Web documents are to be formatted but provides a flexible way of defining the structure of a Web document whose formatting can be described by a CSS style sheet or in DSSSL.

XML introduces the idea of a *well-formed* document to augment the SGML idea of a *valid document*. A valid SGML document is one that can be parsed correctly by an SGML parser, given the appropriate SGML declarations. Since XML prohibits aspects of SGML such as tag minimization and omission, none of the markup in an XML document has to be inferred from context. A well-formed XML document is one in which elements are cleanly nested, meaning that the opening and closing tags for each element occur within the context of some other element. The only exceptions to this are the opening and closing tags for the document itself. An example of a well-formed XML document is the following:

```
<?XML VERSION="1.0"?>
<SAMPLE>
<TITLE>This is a Sample</TITLE>
<PAR>Of course, this could be much more complex.</PAR>
</SAMPLE>
```

The first line of this document identifies it as an XML document and specifies the version of XML that it conforms to. This document is well formed because it is cleanly nested but is not valid because it doesn't provide information about the content of the `<SAMPLE>`, `<TITLE>`, and `<PAR>` elements.

Like any SGML document, a *valid* XML document must contain a DOCTYPE declaration that specifies the DTD to which the document conforms. The element definitions for the document type can either be declared locally or through a SYSTEM or PUBLIC reference. The following example shows a local DOCTYPE declaration:

```
<?XML VERSION="1.0"?>
<!DOCTYPE Sample [
<!ELEMENT Sample (title, par+)>
<!ELEMENT title (#PCDATA)>
<!ELEMENT par (#PCDATA)>
]>
<SAMPLE>
<TITLE>This is a Sample</TITLE>
<PAR>Of course, this could be much more complex.</PAR>
</SAMPLE>
```

Element declarations in XML don't require information about tag omission and minimization, because these features are illegal in XML. An equivalent DOCTYPE statement using a SYSTEM declaration is

```
<?XML VERSION="1.0"?>
<!DOCTYPE Sample SYSTEM "http://www.gethip.com/samples
sample.dtd">
<SAMPLE>
<TITLE>This is a Sample</TITLE>
<PAR>Of course, this could be much more complex.</PAR>
</SAMPLE>
```

Note that the value of the SYSTEM identifier is a URL — exactly the sort of thing you'd expect to find in a form of SGML designed for use on the Internet!

The XML document identifier (the first line of these examples) can contain an optional attribute, known as an RMD (Required Markup Declaration) keyword. This keyword specifies whether an application that reads this XML document must read the DTD or any internal DTD information in order to handle the XML document correctly. Possible values for the RMD attribute are ALL, INTERNAL, and NONE. The value ALL means that the application must read the DTD and any internal DTD subset in order to process the document correctly. The value INTERNAL means that the application must only read the internal subset of the DTD provided in the document (if any) in order to process the document correctly. The value NONE means that the application can process the document correctly without reading any part of the DTD.

Because XML enables Web documents to use arbitrary DTDs, XML is probably the forerunner for the markup language that will be used on the Web in the future. Microsoft has even hinted that future versions of Windows online help may be in XML rather than HTML, as it had previously announced.

XML is being proposed as a standard by the World Wide Web Consortium (W3C). You can find a copy of the current XML standard at `http://www.w3.org/pub/WWW`.

Chapter 8

So Where Do I Get a Document Type Definition?

*T*he previous chapters explain the structure and contents of an SGML Document Type Definition (DTD) and hopefully show you that, if you've ever created a HTML document for the World Wide Web, you probably already know more about SGML than you thought you did.

Now that I've piqued your curiosity about SGML DTDs and shown you how to create a small one in Chapter 4, you may be wondering whether you have to create one yourself or, at least, where you can get one. As I mention earlier in the book, many parts of the documentation industry in which SGML is used already have their own DTDs. These DTDs, many of which took years to develop, provide a specific structure for the documents for that industry, providing the sections, components, features, and tags required to guarantee that documents provide all of the requirements for that field. Various portions of the government, such as the Army, Navy, and the Internal Revenue Service, use DTDs. Many of these DTDs are freely available over the Internet so that contractors working for these agencies can easily obtain and use them.

Other DTDs that are freely available are general-purpose DTDs that have been created as a part of various research efforts, some educational and some as part of the SGML industry itself. As you can see in Part IV of this book, creating a DTD isn't for everyone. Unless you have specific require-ments not met by the freely available DTDs or those DTDs don't fit your documentation model, you have no real reason to create your own DTD. In most cases, you still have to develop a FOSI for these DTDs (or whatever formatting definition your SGML uses), but more about that in Chapter 9!

This chapter discusses some of the more popular DTDs that are available on the Internet, discusses the types of documents that they were designed to address, and provides pointers to where you can get these DTDs so that you can evaluate them for yourself. This chapter is really just the tip of the iceberg regarding the many DTDs that have been created and are available for your evaluation and use!

The Greatest Sites on the Web!

As we all know, the Web provides a huge pool of information on just about anything. Since HTML is just a simple SGML DTD and is the underlying markup language for the Web, it would be surprising if the Web doesn't include a lot of information about SGML. And it does!

The Web provides many excellent starting points for people who are interested in SGML. This section discusses some of my favorites, provides some background information that tells how they're supported and who created them, and discusses some of the types of information that you're likely to find there — including, of course, DTDs!

Robin Cover's SGML Web page

This site (`http://www.sil.org/sgml/sgml.html`) is probably the ultimate Web site for finding out anything you want to know about SGML. The primary location of this site is on the Web server maintained by the Summer Institute of Linguistics, located at the International Linguistics Institute in Dallas, Texas. This site is partially sponsored by SoftQuad, Inc., a well-known vendor of SGML software and services.

The goal of the Summer Institute of Linguistics (SIL) is to "study minority languages and cultures throughout the world" (as it says on its home page). On the SIL home page (`http://www.sil.org`), the link for the SGML page is located in the "Academic Resources" section, under "Document Processing and Publishing." You have to admit that it's amusing to find a central source for information about SGML on a site dedicated to the study of "minority languages and cultures" — I'd like to think that this isn't some subtle commentary on the popularity of SGML! Maybe we can all help change that someday.

After you open the link for this page, you should bookmark it or add it to your list of favorites, depending on the Web browser you use. This page is a smorgasbord of information about SGML! Without listing them all, here are some of the primary topics on this page as I write this chapter:

✔ SGML archive sites: WWW, GOPHER, FTP

✔ SGML bibliography

✔ SGML consortia, users' groups, and SIGs

✔ SGML conferences, seminars, tutorials, workshops

✔ SGML discussion groups and mailing lists

✔ Public SGML software

✔ Commercial SGML software

✔ SGML: general projects and applications

✔ Academic projects and applications

✔ Government and industry applications

As you can see from this list, this Web site provides pointers to online information about most of what's going on with SGML — not just in the documentation industry, but also in the commercial, government, and academic sectors. You can think of this site as one-stop-shopping for SGML fans! It provides lists of many locations on the Internet where you can find other information about SGML, and it also provides lists and reviews of most of the paper resources, such as reference texts and publications, that are available about SGML. If you're looking for general information about SGML software, this site provides a link to Steve Pepper's Whirlwind Guide to SGML Tools and Vendors.

Web-maniacs should take one thing into consideration before surfing to this site — its primary focus is on providing a quickly accessed source of centralized information about SGML. As such, it is primarily a text-oriented site in which the only real graphics you find are in some of the sites that are pointed to from this site. This fact certainly never bothers me, but anyone expecting splashy graphics and animated screenshots of SGML software packages will be disappointed.

The SGML University (SGMLU)

Just because Robin Cover's site provides such an excellent collection of pointers to SGML resources on the Internet doesn't mean that there are no other sites worth visiting. Another of my favorites is the SGML University Web site (`http://www.sgmlu.com`). Unlike Robin Cover's site, the SGML University Web site is sponsored by a commercial entity (the SGML University itself), which is an educational institution that provides actual training in SGML. This site discusses everything from theory to implementation. The SGML University is an accredited academic institution whose courses count as Continuing Education Units (CEUs), which are important in various industries where continuing education is a requirement. The SGML University can perform training at its site or yours, and it seems to be a well-organized firm that can help you explore general concepts and specific aspects of SGML.

One of the more interesting aspects of this Web site is the job postings (`http://www.sgmlu.com/job.htm`). While there isn't always a plethora of job postings, it's always interesting to see that (1) there *are* job postings there and that (2) interest in SGML seems to be on the rise, at least enough to merit the existence of SGMLU. (Wow, would I like to get one of its sweatshirts! I wonder how good its football team is.)

The most interesting portion of the SGMLU Web site for me is its reference page (`http://www.sgmlu/refintro.htm`). This page contains pointers to three different classes of sites:

✔ **Software.** You can find links to a good amount of SGML software that's available on the Internet. This software includes SGML browsers, conversion tools, DTD viewers, editors, parsers, several SGML declarations (discussed in Chapter 4), and some SGML documents you can use to test your SGML applications. One very interesting thing available from this page is a complete set of the entities used in most DTDs. If your SGML software package doesn't already come with these, SGMLU provides a convenient location to get these. A link on this page provides access to all of the DTDs discussed later in this chapter.

✔ **Library.** This page provides a nice collection of FAQs (Frequently Asked Question files), introductions to SGML, and papers about SGML. It provides a centralized reference to papers and other information about SGML-related topics, such as DSSSL and HyTime, and various HTML specifications such as the complete CALS (Continuous Acquisition and Lifecycle Support) specification. (More about CALS later in this chapter!) Like Robin Cover's Web site, the SGMLU Library site also has a link to Steve Pepper's Whirlwind Guide to SGML Tools and Vendors.

✔ **Publications.** SGMLU has its own small press that publishes various SGML-related books and other publications.

Getting a DTD on the Web

This section discusses some of the more common or popular DTDs that are available on the Web. I provide some insight into what they were designed for, provide details on their sizes, and (where appropriate) highlight some of the commonly available SGML software that provides some support for these DTDs. For more detailed information on SGML software, see Chapter 11.

The DocBook DTD

The DocBook DTD is one of the best maintained and most thoroughly researched DTDs that is freely available. Targeted at producing documentation for computer software, the DocBook DTD was originally developed by HAL Computer Systems and O'Reilly and Associates (publishers of the now-legendary series of UNIX reference texts). The DocBook DTD is now maintained by a group of representatives (sponsors) from different software companies that are interested in SGML as a documentation standard. This group is called the Davenport Group, and it contains members from companies such a O'Reilly and Associates, Hewlett-Packard, Sun Microsystems, ArborText, and DEC.

The DocBook DTD is available from the Davenport Group's Web site (`http://www.ora.com/davenport`). If you are interested in participating in or merely observing discussions, you can subscribe to the Davenport Group mailing list by sending e-mail to `listproc@online.ora.com` from any computer account from which you can receive Internet mail. The body of your e-mail message should contain

> subscribe davenport yourname, yourcompany

The focus of the DocBook DTD is software and technical documentation. The DocBook is a very large and complete DTD, so large in fact that many companies use the DocBook DTD more as a starting point than an actual solution — this use is even suggested in the DTD itself. For example, the highest-level element in the DocBook DTD is a set of documents. If you use the DocBook DTD only to create single documents that you do not want to cross-index or cross-reference, you can easily strip out the higher-level elements and use only that subset that you want to use. Similarly, the DocBook DTD contains many lower-level elements that you can also remove from the DTD if your goal is to use an industry-standard DTD but also maintain a fairly small working set of entities or elements. Actually, the DocBook DTD is designed in a highly modular fashion to facilitate using or reusing it in any way. This makes it somewhat hard to read, but you can't have everything!

I discuss how you can use a standard DTD and why you may want to either extend or remove elements from one in Chapter 15. In general, starting with a standard DTD is a great way to get started with SGML and have confidence that you can exchange documents with other companies or reuse the information in other ways. There are obviously maintenance costs associated with segmenting an existing DTD — I address these costs in Chapter 15.

Most software packages that support SGML, such as ArborText Adept, Corel WordPerfect, and Frame+SGML, come with some built-in support for the DocBook DTD. Corel WordPerfect comes with the DocBook 2.4 and 3.0 DTDs, and ArborText Adept and Frame+SGML support DocBook 2.4.1 out of the box.

The IBM IDDOC DTD

IBM's IDDOC DTD is part of IBM's effort to standardize the markup and presentation of the thousands of documents that it produces. You shouldn't be surprised that the company that invented GML and SGML would adopt an SGML solution for its documentation. For the last decade or so, IBM has used an internal GML tool called *BookMaster* to produce its documentation. Unfortunately, this tool only runs on IBM's mainframe operating systems. IBM's move to PCs and UNIX (AIX) workstations, however, has helped motivate it to adopt a more modern solution, which is a set of SGML-related tools that run under OS/2 and AIX. These tools revolve around the IBM IDDOC DTD, which is a huge but tremendously robust DTD. Like the DocBook DTD, most of us will never need to use more than a subset of this DTD. If you need a feature, however, chances are (as the commercials say!) "It's in there!"

The IBM IDDOC DTD is undergoing continual revision. It wasn't really designed for use outside of IBM, but you can get copies of a version of this DTD and its supporting documentation via anonymous file transfer from `ftp://ftp.raleigh.ibm.com/pub/guidesibmiddoc/`. (Use an ftp application to connect to `ftp.raleigh.ibm.com`, log in as the user "anonymous" with your e-mail address as your password, and change the directory to `pub/guides/ibmiddoc`.) Because of its complexity and attention to detail, this DTD and its documentation are an excellent reference even if you are creating your own DTD, especially if you intend to use your DTD to produce software or scientific documentation. A copy of the IBM IDDOC DTD is also available from the SGMLU web site, discussed earlier in this chapter.

The reference manual for this DTD is over 1000 pages long! Don't print it on a whim!

HTML DTDs

As discussed (perhaps to death) in the previous chapter, HTML is indeed just an SGML DTD with a fairly limited set of elements. If you already use SGML software and want to guarantee that your HTML documents fully conform to a specific HTML DTD, you can simply obtain an HTML DTD, load it into your SGML software package, and create your HTML documents in the same software you use for your other SGML documents.

As also discussed in the previous chapter, there have actually been several different HTML DTDs. The most important ones for the majority of the Web browsers and other software that are commonly used on the Internet are the HTML 2.0 and HTML 3.2 DTDs. You can get the HTML 2.0 DTD from `http://www.w3.org/pub/WWW/MarkUp/html-spec` and the HTML 3.2 DTD from the World Wide Web Consortium's Web site (`http://www.w3.org`).

Actually, since HTML is such a well-known DTD and is also so small, most SGML applications come with some version of the HTML DTD. You may want to check your SGML application before you bother to surf for any DTD. Corel WordPerfect and ArborText Adept both come with the 2.0 and 3.2 HTML DTDs.

If you're going to use your SGML application to edit existing HTML documents, you may not always like what you find! As mentioned in the previous chapter, most HTML browsers are much more forgiving than any SGML application. HTML documents created by hand or with HTML editors that don't strictly enforce syntax may contain problems that aren't evident if you just look at the HTML file in a browser. However, if you are generating HTML from SGML source code, installing the HTML DTD provides an excellent way to confirm that your translation process is working correctly and is accurately preserving the structural information in your documents.

The Rainbow DTD

You may come across the name of this DTD fairly often in SGML documents or at SGML luncheons and lawn parties, but the Rainbow DTD really isn't a DTD that you actually want to use when creating a documentation set. The Rainbow DTD is designed to be used as an intermediate step when translating documentation from one format to another. For more information about the Rainbow DTD, see Chapter 21.

DTDs from the Text Encoding Initiative (TEI)

The Text Encoding Initiative has authored a very interesting public-domain DTD called TEI and also provides DTD that implements a simpler subset of the TEI DTD, called TEI-Lite. The Text Encoding Initiative is an international research organization whose goal is to make it easier to exchange machine-readable documents. Rather than being an academic organization, the TEI is sponsored by groups such as the Association for Computational Linguistics, the Association for Computers and the Humanities, and the Association for Literacy and Linguistic Computing. It is funded by grants from the United States, Canada, and various European governments. You can get the TEI DTD and more information about TEI itself at `http://www.uic.edu/orgs/tei`.

The primary use of the TEI DTD is to encode literary works that were previously published in paper form, to preserve these documents, make them readily available on the Internet, and to facilitate linguistic and literary analysis. Because accurate analysis of these documents depends on how completely the SGML versions correspond to the original printed versions, the TEI and TEI-Lite DTDs contain elements that identify things like page breaks and line breaks, which aren't something you'd ordinarily expect to find in an SGML DTD.

Because the goal of the TEI is the easy interchange of machine-readable text rather than documentation, the TEI and its associated DTDs focus on a general description of the structure of any document, not any specific type of document. Nonetheless, the TEI-Lite DTD is an interesting example of how you can apply SGML to different documents that typically have a less well-defined structure than technical documents do, in the name of making it easier to exchange and analyze these documents online.

CALS, Government, and Military DTDs

As mentioned earlier in the book, government agencies were many of the first adopters of SGML. The reasons for this are fairly clear — government agencies deal with thousands of contractors and have to make sure that they can use and maintain the documents they receive from these contractors. Let me see — the former means that they should share a common structure, and the latter means that they must use a common set of markup. SGML to the rescue! It's nice to see our tax dollars going for something useful for a change.

The CALS DTD

CALS is a Department of Defense project designed to standardize the structure and format of documents submitted to the government by contractors and to simplify the maintenance of those documents. CALS originally stood for *Computer-Aided Logistics and Support*, but it now is said to stand for *Continuous Acquisition and Lifecycle Support*. (It also has some more humorous expansions that I won't go into here — you can probably supply some of your own!)

In addition to being one of the most complete and well-documented DTDs available, CALS has introduced the concept of the FOSI (Formatting Output Specification Instance), which is an SGML document that provides a generic way of describing the formatting associated with DTD. In this book, I tend to use FOSI as the generic term for whatever bridges the gap between the pure content and structure information provided by an SGML DTD and its appearance on the printed page. This definition isn't strictly correct because FOSIs are themselves SGML specifications. Now that more graphical tools are available for creating and printing SGML documents, this term is perhaps less accurate and less common in SGML literature — I apologize for the poetic license!

The CALS specification, DTD, FOSI, and many supporting documents and examples are available from various government Web sites or from Robin Cover's Web site at the URL (http://www.sil.org/sgml/gov-apps.html).

The CALS specification and its associated SGML declaration, DTD, and FOSI are invaluable as good examples of how SGML can simplify document interchange and maintenance. If you are contracting for the Department of Defense, there's a good chance that you will eventually use this DTD and FOSI. Even if you don't, the supporting document for the CALS SGML effort (MIL-HDBK-28001) is well worth reading and referring to as a good example of a complete, well thought-out example of using SGML to solve a documentation problem.

The US Internal Revenue Service

Since everyone in the United States has to deal with the IRS, it's interesting to see the DTD that the IRS uses for many of its documents. A large number of its documents are available from ftp://fwux.fedworld.gov/pub/irs-sgml/irs-sgml.htm. I've often had problems getting through to this site, which is a sad but interesting commentary. If you can get through, most of these documents come with the DTD used to mark them up.

By the way, you won't find any tax forms here — you can get those in PostScript, PCL (the printer language used by Hewlett-Packard and other laser printers), and Adobe PDF (Portable Document Format) from http://www.irs.ustreas.gov!

The U.S. Navy

This Web site (http:// navycals.dt.navy.mil/dtdfosi/reposfosi) provides sample documents, DTDs, and associated FOSIs that comply with the CALS standard. You can also get a copy of the CALS specification from this site in WordPerfect format.

The U.S. Army

The Army's Web site is located in acronym heaven because it contains "the U.S. Army Publications and Printing Command (USAPPC) Standard Generalized Markup Language (SGML) Registry and Library (ASRL). The ASRL is part of the Digital Publications Development (DPD) Program, and it is the Army operational site for the DOD CALS SGML Registry (CSR)." (This is a quote from the Army's Web page!) You can find the Army's site at http://www.asrl.com. Like the Navy's site, this Web site contains sample documents, DTDs, and associated FOSIs that comply with the CALS standard.

DTDs for the Publishing Industry

The American Association of Publishers (AAP) has been promoting SGML as an electronic standard for preparing and delivering manuscripts since the adoption of the SGML standard. This "Electronic Manual Standard" was worked on by both the AAP and the Electronic Publishing Special Interest Group (EPSIG) and is now a National Information Standards Organization (NISO) publication. This DTD was designed to satisfy the needs of both authors and publishers. You can get a copy of this DTD from `ftp://info.ex.ac.uk/pub/SGML/APP/`. You can get more information about the EPSIG from their website at `http://www.gca.org/epsig` or by sending e-mail to `epsig@aol.com`.

Since the development of the AAP DTD, the AAP has been working with the European Physical Society (EPS) to develop other DTDs that provide standard ways for marking up scientific documents. These DTDs are the basis for the International Standards Organization's ISO 12083 publication, which describes DTDs for books, articles, mathematical markup, and so on. Versions of these DTDs are available from `ftp://info.ex.ac.uk/pub/SGML/ISO-12083`.

DTDs for Document Archival and Reference

The Encoded Document Archival (EAD) DTD is designed to provide centralized reference sources such as libraries with a standard way of marking up *finding aides*, which are things like inventories, registers, indexes, and guides to the items in their collection. These generally provide standard catalog information as well as detailed information about the history of the item, how to access those items, and any stipulations on the type of access that is available. Though this project was originally started at the University of California, Berkeley, its goals and DTD are now the responsibility of the Network Development and MARC Standards Office at the Library of Congress. You can get more information about the EAD as well as copies of recent beta releases at `http://lcweb.loc.gov/loc/standards/ead/`.

Part III
Defining the Appearance of a Document

The 5th Wave   By Rich Tennant

"QUICK KIDS! YOUR MOTHER'S EXPRESSING
THE VALUE OF AN SGML PARAMETER ENTRY."

In this part . . .

Though separating structure and content from how a document is formatted is a basic feature of SGML, SGML tools wouldn't be very usable if they didn't provide you a way to format and print documents! After all, many people still want paper documents. It's hard to read a Web page on the bus (at least, it is today), and paper documents still provide some basic usability features over online docs.

This part introduces some of the different ways you can associate formatting with the elements, attributes, and entities in an SGML DTD. The only formal standard that exists is the Formatted Output Specification Instance (FOSI), which is the standard way of associating formatting with the CALS (Computer Aided Logistics and Support.

However, the world of SGML is moving too quickly for a single standard to crystallize and take hold. This section also discusses DSSSL, the Document Style Semantics and Specification Language, a leading candidate for the formatting standard of tomorrow, and I provide some examples of defining formatting using DSSSL.

Having discussed some of the standard ways for associating formatting with SGML documents, I conclude by covering the SGML capabilities of some off-the-shelf software that you may already be familiar with: Adobe FrameMaker+SGML, Corel WordPerfect 8.0, and Microsoft Word (through a plug-in, MicroStar's Near & Far Author).

Chapter 9

Introducing SGML Document Formatting

* *

In This Chapter

▶ What's a FOSI?

▶ Designing a FOSI

▶ The FOSI and DSSSL Standards

▶ Other ways of formatting an SGML document

* *

*I*f you've been reading this book sequentially, you're probably thinking "this SGML stuff is all well and good, but I really do have to print my documents and make them look good in the process. How am I supposed to do that?"

Excellent question — precisely the topic of this chapter!

Most people associate the phrase *Formatting Output Specification Instance* (FOSI) with SGML because it is the classic way of defining how an SGML document is formatted. FOSIs are used in pure SGML tools. Desktop publishing and word-processing software packages tend to define how an SGML document is formatted slightly differently. As SGML becomes more popular and additional SGML applications become available, even the FOSI concept is being replaced by newer and more effective approaches to software-independent formatting descriptions, such as DSSSL.

This chapter discusses the approaches that different software packages take to bridging the gap between SGML content, markup, and the printed page. I start by discussing FOSIs because they are a standard SGML approach to associating formatting with markup. I also provide an overview of the approaches taken by several WYSIWYG publishing packages that provide SGML support. For more complete information about how some common desktop publishing and word-processing packages that support SGML deal with formatting and printing issues, see Chapter 11.

What's a FOSI?

The FOSI was proposed as part of the CALS standard, which set much of the stage for the development and popularity of SGML as we know it today. A FOSI allows you to describe the formatting of the SGML elements in a specific DTD. FOSIs are software-independent formatting descriptions, meaning that any application that can read and interpret a FOSI should be able to format any document that uses that FOSI. Since the FOSI is not directly contained in a DTD, you can associate multiple FOSIs with a single DTD. Each FOSI is just an output *instance,* meaning that it's just one possible way to prepare output from a given DTD, just like an instance of an element is just one set of the beginning and ending tags for that element. Usually only a small number of FOSIs (often only one!) is associated with a given DTD. You may associate more than FOSI with a DTD because you want to provide output in different formats at different stages of the writing, editing, and publishing processes. For example, you may want to create separate "draft" and "final" DTDs to use more of the space on the printed page when reviewing; there's no reason to waste paper during the document review cycle if your printer can produce $8\,1/2 \times 11$ output but the size of your final documents is a smaller size, such as 7×9.

The primary reason that usually only a small number of FOSIs are associated with a single DTD is that it takes a significant amount to create multiple descriptions of how to produce output from a single DTD. This is understandable, since FOSIs provide formatting instructions like "the margins are so wide, a level one heading has so much space before and after it," and so on. You can see that producing even two of these for a single DTD requires some effort, especially considering things like line-wrapping, font sizes (smaller page sizes can usually use slightly smaller fonts), and so on. However, if you have the time, the resources, and are required to work in an SGML environment where FOSIs are used, creating multiple FOSIs can be useful and also show you how flexible SGML can be.

So what exactly is a FOSI? In an interesting example of recursion, a FOSI is an SGML document that associates formatting characteristics and values with each of the elements in a specific DTD. Technically, a FOSI is an instance of the *outspec* (Output Specification) DTD discussed in the CALS standard (government document number MIL-STD-28001, available at http://www.acq.osd.mil/cals/specstds.html).

Because FOSIs use SGML syntax to describe the formatting of SGML documents, you have two significant reasons for using a FOSI or similar type of formatting definition:

✔ An SGML parser can parse and verify the syntax of a FOSI just like any other SGML document.

✔ Like SGML, FOSIs provide a software-independent solution for describing the formatting of an SGML DTD.

Interpreting the FOSI and mapping the description of how the elements in the associated DTD should be formatted is the responsibility of the application that actually does the formatting. This is usually either a one- or two-step process. In a one-step process, the formatter can actually read the FOSI and perform the specified formatting. In a two-step process, a pre-processor maps instructions in some low-level formatting language to the FOSI instructions, creating a temporary document which it then hands off to the low-level formatter. ArborText Adept takes the two-step approach, using TeX as its low-level formatter to process a temporary file that it creates by embedding specific TeX instructions around each instance of the elements in an SGML document.

FOSI syntax

A sample section of a simple FOSI looks like the following:

```
<outspec>
<rsrcdesc>
<counter initial="0"
         style="arabic"
         enumid="pagect">
<pagedesc>
<pageset id="stdpage">
  <rectopg width="55pi"
           nomdepth="70pi"
           bind="1left">
   <pageres>
   <enumerat enumid="pagect" incremen="1">
<styledesc>
   <e-i-c gi="par" context="list">
   <charlist>
   <font style="serif" size="12pt">
   <indent leftind="2pt"  rightind="0pt">
```

This simple extract from a FOSI shows three sample sections of the outspec DTD:

- ✔ <rsrcdesc>, the resource description section, in which you declare variables used throughout the document
- ✔ <pagedesc>, a page description section, where you define the characteristics of different types of pages in your document
- ✔ <styledesc>, the style description section, where you define the formatting characteristics of certain elements in various contexts

For example, the resource description section of this sample FOSI section defines a single numeric counter used for counting pages. It then defines a type of page called `stdpage`, whose right-hand pages (the odd-numbered pages that appear on the right-hand side of a book) are 55 picas wide by 70 picas high and have a binding margin of 1 pica on the left side of the page. Each time a page is produced, the page counter is incremented. The `styledesc` section shows a sample description that defines the font and indentations used for paragraphs that appear when they occur within lists.

Creating a FOSI

The first and most important step in creating a FOSI is a conceptual one — understanding the structure of a document as expressed in the DTD. If you use an existing DTD, you can (hopefully!) locate the reference manual for that DTD. The reference manual should describe each tag in that DTD. Even if the reference is not 100 percent complete, it should at least provide information about the basic elements in the DTD, the relationships between those elements, and the context in which different elements can occur. If no reference manual is available, you can always use the DTD itself. Since the DTD defines all of the elements and their context, it is the final arbiter of how things work in your documents. DTDs can be slow reading, however — make sure you have plenty of coffee or tea available if you must read the DTD!

When you're comfortable with the structure of your documents, you need to understand the formatting requirements for each way in which you want to produce output from your documents. If you are lucky enough to be migrating an existing set of documents, want to preserve the current output format, and your primary output format is still paper, you probably shouldn't have a problem understanding the formatting requirements; you can get much of the formatting information by simply comparing an existing document with the SGML version of the same document. You can use a local style guide, if you have one, to tell you how different types of things in your documents should be formatted. Many of the items discussed in your current local style guide may well map to specific elements in your DTD.

Even with a local style guide, you need a much deeper analysis of your documents than a style guide typically provides in order to create a FOSI. A FOSI must contain a page description for each type of page that appears in your document, such as blank fill pages, the first and subsequent pages in your table of contents, body, index, appendixes, and so on. You must also provide information for how to lay out and orient left (even) and right (odd) pages for each of these parts of your document.

The most time-consuming part of creating a FOSI is actually entering all of the information for all of the elements, types of pages, and structural portions of your document. Although you can create a FOSI with a text editor and verify it against the outspec DTD with an SGML parser, you can

Creating FOSIs fast

When creating a FOSI, I've found that it's fastest to first create a simple page layout that you can use throughout the document while you're first developing the FOSI. I typically create the right-hand (the odd-numbered pages in a two-sided document) first. I then create output specifications for each of the primary elements in the body of your document using these single-sided pages. I then create the left-hand pages for this primary section and finally move onto creating page descriptions for successively more complex (and smaller) portions of your document. In other words, first resolve the basic layout of the majority of your document (hopefully its body!), and then continue to expand and refine the layout until you have created all of the page format necessary for your document. Using this method, you begin to see results almost immediately, which can help reduce the impact of the sizable task in front of you.

take comfort in the fact that SGML tools that use FOSIs (such as ArborText Adept) provide software that simplifies writing and validating a FOSI. I invite you to take a look at this particular tool in more detail.

Example: ArborText's FOSI Editor

ArborText's FOSI Editor is a part of ArborText's excellent Adept series SGML software package, which primarily runs on UNIX and Windows systems. Some parts of the Adept package, like the editor, are also available for other platforms, such as OS/2. The Adept software provides a complete SGML solution, allowing you to do everything from creating a DTD and a matching FOSI, to authoring in SGML using arbitrary DTDs, to formatting and printing your documents. In terms of functionality, Adept is the same as other SGML software packages, such as Corel WordPerfect or Frame+SGML, discussed elsewhere in this book, but ArborText's software strictly adheres to existing SGML specifications such as CALS (discussed in the preceding chapter). In other words, if you produce documents in an environment that requires that you produce a FOSI or use an existing one, ArborText's Adept software is probably the best package you can buy. Definitely bring your wallet — ArborText's software is not cheap, but it is a complete solution. As you see later in this chapter, other SGML software packages provide the same capabilities, but do so in their own ways.

The ArborText SGML software consists of three basic modules:

✔ Adept Editor — an SGML editor that enables you to author using a DTD and FOSI that are provided or which have been compiled for you

- Adept Publisher — the Adept Editor plus a formatter that enables you to format and print documents using DTDs and FOSIs that are provided or have been compiled for you

- Document Architect — a package that enables you to create DTDs and FOSIs and compile them for use with the Adept Editor or the Adept Publisher

I provide more information about the Adept Editor and Publisher in Chapter 20. I discuss the Adept FOSI Editor here.

The FOSI Editor, a part of the Adept Document Architect, provides a graphical interface for FOSI design. To use the Document Architect, you (basically) must follow these steps:

1. **Create or import a DTD.**

2. **Analyze and mark up some documents that show the type of formatting you want to see.**

3. **Create an associated FOSI.**

4. **Install either or both of these for use with the Adept Editor or Adept Publisher.**

When you create or import a DTD, the Document Architect automatically creates a trivial FOSI for that DTD. Therefore, you can install the DTD as soon as you're done with it, and writers can use it even before you're done with the FOSI. If you try to print a document with this default FOSI, you'll be pretty disappointed about its appearance because it's not very sophisticated at this point, but at least you can start working with your SGML documents right away!

ArborText's FOSI Editor is especially handy because it provides an easy-to-use graphical front end for many of the more obscure aspects of a FOSI. As you can see in the sample FOSI syntax shown earlier in this chapter, FOSIs aren't always easy to read or work with because their syntax can be pretty obscure. ArborText's FOSI Editor prevents you from having to remember all of the different aspects of a FOSI because they're all encapsulated in the FOSI Editor's graphical interface. A sample screen from the FOSI editor is shown in Figure 9-1.

As you can see from Figure 9-1, ArborText's FOSI Editor automatically parses your DTD and displays templates for FOSI creation that contain the attributes that you can associate with each element in your DTD. By selecting various panels and menus, you can specify the formatting of all of the elements in your document, as well as define things like page size, headers and footers, and so on.

ArborText's SGML software provides an excellent, complete solution to SGML publishing. If you are working with CALS documents or other documents that

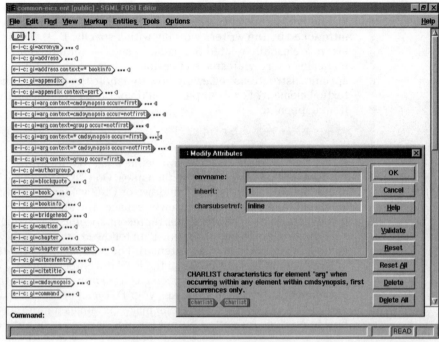

Figure 9-1:
A sample
screen from
ArborText's
Graphical
FOSI Editor.

require that you produce a FOSI, you should definitely evaluate ArborText Adept. If you need to produce or work with a FOSI, you may not be able to afford to be without it (even though it is fairly expensive)!

FOSI subtleties

Here are a few tips on creating a FOSI. These are largely dependent on how your SGML software works, but they're things to keep in mind:

✔ Element context, element context, element context! The syntax of a FOSI enables you to define the way in which an element should be formatted based on the context in which it appears. For example, a paragraph appearing within in a list should follow the prevailing indentation and any hanging margin for that list, while paragraphs that don't appear within a list simply respect the prevailing margin. The FOSI's ⟨e-i-c⟩ characteristic description provides you with the power to format elements. Always consider the context in which an element can appear, especially if your goal is sophisticated formatting.

✔ When creating a FOSI, you want to try to think of the characteristics of various tags as meaning something like "this element should be bold," not "feed the following formatting codes to your formatter." You may not be able to think like this if your SGML software doesn't provide a level of abstraction between the FOSI and the underlying formatter.

✔ When designing a FOSI, you must also consider whether the FOSI should try to correct certain types of errors that may have been introduced by the writers working with a specific DTD. These types of errors are usually related to spacing issues — should your FOSI automatically insert whitespace at certain points, or should it include specific instructions regarding how to handle the end of each SGML or textual element? For example, should your FOSI prevent the following from happening:

```
the filename is<FILENAME> myfile.txt </FILENAME>, and
```

As another example, assume you define a tag that identifies the character used as a path-separator in filenames. On UNIX systems, this character is /, and it is \ on Windows or OS/2 systems. You often shouldn't follow such tags with whitespace. You should, however, follow entities or other tags that represent specific text strings by a space unless those tags or entities are followed by a period (which could indicate the end of a sentence). The responsibility for these types of rules should be split between the FOSI developer, the DTD developer, and the writers working in a specific DTD. If you can ensure that elements in a document that uses your DTD can't end in a space or the carriage-return character, you can make certain assumptions about how to produce formatted output for these elements or entities.

The DSSSL and FOSI Standards

The Document Style Semantics and Specification Language (DSSSL) has been developed over the past few years to provide a generic method of defining the formatting of SGML documents. It addresses some of the shortcomings of the FOSI standard, while providing an enhanced version of the software-independent approach to associating formatting with the elements in an SGML DTD.

DSSSL actually consists of three basic components:

✔ A transformation language that defines how to convert SGML documents that conform to one DTD into SGML documents that conform to another DTD

✔ A query language, the Standard Document Query Language (SDQL), that lets you extract or identify specific portions of an SGML document

✔ A style language that enables you to associate style information with the elements in a document associated with any SGML DTD

DSSSL applications that perform transformation, queries, and style mapping are usually referred to as DSSSL processors. The transformation language is actually optional — for example, the popular Jade DSSSL processor doesn't currently support a transformation language. Not all DSSSL processors support the full SDQL language — this is only available in DSSSL processors that identify themselves as supporting the "Query Feature."

SGML documents are naturally hierarchical because they provide a structural description of your document. The DTD describes the context in which various elements can appear and therefore describes the relationships between different types of elements. The core of DSSSL is its ability to intelligently process hierarchical SGML input files and transform that hierarchy into a corresponding series of *flow objects*. Flow objects are the DSSSL term used to describe layout constructs such as pages, paragraphs, lists, and graphical objects.

DSSSL extends SGML's hierarchical document model by considering SGML documents to be sets of nodes that are organized into trees. These trees represent SGML elements and their associated attributes and are themselves organized into groves, which are essentially trees of trees. This provides a completely hierarchical model of an SGML document which is easily parsed and transformed into flow objects with specific formatting for the target output format.

DSSSL style sheets consist of statements that define the formatting associated with different structural elements found in the SGML document. These are often referred to as construction rules because they enable you to build a formatted document from an SGML document. Here is a sample construction rule:

```
(element par (make paragraph
       font-family-name: "Helvetica"
       font-size: 10pt
       space-after: 12pt ))
```

This construction rule tells the DSSSL processor that, as it encounters <PAR> elements in the SGML input file, it should create corresponding paragraph flow objects with the specified font-family-name, font-size, and space-after attributes.

Some basic advantages of the DSSSL approach over FOSIs are

✔ DSSSL is truly an international standard, whereas the FOSI standard was developed as a stop-gap for use in specific industries, such as the U.S. government. Though the FOSI standard was the first software-independent mechanism for describing SGML formatting, as a non-ISO standard, it has never been accepted by a majority of SGML software vendors.

✔ DSSSL is built on top of the Scheme programming language, which provides a general purpose programming interface for extensions to DSSSL's transformation, query, and style languages.

✔ DSSSL's transformation, query, and style languages let you dynamically perform document processing, rather than limiting you to the static SGML-to-style hierarchical mapping that FOSIs provide.

Several public-domain DSSSL processors are already available. Probably the best known freely available DSSSL processor is Jade, by James Clark, who has authored many excellent SGML tools and was a major contributor to the DSSSL standard. Jade lets you transform SGML documents into output formats such as HTML, RTF, and TeX, and is available at `http://www.jclark.com`.

You can obtain the current DSSSL standard in Postscript, SGML, or Adobe PDF formats from `ftp://ftp.ornl.gov/pub/sgml/WG8/DSSSL`.

Other Ways of Formatting an SGML Document

As mentioned earlier, more and more word-processing and desktop publishing packages are adding SGML capabilities. Since these packages are already WYSIWYG, they usually take different approaches to DTD creation, SGML document creation, and associating formatting information with SGML documents.

This section discusses two such software packages, Corel WordPerfect and Adobe's Frame+SGML. Each of these are well-known tools with large numbers of existing users.

SGML formatting in Corel WordPerfect v8.0

Corel's WordPerfect product provides off-the-shelf support for SGML. When you open an SGML file in WordPerfect, it automatically recognizes it as an SGML document and lets you select the appropriate DTD.

To provide a real SGML solution, WordPerfect comes with several other tools that provide the support you need to work with SGML documents. I discuss these tools in detail in Chapter 11. In this section, I focus on the WordPerfect tool that lets you create the formatting information associated with the elements and attributes in your SGML documents.

No, I don't hate Microsoft!

Microsoft fans or users may notice that I'm not explicitly discussing any SGML solutions for Microsoft Word. I am not prejudiced against Microsoft Products! The difference between the products I discuss in this section and the Microsoft Word add-ons that support SGML is that the latter are simply add-ons for Word. Software packages like Corel WordPerfect and Adobe's Frame+SGML provide off-the-shelf, integrated support for SGML. Some of the SGML add-ons for Word are discussed in Chapter 11. However, companies such as Corel, Frame, and Interleaf actually support SGML themselves, and they are therefore worthy of special notice as far as I'm concerned.

WordPerfect has a tool called the Layout Designer that enables you to associate formatting with the elements in an SGML DTD (see Figure 9-2). See Chapter 11 for details on importing and compiling a DTD in WordPerfect.

By separating the process of creating a DTD from the process of defining the formatting associated with elements and their attributes, Corel provides a nice set of tools for working with different aspects of SGML documents. You can import a DTD, compile it, and get users started working in that DTD while you're still working on perfecting the formatting associated with that DTD. The downside, of course, is that you (or whoever develops your company's SGML solution) have to learn to use several tools.

WordPerfect's Layout Designer provides an intuitive, graphical interface for defining the formatting associated with the elements in your SGML documents. The Layout Designer lets you define the formatting codes that are associated with each of the elements in your SGML documents. You can associate specific formatting with three different points of an SGML element:

✔ When you encounter the opening tag for an SGML element.

✔ When you encounter the closing tag for an SGML element but before you exit the environment implied by that tag. For example, when a closing tag is encountered, any font change specified for the matching opening tag automatically reverts to the font that was used before the opening tag was encountered.

✔ After encountering the closing tag for an SGML element and after you exit the environment implied by that tag

Allowing you to associate specific formatting with these three different points in your documents simplifies many common formatting issues, such as automatically changing the spacing after the last item in a list. Many standard word-processing or desktop publishing tools use a separate tag to correctly set up the spacing between the last item in a list and the following paragraph. WordPerfect's Layout Designer makes this task easy — along

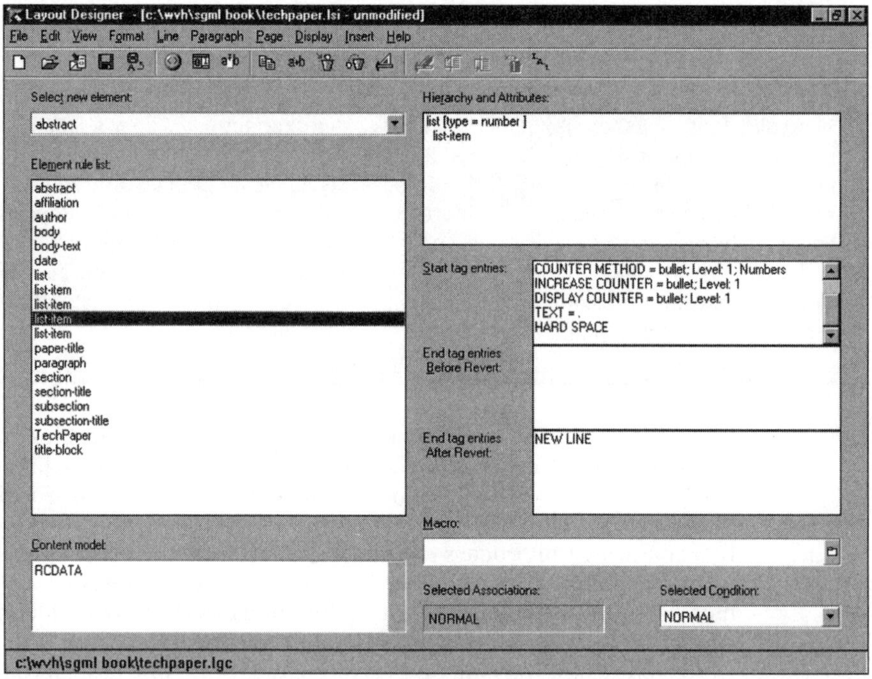

Figure 9-2:
WordPerfect's
Layout
Designer.

with the fact that you're using a structured input format (SGML) in the first place! WordPerfect users who are familiar with defining and using styles will probably be quite comfortable with the Layout Designer.

The Layout Designer lets you associate different formatting with the same elements, based on the context in which they occur. You can change the formatting of elements based on their attributes or the values of those attributes. You can also create macros, which are sets of WordPerfect formatting commands that are automatically executed when an instance of an element is inserted in your document.

The Layout Designer saves the rules you create in Layout Specification Instance (LSI) files. As you can with FOSIs and FrameMaker+SGML, you can create multiple LSI files for one DTD and switch between them while you are writing your documents. You can therefore use different LSI files to provide different page layouts while you are writing your documents, in copies of your documents that you send out for review, and for final printing of your documents. The Layout Designer makes this task fairly easy to do.

WordPerfect includes a large number of sample SGML DTDs and associated formatting definitions to help you get started using SGML. These include the DocBook 2.4.1 and 3.0 DTDs, several HTML DTDs, and the TEI-Lite (Text Encoding Initiative) DTD, all of which are discussed in Chapter 8.

SGML Formatting in FrameMaker+SGML v5.1.1

FrameMaker+SGML (Frame+SGML) is a version of the popular FrameMaker desktop publishing application that understands structured documents such as SGML. If you're already familiar with FrameMaker, Frame+SGML should look pretty familiar to you, since it uses the same user interface as FrameMaker, with all of the familiar menus in all the standard places. Of course, it also provides new menus for SGML-specific features, but if you're already a Frame user, you shouldn't have any big surprises when you first start Frame+SGML. See Chapter 11 for more detail on FrameMaker+SGML. This section discusses how FrameMaker+SGML formats SGML documents so that you can compare and contrast its capabilities with FOSIs and the approach used by Word Perfect.

Because Frame+SGML is based on FrameMaker, its developers were presented with an interesting problem — how to add SGML and other structured documentation capabilities without alienating their existing users. They decided to use a translation model, in which SGML documents can be translated into Frame+SGML documents, and vice versa. Frame+SGML lets you create SGML applications that contain sets of read/write rules for converting between standard SGML documents and Frame+SGML documents. Once an SGML document has been converted into a Frame+SGML document, Frame+SGML uses an *Element Definition Document* (EDD) to define the contexts in which different elements can appear, specify how to handle element attributes, and define the formatting associated with those elements and attributes.

If you already have a DTD that you'll use with Frame+SGML, you can create a template EDD file from the DTD by opening that DTD using Frame+SGML menu commands. This defines the basic set of elements present in your document. If you are not starting with a DTD, you also have to plan to spend some time creating both the DTD and the read/write rules that will produce SGML documents from your Frame+SGML document, and vice versa. I strongly suggest that you create your DTD and validate it before starting to work with an EDD. Doing so guarantees that your elements and attributes will conform to SGML naming conventions, maximum lengths, and so on. More about this stuff in Chapter 11!

After you create an EDD, you can use commands on Frame+SGML's Developer Tools (a submenu off the File menu) and Elements menus to modify element and associated attribute definitions, associate formatting with those elements, and so on (see Figure 9-3). Like FrameMaker, FrameMaker+SGML has a nice user interface that makes it easy to associate complex formatting rules with the different parts of your documents.

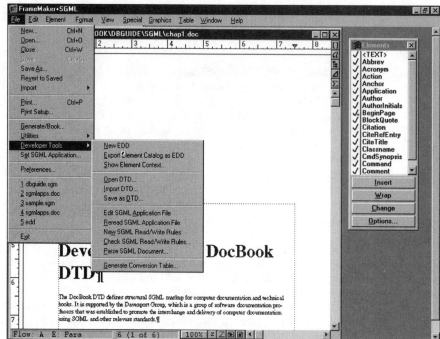

Figure 9-3:
FrameMaker+
SGML's
Developer
Tools Menu.

FrameMaker+SGML's translation model can increase the amount of time that it takes to get your users up and running in an SGML environment, because it can require a significant amount of time for you (or a documentation tools developer) to create the EDD and the translation (read/write) rules, and to perfect the formatting. Surprisingly, Frame+SGML doesn't come with many samples of how to do this — it only provides a single large template, which is based on version 2.2.1 of the DocBook DTD. However, if you or the writers you work with are already familiar with FrameMaker or already have existing documents in FrameMaker format, using Frame+SGML can save you from having to retrain everyone to use a new tool when you move to an SGML environment.

Chapter 10

How to Include Specific Formatting Instructions

● ●

In This Chapter

▶ Defining a processing instruction

▶ Using processing instructions only when you have to

▶ Looking at the future processing instructions

● ●

*T*he mantra for this book (and most other SGML books) is "separation of content and formatting, absolute separation of content and formatting." Repeat that a few thousands times if you're not comfortable with it — after all, this core SGML concept frees you from the constraints of a specific output format or output device. However, at the same time that I like to stand up for intellectual and moral purity, I also like to stress that SGML doesn't remove the primary responsibility of most writers and documentation groups to produce books — on paper or in other formats! With the advent of the Web, many people may be willing to accept electronic books, but lots of people still want paper ones. After all, it's hard to read a manual over the Web while you're riding home on the bus — at least it is as I write this.

This chapter discusses one of the more "unpopular" aspects of SGML, which is its support for ways to pass specific formatting hints to other applications that use your SGML input files, such as the formatters that produce different types of output. This chapter shows that formatting hints are not just a necessary evil or a sign of immaturity in SGML and that you can use them in some interesting ways that can actually add value to your SGML working environment.

What Is a Processing Instruction?

You can think of these as the basic steps in developing an SGML document:

1. You write your SGML files.

2. The parser validates those files.

3. Another application uses the information in your validated SGML files. For example, a formatting application produces output in a specified format.

These steps are highly simplified since each step usually contains multiple loops. However, these steps provide a basically accurate outline of how the information you produce flows through one or more SGML applications.

People commonly use processing instructions in SGML to pass information from their input files, through an SGML parser, to some application on the other side. Processing instructions literally contain hints about how the "application on the other side" should process the part of the document where the processing instruction appears. In many cases, the application on the other side is a formatter designed to produce output that's suitable for printing, but (as you see later in this chapter) that isn't always the case. An SGML parser does not interpret processing instructions; it passes them through, intact, to the application that reads the output of the SGML parser.

Here is the basic SGML syntax of a processing instruction:

```
<?CDATA>
```

A processing instruction is anything that begins with the characters <? and ends with a closing >. Many people have joked that the fact that a processing instruction begins with the expression <? shows just how dubious the use of this sort of instruction is. Even the SGML standard (Goldfarb) suggests that you minimize the use of processing instructions.

Okay, I confess — the most obvious use for a processing instruction is to pass a specific processing command to a formatting application. Although this use appears to refute the most basic principle of SGML (our mantra "separation of content and formatting . . ."), face it — because paper is the most common output format, you probably need to embed this sort of instruction now and then. Because formatting applications aren't perfect and you sometimes need to add a linebreak or pagebreak for emphasis or aesthetics, people who produce paper documents occasionally need to embed an explicit linebreak or pagebreak.

Because you often use processing instructions to pass explicit commands to a specific formatter, you should be able to see why you shouldn't use them. Because processing instructions provide specific instructions in the markup or formatting language used by a specific formatter, they limit the portability of your SGML documents, which is one of the primary goals of SGML.

You commonly see processing instructions in SGML documents that have been translated from another markup language. It's easy to see why — since most non-SGML markup languages are unstructured, nothing forces documents in these markup languages to follow a specific style. There is probably a style-sheet or a set of recommended markup symbols that writers should use, but nothing forces anyone to adhere to either one. For this reason, documents in non-SGML markup languages often contain explicit formatting instructions, such as explicit font and font-size changes and line- and pagebreaks. Because the application that converts non-SGML documents into SGML can't recognize every possible markup element and there may not actually be an appropriate SGML element to map each of these to, explicit formatting commands are usually translated into processing instructions.

Processing instructions form a weird bridge between SGML and specific types of formatting because they are a necessary evil. You should use processing instructions that mandate specific types of formatting only when absolutely necessary, and even then you should think long and hard about whether they really are absolutely necessary.

Creating entities for "official" processing instructions

As mentioned in the section of Chapter 6 on entity declarations, SGML's entity declaration syntax supports the creation of entities that are identified to the system as processing instructions. The general syntax of this type of entity is the following:

```
<!ENTITY name PI "contents" >
```

Here is an example of a processing instruction declared in this syntax:

```
<!ENTITY linebreak PI ".br" >
```

Because the system understands this type of entity as a processing instruction, you can use it in the text of your documents as `&linebreak;`, and the system automatically supplies the opening and closing tags for the processing instruction before passing it on to the SGML parser. This entity therefore expands to the following:

```
<? .br >
```

If you have a set of processing instructions that are officially sanctioned for use in your documents, you may want to declare them in this way in your DTD or in the local declarations section of your `DOCTYPE` statements. Doing so makes it easy for you or any writers you work with to use a selected set of processing instructions that are useful in your environment. It also makes it easy for you to identify any "unofficial" processing instructions that writers might add in the frenzy of the release cycle, as these still look like standard processing instructions rather than entities.

Using processing instructions for multiple formatters

Because processing instructions contain information specific to a particular formatter, they limit the portability of your SGML documents. If you format your SGML documents with several different formatters, each of which needs some processing instructions, you have to come up with several different types of processing instructions, each uniquely identifiable by the formatter that needs to use them.

As an alternative, you can use marked sections to include specific sets of processing instructions while excusing others. As discussed in Chapter 6, marked sections are regions in an SGML document that the SGML parser either ignores or includes based on the value of the keyword inside them. As a quick refresher, a typical marked section looks like this:

```
<![ IGNORE [ This text will be ignored in this document,
since the whole marked section is ignored by the SGML
parser.]]>
```

Because you typically use marked sections to hold system-specific text in a document, you can combine marked sections with an entity to minimize the number of places you have to activate specific marked sections. By changing the value of the entity, you can activate the correct sets of these throughout your document, as in the following example:

```
<!ENTITY % hp "IGNORE">
<!ENTITY % ibm "INCLUDE">
<!ENTITY % sun "IGNORE">
<!ENTITY % win95 "IGNORE">
...
<![ %hp; [
Insert the distribution media and run sam, the system
administration manager, to begin installing your software…
]]>
<![ %ibm; [
Insert the distribution media and run smit, the system
management interface tool, to begin installing your
software… ]]>
<![ %sun; [
Insert the distribution media and run pkgadd to add the
specific software package to your system… ]]>
<![ %win95; [
Insert the distribution media and click the Control Panel's
Add/Remove Software icon to begin installing your software…
]]>
```

You can do the same thing with marked sections and different sets of processing instructions. For example, suppose you use troff and LaTeX — two formatters that certainly format your document differently — to format your documents. Assume that you want to insert a linebreak in a specific, but different, part of your documents for each formatter. You can do something like this:

```
Now is the time for all good men to come to the aid of
their country.<![ %troff; [<? .br >]]> Ask not what your
country can do for you, ask what you can do for your
country. <![ %html; [<? &lt;BR&gt; >]]>
```

If you produce the version of this document to be formatted with troff, the entity declarations section of the DOCTYPE statement in your SGML document contains these statements:

```
<!ENTITY % html "IGNORE">
<!ENTITY % troff "INCLUDE">
```

The resulting portion of your document from the SGML parser looks like this:

```
Now is the time for all good men to come to the aid of
their countrymen.
.br
Ask not what your country can do for you, ask what you can
do for your country.
```

You can even take this sort of thing one step further. If you want to insert formatter-specific processing instructions at the same point in your document and have these instructions be specific to your formatter, you can insert a generic entity reference at the right point in your document but change the value of the entity based on the formatter you use. Here's an example. The DTD or entity declarations section of the DOCTYPE statement in your SGML document would contain these statements:

```
<![ %html; [ <!ENTITY newline PI "<BR>"> ]]>
<![ %troff; [ <!ENTITY newline PI ".br"> ]]>
<!ENTITY newline "">
```

In the previous example, note that the final ENTITY declaration for "newline" is always defined. This is necessary in case both html and troff are defined as IGNORE. In SGML, the first declaration of an entity is the definitive declaration — subsequent declarations of the same entity are ignore, but are not illegal.

The text in your document could now read:

```
Now is the time for all good men to come to the aid of
their country.&newline;
```

If you use the values for the html and troff entities specified previously, your output looks like this:

```
DTD Section: <!ENTITY newline PI ".br">

In Text: Now is the time for all good men to come to the
aid of their country.&newline;
```

Although these uses of processing instructions are clever, you should use processing instructions as infrequently as possible. The next section discusses some clever uses for processing instructions.

When Is a Processing Instruction Okay?

The most obvious case when a processing instruction is useful is when you want to encode information that is important to a specific formatter, as discussed in the examples earlier in this section. This is most important for issues like widow and orphan control in printed documentation. In the future, as formatters improve and paper becomes less critical as an output format, processing instructions should be used even less frequently than they are now.

Just because the most common use of processing instructions is for formatting purposes doesn't mean that there aren't some bonafide, long-term uses for processing instructions. Don't forget that SGML is still in its infancy. For this reason, many companies that currently use SGML have written proprietary applications that they use to post-process and transform their SGML information. Because processing instructions pass straight through an SGML parser, you can use them to provide "downstream" applications with useful information that you may have no other way to easily represent. Some DTDs provide attributes (such as the DocBook DTD's remap and role attributes) that serve as catch-all ways of attributes containing information used to hold information — information that would otherwise be represented by processing instructions.

In some cases, the application that uses a processing instruction is the same one that generates it. For example, take ArborText's Publisher product, the previous generation of the ArborText Adept series software discussed elsewhere in this book. Though essentially a GML product (Generalized Markup Language — the predecessor of SGML) rather than a pure SGML product, ArborText Publisher can write SGML files from its interactive editor (the analogue of the Adept Editor in the Adept series of products). Because Publisher is a graphical editor, it writes certain information specific to the GUI, such as the current cursor position, to the SGML files as a processing instruction. Because you can also reload these files into the Editor, the editor uses these processing instructions to correctly reposition the cursor when the file is reloaded.

Processing instructions have another interesting use — they provide a way to protect SGML documents from enhancements that may not be supported by the application that uses them. For example, XML (discussed in Chapter 7) uses a processing instruction to "hide" the XML version declaration in an HTML file:

```
<?XML VERSION="1.0"?>
```

An HTML browser that doesn't understand XML will ignore this directive, and one that uses XML will use it to identify the set of XML features that the document follows. This is an interesting example, because XML is an up-and-coming standard that essentially depends on processing instructions. Hmmm . . . maybe we're not quite ready to punt processing instructions just yet.

The Future of the Processing Instruction

As the applications that can accept output from an SGML parser increase and improve, the number of times that you should have to use processing instructions for formatting purposes should decrease. In a suite of truly SGML–aware instructions, you can reduce the need for processing instructions by expanding the attributes associated with the element in your SGML documents — you can use attributes to provide the same sort of "hints" for various types of SGML elements without using processing instructions.

Though processing instructions are unpopular and are often abused in SGML documents, at least the creators of SGML were farsighted enough to see that even features that are somewhat contrary to the spirit of SGML have their place in the SGMLs specification.

Chapter 11

SGML Tools That You Probably Already Know

● ●

In This Chapter

▶ Corel WordPerfect and SGML

▶ Adobe FrameMaker+SGML

▶ Microstar's Near & Far Author for Microsoft Word

● ●

This chapter discusses some common word-processing and publishing software packages and their approaches to SGML. You can tell that interest in SGML is on the rise because so many common software packages support it. This chapter shows you how you can begin using SGML by learning a specific approach provided by word-processing and publishing software that you may already know! All of these word-processing and publishing packages (WordPerfect, Frame, and Word) were available before SGML was popular, so the extent to which SGML support has been integrated is different for each package.

In each of the following sections, I discuss any DTDs that are included with each application and take you through the steps necessary to get the sample TechPaper DTD (created in Chapter 4) up and running in each software package. Discussing these two aspects of various SGML software packages provides a useful comparison of any built-in support provided by these packages and also shows what may be required if you decide to implement your own DTD and use it with each package.

Corel WordPerfect v8.0

WordPerfect lets you open an SGML document that uses any document type that it recognizes. WordPerfect comes with several DTDs, including the DocBook, TEI-Lite, and HTML 2.0 and 3.2 DTDs. You can use three WordPerfect tools to help you build DTDs, compile them into WordPerfect's internal format, and associate formatting with the elements in your DTD:

- ✔ **Corel Visual DTD Builder.** You can build a DTD graphically with this tool. If you have an existing DTD in text format, you don't have to use this tool.

- ✔ **Corel WordPerfect DTD Compiler.** This tool compiles your DTD into WordPerfect's internal format, called LGC (LoGiC) files.

- ✔ **Corel WordPerfect SGML Layout Designer.** Use this tool to associate formatting with the elements and attributes in your DTD, creating LSI (Layout Specification Instance) files used by WordPerfect when formatting SGML documents.

The next few sections show how you can use these tools to import the small the Technical Paper (TechPaper) DTD created in Chapter 4. For more detailed information about using any of the tools discussed in this section, see the Corel WordPerfect documentation.

Using the Visual DTD Builder

In an interesting twist, some portions of Corel's Visual DTD Builder are licensed from Microstar, whose Near & Far product is discussed later in this chapter in "Microstar's Near & Far Author for Microsoft Word."

If you have a text-format DTD that you want to use with WordPerfect, you don't need to use the Visual DTD Builder, since you can compile that DTD with the DTD Compiler (discussed in the next section). However, if you're creating a DTD, you may want to look at it in the Visual DTD Builder. The Visual DTD Builder shows you the structure of your DTD and lets you print a graphical view of all or just a portion of it. Figure 11-1 shows the sample TechPaper DTD in the Visual DTD Builder.

To begin creating a DTD using the Visual DTD Builder, select the New command from the File menu. When you do this, a new window, labeled Untitled1, appears. You can select the sample element that represents the root element for your DTD and use menu commands to define or modify its content model and attributes, and then you can use other menu or toolbar commands to add other elements.

Using the DTD Compiler

Once you've created or obtained a DTD, you have to convert it into an LGC file, the internal format used by Corel WordPerfect to store DTDs. To do so, start the DTD Compiler from the WordPerfect Office Suite's Tools menu, and the DTD Compiler appears.

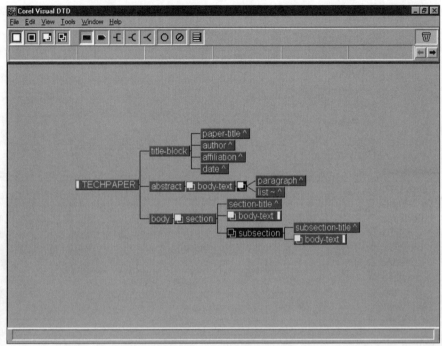

Figure 11-1:
The
TechPaper
DTD in
the Corel
Visual DTD
Builder.

Compiling a DTD means to produce a binary representation of the information in that DTD. Applications can usually load binary representations of information more quickly than they can reprocess a DTD in text form and generate the appropriate internal representation — since the binary version exists, it can simply be loaded with no verification, because the DTD must previously have been successfully processed in order to create the binary version. Just as many word-processing and publishing packages store documents in a proprietary binary format, many SGML editors compile DTDs to expedite subsequent processing.

Enter the name of your DTD in the DTD (Input) File input box or click on the icon to the right of the input box to browse your machine for the file's location. (See Figure 11-2.) If your DTD requires different declarations (discussed in Chapter 4) for any of the SGML defaults, enter the name of the file containing your SGML declarations in the SGML Declaration File input box. Similarly, if your DTD uses any special entities that it doesn't declare internally, you have to enter the name of a file that contains them in the Entity Mapping File input box. The Entity Mapping File is essentially the "catalog" file discussed earlier in this book. For more information on entities and how different software packages locate them, see Chapters 4 and 6.

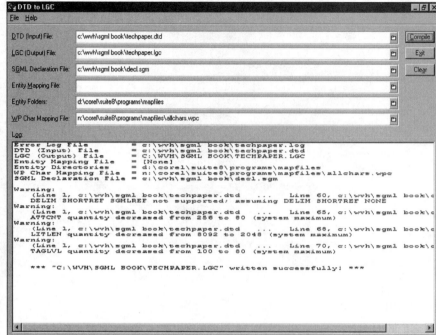

Figure 11-2:
Word-
Perfect's
DTD
Compiler
after
compiling
the
TechPaper
DTD.

After you've provided all this information, you enter the Public Identifier by which your DTD will be identified, and click the Compile button to compile your DTD. As WordPerfect compiles your DTD, any syntax errors or warnings appear in the Log window. A final dialog pops up to congratulate you if the compilation is successful or to inform you of any errors that prevented your DTD from compiling. If errors were encountered, resolve them and then recompile the DTD.

Using the SGML Layout Designer

After you compile a DTD with WordPerfect's DTD Compiler, you use the SGML Layout Designer to specify how the elements in your DTD will be formatted. You can start the Layout Designer from the WordPerfect Office Suite's Tools menu. The Layout Designer saves the rules you create in a Layout Specification Instance (LSI) file. LSI files are known as *layout specification instances* because each LSI file is just one possible way of formatting a document for that DTD. You can create multiple LSI files for one DTD and switch between them while you write your documents. Therefore, you can use different LSI files to provide different page layouts at different times while you are developing your document and to define different layouts for other media, such as online documentation. Figure 11-3 shows the Layout Designer displaying an LSI file for TechPaper DTD.

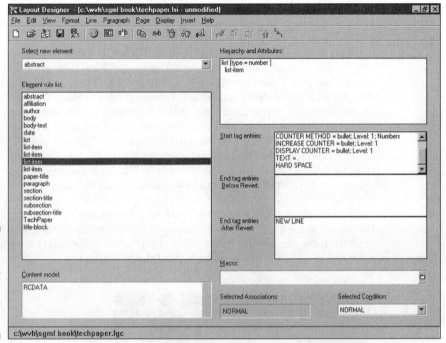

Figure 11-3:
Defining a
layout
for the
TechPaper
DTD.

The Layout Designer lets you associate formatting with specific elements,
the context in which a specific instance of an element occurs, and the
attribute values of a specific element. You can also attach specific formatting to SGML elements at three different points:

- ✔ When you encounter the opening tag for an SGML element (the Start
  tag entries field at the lower right of the dialog box).

- ✔ When you encounter the closing tag for an SGML element but before
  you exit the environment implied by that tag (the End tag entries Before
  Revert field at the lower right of the dialog box).

- ✔ After encountering the closing tag for an SGML element and after you
  exit the environment implied by that tag (the End tag entries After
  Revert field at the lower right of the dialog box).

Aspects of formatting such as font changes are applied after the start tag for
an element has been encountered. You don't need to explicitly revert to a
previous font when you encounter the closing tag for an element. Once you
encounter the end tag for that element, the font automatically reverts to
whatever it was before. Allowing you to specify formatting that takes place
before and after you revert to the previous environment provides you with
more granular control over the formatting of your SGML documents.

The dialog shown in Figure 11-3 provides a list of the elements in your DTD. You can see any current formatting and context information associated with any element by selecting the name of that element in the Elements Rule List dialog box at the upper left of this screen. To specify or modify the formatting for these aspects of an element, double-click on the name of an element in the Elements Rule List dialog box. Figure 11-4 shows the dialog box in which you specify the formatting for these different aspects of an element. The three fields at the lower left of this dialog box correspond to the three fields for element rules shown on the dialog box in Figure 11-3. Allowing you to associate specific formatting with these three different points simplifies many common formatting issues, such as automatically changing the spacing before or after lists and figures, which many standard word-processing or desktop publishing tools use separate tags to achieve.

Figure 11-4 shows a fairly complex set of rules to apply when you encounter the start-tag for a <LIST-ITEM> element. These rules force a new line to be printed, then change the indentation, increment and display a counter for each <LIST-ITEM>, followed by a period and a space.

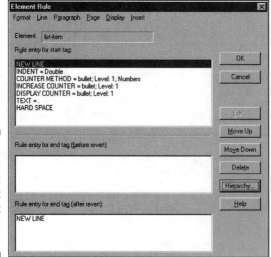

Figure 11-4:
Use this
dialog box
to set
element
and tag
attributes.

Clicking the Hierarchy button on the dialog box shown in Figure 11-4 displays the dialog box shown in Figure 11-5. This dialog box lets you associate specific formatting based on the context of a specific element or the values of its attributes.

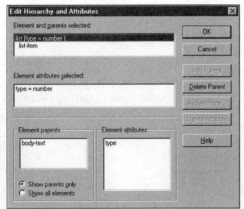

Figure 11-5:
Use this
dialog box
to define
formatting
by context
or
attributes.

The dialog box shown in Figure 11-5 shows how you use the Hierarchy and Attributes dialog box. This dialog box says that the rules shown in Figure 11-4 are only applied to a <LIST-ITEM> element if that item appears within a <LIST> whose TYPE attribute has a value of number. Different rules apply if the TYPE attribute has any of the other values used in the TechPaper DTD, such as alpha, bullet, or none.

To acknowledge specific formatting requirements, the Layout Designer also lets you attach macros to the elements in your DTD. *Macros* are sets of WordPerfect formatting commands that are automatically executed when an instance of an element is inserted in your document. By attaching macros, you can take advantage of specific WordPerfect commands and features with which you are familiar.

Once you've created an LSI file, save it. You can specify which LSI file you want to use when you open an SGML document in WordPerfect, as explained in the next section.

Using WordPerfect with SGML files

Once you've compiled a DTD into an LGC file, you can use WordPerfect to work on SGML documents that use that DTD. It's helpful to have at least created some sort of Layout Specification Instance to accompany that DTD, but you don't need one — your output just won't look very nice until you have one! As mentioned earlier in this section, you may find it useful to define multiple LSI files for a single DTD. For example, you can define a structure-oriented LSI file that you can use when editing your SGML files and define a formatting-oriented LSI for use when producing printed copies of your SGML documents. Word Perfect makes it easy to switch between different LSI files when working on an SGML document.

In order for WordPerfect to work with an SGML document, you must define that document type in WordPerfect. To do so, select the Document Types command on the Tools menu's SGML submenu.

After selecting this command, the Document Types dialog box appears, as shown in Figure 11-6. To define a new document type, click New, and the Document Type Entries dialog box appears, as shown in Figure 11-7.

Figure 11-6:
WordPerfect's
Document
Types
dialog box.

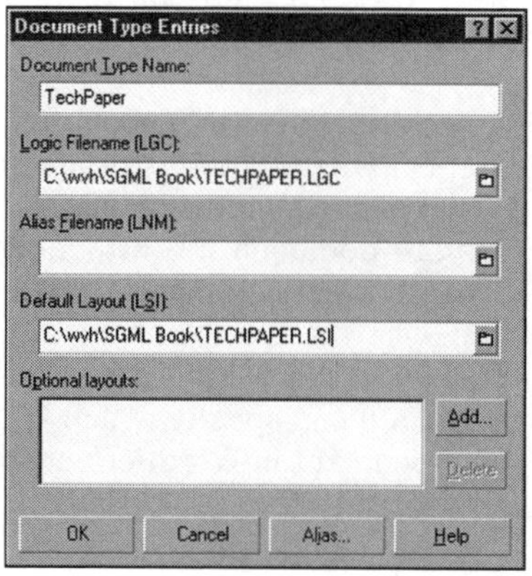

Figure 11-7:
WordPerfect's
Document
Type
Entries
dialog box.

In the Document Types Entries dialog box, enter the name you want to associate with the new document type and the location of the compiled DTD (LGC) file for that document type. If you've already prepared a Layout Specification Instance (LSI) file for that document type, you can also specify it here. If the LSI file isn't ready yet, you can enter it later. The Aliases field on this dialog lets you specify a file that contains alternate names for the elements in your DTD, which is one way of assigning more meaningful names to elements whose names would otherwise be cryptic — perhaps because they conform to the name length limitations imposed by the default set of SGML declarations.

The Document Type Entries dialog box ties together all of the files that you've previously created for use with SGML documents that conform to a specific DTD. Click OK to add the document type definition to the list that WordPerfect knows about.

Use the File menu's Open command or the Open SGML File command on the Tools menu's SGML submenu, select the appropriate document type, and you're off! Figure 11-8 shows a sample SGML document in the TechPaper DTD as it appears in WordPerfect.

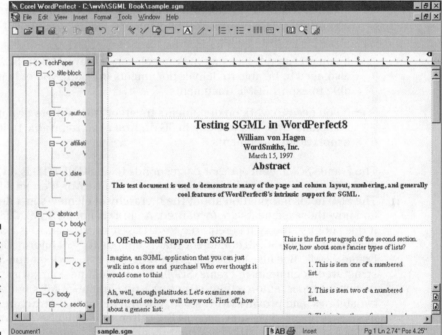

Figure 11-8: A Sample SGML Document in Word-Perfect.

FrameMaker+SGML v5.1.1

FrameMaker+SGML (Frame+SGML) provides a nice environment for working with SGML files and existing SGML document types if you're an existing FrameMaker user. The interface should be familiar because it's very similar to the existing FrameMaker interface — the only real differences are some special commands and dialog boxes that provide SGML support.

As introduced in Chapter 9, Frame+SGML supports SGML and other types of structured documents. Frame+SGML provides a translation model for SGML documents rather than providing actual support for SGML. You can import SGML documents to and export SGML documents from Frame+SGML, but you are actually working in a Frame+SGML document while you're working in Frame+SGML.

Frame+SGML's translation model gives you three possible ways to work with structured documents:

- ✔ If you have SGML documents that are produced and managed by another SGML application but want to use Frame+SGML's formatting and printing capabilities, you only need to be able to import the SGML documents into Frame+SGML.

- ✔ If you are already working in FrameMaker or FrameMaker+SGML but also need to be able to deliver documents in SGML, you only need to be able to export SGML documents.

- ✔ If you need to work on documents together with writers or partner companies who are working in SGML, you need to be able to import and export SGML documents.

The Frame+SGML concept that corresponds to an SGML DTD is an *Element Definition Document* (EDD), which is also similar to WordPerfect's LSI files. The EDD holds information about the hierarchy of elements in a document and how those elements are formatted. An EDD is not an SGML DTD because it does not use the syntax required for DTDs. Instead, an EDD is a specially organized Frame+SGML document that is a repository of information for Frame+SGML. Because an EDD is not a DTD, you can work on non-SGML structured documents in Frame+SGML. You can define your own structured document types, enforce their structure using Frame+SGML's built-in capabilities, and provide writers with a template for that structured document type. Figure 11-9 shows a new EDD after importing the TechPaper DTD, but before much formatting information has been supplied.

The primary goal of an EDD is to provide a way of defining a structured documentation environment that you can use with the existing FrameMaker interface. If you have a large group of writers who are already familiar with the FrameMaker interface, you can certainly save a lot of retraining time by using Frame+SGML as your SGML environment.

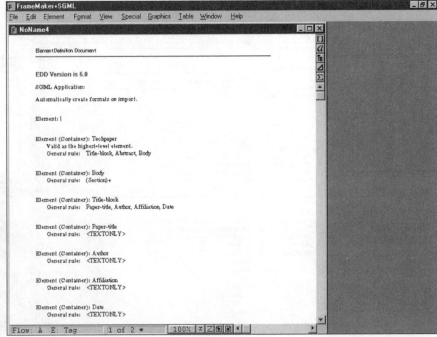

Figure 11-9:
A New EDD after importing the TechPaper DTD.

Planning a FrameMaker+SGML Application

When using Frame+SGML, a DTD, EDD, a set of rules to convert between the two (known as *read/write rules* in Frame-speak), and any sample documents you provide make up an SGML application. Like its EDD, Frame+SGML stores information about its SGML applications in a specially structured Frame+SGML file. This file is called `sgmlapps.doc` and is located in the `sgml` subdirectory of the directory where you installed Frame+SGML. To modify this file, select the Edit SGML Application File command from the File menu's Developer Tools submenu. Figure 11-10 shows the structure of this file, with some appropriate definitions for use with the TechPaper DTD, as well as the default settings, which are for a version of the DocBook DTD.

As with the other SGML tools discussed in this book, you need to do a significant amount of development to be able to use Frame+SGML in an SGML environment. Creating an SGML application for Frame+SGML is analogous to creating a FOSI for the ArborText Adept series tools (discussed in Chapter 9), creating a Layout Specification Instance in Corel WordPerfect (discussed earlier in this chapter), or associating Microsoft Word formatting with a DTD in Microstar's Near & Far Author (discussed in the next section).

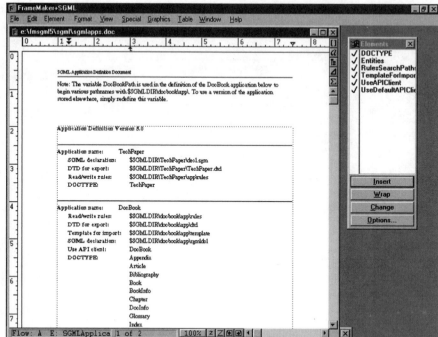

Figure 11-10:
Editing the
Frame-
Maker+SGML
file that
defines
SGML
applications.

The more an application supports SGML, the less work you have to do in order to create an SGML document that works in that application. The ArborText Adept tools provide pure SGML support and use an established standard (the FOSI) for their formatting definition. Corel WordPerfect provides intrinsic support for SGML after you compile it into a format that WordPerfect can use and after you use a separate tool to define the formatting associated with the elements in your DTD. Near & Far provides a complete environment for importing DTDs and mapping their elements to Microsoft Word styles. You need to do more work to use Frame+SGML than you need for either ArborText Adept or Corel WordPerfect, but you can minimize the amount of work you have to do by planning your SGML application carefully.

The key to using Frame+SGML is determining which of the translation scenarios listed in the previous section best describes your situation:

✔ If you have SGML documents and only want to import them into Frame+SGML, you must already have a DTD. You can import that DTD into Frame+SGML and then create read/write rules to convert between the SGML elements and the existing elements in your EDD.

✔ If you are (or want to be) working in Frame+SGML but need to provide SGML documents, you need an EDD. If you don't have one, you should create one. You can then create a DTD from that EDD and create any read/write rules that you want to use to remove any Frame-specific items, such as markers, system variables, and so on, that you don't need to preserve.

✔ If you need to exchange documents with other writers or companies who work in SGML and Frame+SGML, you need to produce read/write rules to go in both directions: from the DTD(s) that they use into your existing Frame+SGML environment, and from your Frame+SGML environment back into their DTD(s). You need to discuss the DTD(s) that they use and get copies of them. If the other writers or companies use a single DTD and you are very familiar with creating an EDD, you may be better off importing their DTD to create an EDD that contains elements with the right names and then specifying the formatting. If you and any writers you work with are very familiar with your existing elements, you may be better off creating the appropriate read/write rules to convert between your existing elements and those in the SGML DTD(s).

In my opinion, Frame+SGML's translation model can make Frame+SGML more cumbersome to work with than other common SGML applications. However, many people prefer to learn the intricacies of the EDD and read/write rule files in order to use the FrameMaker interface and its sophisticated printing capabilities. For a complete discussion of how to create SGML applications for Frame+SGML and how to create read/write rules, see Adobe's *FrameMaker+SGML Developer's Guide*.

Microstar's Near & Far Author v2.0 for Microsoft Word

Microstar's Near & Far Author is a plug-in for Microsoft Word, which means that you must have a copy of Microsoft Word in order to use it. If you're already a Microsoft Word aficionado, Near & Far Author provides support for SGML in an environment that you're already familiar with! Near & Far creates an additional Word menu that contains all of its commands, installs templates for some basic SGML document styles, and includes toolbars that provide easy access to Near & Far commands from within Word. Figure 11-11 shows a sample SGML document that was imported into Microsoft Word using Near & Far Author.

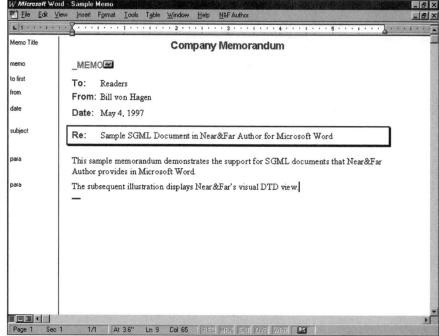

Figure 11-11:
An SGML
memo in
Microsoft
Word using
Near & Far
Author.

Near & Far Author comes in two flavors — a standard edition that lets you use existing Near & Far document templates, and a Manager's Edition that lets you import DTDs, associate formatting information with the elements in a DTD, and save these DTDs as Near & Far document templates. Once you create these templates using the Manager's Edition, you can distribute them to any writers who have the standard edition of Near & Far installed on their systems.

As you might expect, you have to do some work in order to integrate Near & Far into the Word environment. After importing a DTD using the Manager's Edition, you must create a *map* that links the elements in your DTD to Word styles. A map specifies which Word styles will be applied to each element in your DTD by defining a one-to-one relationship between those elements and different Word styles. These styles are automatically created for you when you import a DTD, but they are all initially created as clones of Word's default paragraph style.

Near & Far's Manager's Edition makes it easy for you to create specific styles to be used when commonly used elements, such as paragraphs, appear in different contexts. It also lets you associate different styles with the first instance of an element in a specific context and with subsequent instance of that element in the same context.

To help visualize your document when creating style mappings, Near & Far's Manager's Edition includes the Near & Far Designer, which is a Visual DTD Builder that shows you the hierarchical structure of your SGML documents at any point. You can collapse or expand any portion of the DTD and print different views of your DTD (see Figure 11-12). These printouts can be useful at planning meetings or as part of any training material that you produce for the writers who will use the SGML document templates that you create.

As mentioned earlier in this chapter, some portions of Corel WordPerfect's Visual DTD Builder are licensed from Microstar — this will be obvious if you have occasion to use both products. That's an interesting endorsement, coming from a competitor!

To create an SGML template for use with Near & Far Author, simply follow these steps:

1. **In Word, create a new document template based on Near & Far's** `sgmlnfa.dot` **template.**

2. **From the Near & Far menu, either attach an existing DTD or attach a visual DTD that you created using the Near & Far Designer.** This creates a default map and set of Word styles for the elements in the DTD.

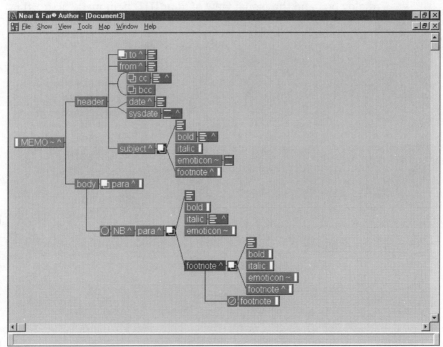

Figure 11-12:
The DTD for the SGML Memo in the Near & Far Designer.

3. **In the Near & Far Designer, use the Edit Element Type menu command to set the type of any elements in your DTD that do not map to Word styles.** Other types of elements that may not have one-to-one mappings to Word styles are graphics objects, tables, equations, footnotes, and cross-references.

4. **In the Designer, use the Edit Element Map menu command to begin associating formatting information with the elements in your DTD and their corresponding styles.** You can add automatic text and counters, and differentiate between the first occurrence of an element and subsequent occurrences. You can also define the possible elements that can follow — these will be appear in a Next Style dialog box when someone uses your template, making it easy for that person to select specific elements for insertion.

5. **Use the Designer's Publish Map menu command to validate your map and export it back into Word until you're satisfied with the results.**

6. **Save the new document template as a Word document template with an appropriate name.**

That's basically all there is to it! Near & Far is a useful piece of software in word-processing and publishing environments that are heavily committed to Microsoft Word. My only real gripe about Near & Far is that it doesn't show SGML container elements in the Word Style window, but the Next Style dialog box and the visual view of your DTD help make up for this.

Part IV
Developing a Document Type Definition

The 5th Wave   By Rich Tennant

"Hey Dad- guess how many elements fit inside your SGML DTD."

In this part . . .

In this part, I examine when, why, and how you may want to write your own DTD. I look at some of the costs involved in developing and supporting your DTD — not just in terms of potentially hiring someone to do the work, but in terms of some costs that you might not have thought of.

I then discuss document analysis, which is the cornerstone of moving your documents to any DTD or of designing your own. On the surface, document analysis seems simple — you just look at your current document set, figure out the general types of organization in each type of document that you need to produce, and then either map that to an existing DTD or design one that fits your needs. Simple, right? Actually, no. Document analysis is a cooperative effort than involves representatives from every group in your company affected by moving your documents into SGML.

I then move on to some specific tips about designing a document type definition. I conclude this part by covering ways you can save yourself a lot of time and effort by extending and enhancing an existing DTD. Part III identified some freely-available DTDs and the industries in which they were used. If one of these DTDs is already in common use in your industry, or is very close to your requirements, this part shows ways to extend that DTD to provide the additional features you require.

Chapter 12

Developing a DTD — It's Not for Everyone

Developing a DTD is one of the most time-intensive aspects of SGML — after all, the DTD shapes the structure of your documents and therefore provides the hierarchy on which you or your company hangs its information. Developing a DTD is a big responsibility, but it's also a great chance to be a hero. However, as the old saying goes: "Discretion is the better part of valor." Therefore, before you develop a DTD, you first must determine whether you have to develop one or whether you can use or adopt an existing DTD. Make sure you read the discussion of some of the DTDs that are publicly available and the types of documents and industries that they were designed for in Chapter 8 before jumping headlong into DTD development.

I don't want to discourage you; I just want you to be realistic. DTD development is a complex, iterative process that requires significant input from other potential users of the information that you are structuring. Developing a DTD requires substantial analysis of your existing documents, as well as a thorough understanding of what you're trying to achieve by converting to SGML. See Chapter 13 for a discussion of *document analysis,* including how to examine your current documentation and develop an SGML structure that satisfies your current and future needs, and whom to involve in this analysis.

This chapter sets the stage for document analysis by discussing how to analyze existing DTDs and the major reasons why you might want to develop your own DTD. I tell you what you need to know in order to develop and support a DTD, and I examine the types of resources you need to have (or contract for) if you want to develop a DTD, train writers to use it, and support it in the future.

Do You Need to Develop Your Own DTD?

You need to consider why you're moving to SGML when deciding whether to use an existing DTD or develop your own. You should ask yourself a few fundamental questions before you decide to develop your own DTD:

- ✔ Are you moving to SGML to improve your documentation process, or because SGML is a delivery requirement, or both?
- ✔ If SGML is a delivery requirement, does the industry you're working in require a specific DTD or just SGML delivery?
- ✔ If you have some freedom in choosing a DTD, do any existing DTDs provide the functionality that you need?
- ✔ If you have some freedom in choosing a DTD, what software do you want to be able to interface with your SGML documents? What groups are going to be sharing the documents?

There are also some more practical concerns to consider:

- ✔ Are you required to use a specific software package? What DTDs does that software support? Does that software support arbitrary DTDs?
- ✔ If you have some freedom in choosing a DTD, do you have the time to develop a DTD and still do forward development of your documentation at the same time?

SGML as a delivery requirement

A *delivery requirement* is a fancy way of identifying any of the contractual requirements for the successful completion of a project. When working for a company or government agency that requires documentation in SGML form, you need to find out whether you're required to use a specific DTD or are just required to provide documentation in SGML. Even if your clients do not require that you use a specific DTD, they almost always have a specific DTD in mind.

If you or your company have to use a specific DTD, you don't have to develop it. The company or agency that you're working with should provide it, or you may have to purchase a copy of the DTD and its documentation from whatever group supports it. This doesn't mean that you're home free, but you're off to a good start! You still have to learn how to work in that DTD, but this is (hopefully) simpler than going through the entire document analysis, DTD design, and DTD development process.

Even if you must work with a specific DTD, you can't be sure that your SGML software provides support for that DTD. If you're already working in an SGML software environment, you may still have to integrate the DTD with your SGML software and develop a formatting environment for that DTD. As discussed in Chapter 9, there is no single standard for how SGML application formats SGML documents. The formatting environment you develop also depends on the output formats in which you're required to deliver your documents.

If you are moving to an SGML environment because it is a delivery requirement and are not already working in SGML, the company or agency you work with probably has some experience in using a specific SGML application. It may have already received documentation for other projects in SGML and may be able to provide you with a FOSI or other SGML formatting description. It may also be able to point you to other firms from whom you may be able to get suggestions or other forms of assistance. If you're totally working in the dark, Chapter 19 discusses how to identify and select the types of SGML software that you need to use to complete your project.

Evaluating existing DTDs

If you are moving to SGML to improve your documentation process or are working on a project for which SGML is a delivery requirement without a specific DTD, you should evaluate the existing DTDs that are publicly available before you consider developing your own. After all, these DTDs were developed for various purposes, usually over a long period of time. Chapter 8 discusses some of the more popular DTDs that are freely available and the reasons that they were created. For example, if you are preparing software or other technical documentation, you should consider using the DocBook DTD, available from the Davenport Group. If you are working in an industry where you know that other companies are using SGML, try to find out what DTD they use. You may have trouble obtaining this information from a competitor, so you may need to consult trade publications, special interest groups, or Web sites to get this information. You should certainly check some of the resources mentioned in Chapter 21 of this book.

Avoid the Not-Invented-Here syndrome!

In many cases, other writers and documentation groups have faced the same decisions and problems that you face today. I've worked for various software companies over the years, several of which have had problems adopting other people's solutions to common problems. This is known as the Not-Invented-Here (NIH) syndrome, meaning that if the solution wasn't invented here, it can't be right. If you feel this way, slap yourself! This sort of perspective is especially silly in the world of SGML because SGML is supposed to facilitate document and information interchange.

You should consider using existing DTDs that were developed for the industry in which you work. If those DTDs don't meet your needs, then don't use them. However, don't reject them out-of-hand simply because you didn't write them. As you see in this chapter (if you don't already know!), developing and supporting a DTD can be an expensive proposition. If you can use an existing solution, you can reduce your costs. You may be able to further reduce costs by leveraging existing books or training materials, or by hiring writers who already have experience with that DTD.

If your documents are a circular peg and a publicly available DTD provides a square hole, you shouldn't just hammer your documents into that DTD to get the selection process over with. After all, you move your documents to SGML in order to make your information more standardized and manageable, and you will have to live with the results of your decision for some time to come. Choosing the wrong solution for some of the right reasons isn't really progress — if you take the time to do it right the first time, you won't have to take the time to do it over in the future.

Preliminary analysis of an existing DTD

If you've identified one or more DTDs that you believe may meet your needs, you should get a copy of each DTD and any reference material that's available for it. Once you've become one with a DTD and its reference information, you need to perform a round of document analysis in miniature to determine whether the DTD really suits your needs. This section helps you evaluate existing DTDs. For more complete information about documentation analysis, see Chapter 13.

If you are responsible for recommending which DTD to use, you may have to do all of the preliminary analysis yourself. If you are working with others to select a DTD, you may be able (or may simply have to) distribute responsibility for evaluating different DTDs to different people. Regardless of who's involved, the steps at this stage of the process are the same:

✔ If you already have an existing documentation set that you're migrating into SGML, select one or two representative samples of different types of documents. Analyze how well the existing DTD matches the structure of your existing documents, while considering whether the structure provided by the DTD may be superior to the current organization of your documents.

✔ Take some small subset of these existing documents and map it into corresponding portions of each proposed DTD. Determine whether the DTD provides all of the information that you believe that you'll need and also whether the DTD is reasonable to work with. You should consider whether the structure of the DTD prevents you from doing anything that you may already depend on in your existing documentation set or whether it forces you to do too much work to accomplish simple tasks.

✔ Verify that the SGML software that you will be using supports each DTD under consideration or whether it can at least be made to work with that DTD.

If the DTD "passes the audition" at this point, you should create a small sample document from scratch using the proposed DTD. If you're already using an SGML package that doesn't provide built-in support for this DTD, you may have to do some work with that tool to be able to use the new DTD. If you are going to be converting existing documents into SGML, it's also a good idea to try converting a section of an existing document into that DTD, to verify how well it actually works with your existing document models.

As you create or convert your sample documents, you may have to refer to the documentation for the proposed DTD frequently. As you do this, try to consider whether you are referring to the documentation to learn the names of tags, or whether you're using the documentation to resolve confusing aspects of the DTD.

If, after performing all this analysis, you still believe that you may be able to use an existing DTD, you need to bring some of the people who will have to work with the DTD, use your documents, or both, into the process.

Welcome to the next level!

You use SGML so that you or other groups that you work with can re-use the information in your documents. You document information in order to provide all the information that your company and its customers need to be able to use your products. The next step in analyzing an existing DTD is to determine whether that DTD satisfies those requirements.

✔ Contact other groups in your organization that may want to share information that's currently in your documents. Show them how one of your sample documents marks up information that they may want to share, and ask them whether that markup meets their needs. Suppose the marketing department wants to be able to use some of the introductory material in your documents in one of its white papers or in technical marketing materials. If the marketing department believes that the markup is more complex than what it needs, try to determine whether it can extract the information from your documents and filter out the excess markup.

✔ Contact groups in your company, such as the customer support group, that have to use your documents to determine whether the information in a sample document that uses the proposed DTD meets their needs. If you have existing documents and did some small sample conversions into the new formats, verify that the mapping between your old documents and the elements in the proposed DTD still provides the information that they need.

If you have an existing set of documents and have converted some samples into the proposed DTD, make sure that you take any comments you receive from other groups with a grain of salt. It is the responsibility of each writer and documentation group to make the final decisions on how information is presented and organized. Make sure that any negative comments you receive are actually based on how information in the proposed DTD is organized and not on how it is formatted. After all, SGML frees documents from the chains of formatting. You can always modify the formatting of your documents later.

If the proposed DTD has passed this second audition, it's time to seriously consider using this DTD. If you've been able to get everyone to agree on a specific existing DTD, you should propose to your management that you adopt this DTD. If you have multiple DTDs that seem to meet your needs, you have two choices:

✔ Re-evaluate whether your selection criteria was tough enough. If you end up with too many candidates at this point, you may not select sample documents that were different enough to illustrate low-level differences between them. Repeat the evaluation process with a more detailed sample document, if necessary.

✔ Choose one of the DTDs.

All for one or many for all?

If the company for whom you're selecting a DTD produces a wide range of products or information, you may not be able to select a single DTD that meets everyone's needs. There's nothing wrong with using more than one DTD at a company or using different subsets of a single, large DTD for different purposes. For example, the DocBook DTD was designed to support documentation sets and individual books, but it also contains a subset for simple articles. If a single large existing DTD doesn't meet your needs, use different DTDs for different types of documents. If you're going to be sharing information between documents that use different DTDs, you'll have to develop some sort of filter or extraction method that translates tags between the two without losing meaningful information. The cost of doing this, however, may be less than the costs of shoehorning different types of information into the same DTD or developing your own monster DTD that handles every documentation need for your company.

Existing DTDs and information interchange with other companies

When selecting a DTD, you also need to determine whether you will need to share information with other companies who may already be working in an SGML environment. If so, you need to contact someone in the documentation group at those companies and get information about the DTD that the company uses. If you're working closely with another company, you should consider using the same DTD that it uses. That company probably went through the same sort of evaluation and selection process that you're currently in the middle of, and you should be able to get some information about why it selected a specific DTD.

In general, companies usually select an existing DTD for one or more of the following reasons:

- ✔ The DTD is a project or industry requirement.
- ✔ An existing DTD suits the type of documentation that they produce.
- ✔ The SGML software they are using supports the DTD they selected or can be made to work with that DTD.

I have discussed the first two points in the preceding two sections, but the last point is an interesting one to consider here. Make sure that you understand and agree with the reasons why any other companies that you're working with selected the tools and DTD(s) that they use. Some companies require that certain software packages be used without consulting all of the potential victims (users) of these software packages. Mandating the wrong tool can, in turn, require the use of the "wrong" DTD simply because the specified tool doesn't support the "right" DTD. Hopefully, this isn't the case for any companies that you work with, but you won't know unless you ask why a specific DTD was chosen.

If you will need to exchange documents with other companies and you choose not to use the same DTD that they use, make sure that you have good reasons for doing so. You or the other companies will have to develop translation tools to go from one DTD to the other without losing any significant information. This process can be both time-consuming and expensive, which you should factor into your decision. However, if you have to exchange documents with a company that uses an SGML tool or DTD that you believe to be inadequate, your costs in developing translation tools may be much less than the cost to your company of using the wrong tools. Remember who you work for! It doesn't help if you're a hero at some other company but your name is mud at your own.

Extending an existing DTD

Before you decide to create your own DTD, you should consider whether you can extend an existing DTD to provide the additional features that you require. The mechanics of extending a DTD are discussed in Chapter 15 — this section introduces some of the logistical reasons that you may want to consider extending an existing DTD rather than writing your own from scratch.

If an existing DTD almost meets your needs but is missing a few key features, you may be able to extend that DTD to meet your needs. If an existing DTD is that close to your requirements, you should first consider whether your additional requirements are really that critical, especially if the existing DTD is one that's widely used throughout the rest of the industry you work in and no one else that you know has modified the DTD.

Before beginning to develop a set of extensions to an existing DTD, consider the following:

✔ Can you get the same results by overloading the meaning of tags that are already present in the existing DTD? For example, if you have an existing application that converts your current documentation into other formats based on styles in your existing documents, you may be able to modify that application to convert other styles or elements to tags that are already present in the DTD. (Generally not a good idea, but sometimes necessary!)

✔ Are the "missing" structural elements actually critical? Do they actually add meaning that is significant, or is this extra meaning currently unused? For example, if you are working in the software industry and your current documents tag commands, function names, and data types differently but the existing DTD does not, are you actually doing anything with that information? If you aren't, you may be able to simply drop the differences and use the same tag for each of these.

If you feel that the differences between your requirements and an existing DTD are important, you should consider extending the DTD. Extending a DTD isn't all that difficult to do, and some standard DTDs (such as the DocBook DTD) even encourage you to do it. Make sure you consider these things:

✔ If you work in an industry that requires the use of a specific DTD, can you extend that DTD and still satisfy the terms of your contract? If you have to submit documentation in a specific DTD, the company or agency you work for may not be able to format those documents because its SGML software doesn't have formatting information for the additional elements in the DTD extension.

✔ Writers who are familiar with the existing DTD will have to learn your extensions even if they are thoroughly familiar with the DTD. The cost of training these people to use your extension, however, should be substantially less than the cost of training them to use your own, custom DTD.

✔ You will have to make sure that you modularize your extensions so that you can easily provide them to any companies that you have to ex-change information with. If possible, you should also modularize the formatting information for those elements so that you can provide that as well. This is easier in SGML software that uses standard, software-independent formatting descriptions such as FOSIs, DSSSL, and so on.

For more information about the ways in which to extend an existing DTD, see Chapter 15.

Developing your own DTD

So you don't have to use a specific DTD, and no existing DTD meets your requirements. Congratulations — you're about to join the few, the proud, the DTD developers!

Developing a DTD is a complex process, but you should do it if no existing DTD can satisfy your specific information requirements. These can range from requirements imposed by specific software packages that you want to use, to detailed types of tagging that you would like to be able to do to facilitate using your documents as efficiently as possible.

Much of the work involved in creating a DTD revolves around understanding the structure of any existing documents that you have or the way in which you want to structure any new documents that you create. Those aspects of creating a DTD are discussed in Chapter 13. The mechanics of actually developing a DTD are discussed in Chapter 14. The remainder of this section discusses some general issues in developing your own DTD.

Documenter, document thyself

When you write a DTD, you should document the DTD as you go along. Even after you're "done" with the DTD, you're going to have to revisit it some day. Unless your memory is much better than mine, at some point you'll find yourself staring at some part of the DTD and thinking "why did I do that?"

Well-documented DTDs require at least two types of documentation:

> ✔ A reference guide to the elements in the DTD, their intent, and how to use them
>
> ✔ Internal documentation in the DTD itself

The second point sounds trivial, but it's often the most important aspect of documenting a DTD, especially if you use some conventions for naming your entities, elements, and attributes. For example, assume that you created a set of elements that can be used only in paragraphs and identify these elements by using the p. prefix. These sorts of conventions make it much easier for writers to work with a DTD, because the names of the elements provide some insight into where and how they can be used. You should document these conventions both in the reference document and in the DTD itself. In many cases, the person who writes the DTD does not actually use the DTD daily.

Reference information and a well-commented DTD are best developed in parallel with the DTD itself. In many respects, developing a DTD is much like developing software, in which having a specification before you begin coding is almost always critical to a well-organized and successful project. As discussed in Chapter 13, you may want to develop a preliminary reference manual for the DTD during the document analysis phase of your DTD development effort. The reference manual can serve as a guide to whoever is actually writing the DTD or as a check that the DTD implementation satisfies the original project requirements, and you can even use it to train writers to use the new DTD.

You don't need a union to be well organized

A well-organized DTD is one in which related elements are grouped together and whose organization reflects the structure of the documents. Organization is an aesthetic issue for many DTD developers, so the beauty of any DTD may lie in the eyes of the beholder. But here are some suggestions that work for me:

- Group entities together based on how they're used and list these as early as possible near the beginning of the DTD. Since you can't refer to an entity before it has been declared, you should organize these together, from lowest level to highest level.

- Organize the structural elements in a DTD in the same way that you might expect to encounter them in a document.

- Include attribute lists immediately after the elements that they modify so that you can see how the attributes provide extra information about the elements they're associated with. Being able to see the content model for an element along with its attributes also makes it easier to identify why attributes were defined in the first place.

- Group elements together that are associated with specific constructs, such as figures and tables.

Once again, these are just my suggestions (and you can certainly find opposing viewpoints in other books on SGML). I say "Tomato," you say "Tomahto" — whatever works for you is the right thing to do.

Using meaningful element and attribute names

Anything that helps users understand how and when to use different tags makes your DTD easier to use by providing a way for users to infer when they should consider using a certain tag. Unfortunately, the default SGML declaration defines the maximum length of names and attributes at eight characters, which really isn't enough for many meaningful names. "Chapter" fits, as does "Section," but something as simple as "SubSection" does not. Sigh!

If you're creating a DTD, you can make your DTD more readable by increasing the value of the NAMELEN (maximum name length) and LITLEN (maximum attribute name length) values to something more reasonable, like 16. You then can create names that anyone can read and understand the purpose of, which makes the DTD easier to maintain in the future and also helps you and other writers get up to speed in using the new DTD as quickly as possible.

Make sure that every SGML package that you plan to use supports changes in the SGML declaration. Not all SGML software lets you modify the default SGML declaration or supports modified values. If you have to exchange documents in your DTD with other companies, you must also provide them with a copy of your SGML declaration. You can't be sure that the SGML software that they use supports modifications to an SGML declaration.

Even if you change values in your SGML declaration and later have to use other SGML software that doesn't support them, you should have little trouble writing a small UNIX shell-script or using a DOS utility to replace all of the extended tag names in your documents with some shorter abbreviation. You'll probably still be ahead if you've been able to work for a while using tags that actually provided useful information via their names.

If none of the items in the previous paragraph are the case, go for it. The eight-character limitation on names dates from the days when each byte of memory was precious. The advent of cheap memory and virtual memory have put those days behind us, so why shouldn't you?

When creating meaningful element names, you should balance the value of having a truly meaningful name with the number of times that people might have to manually enter the tags for that element. For example, a <PARAGRAPH> element is more meaningful than a <P> element, but since you will probably type opening and closing <P> tags a zillion times per document, you may want to keep that one short. It's almost always useful to assign meaningful names to infrequently used elements, because you don't use them that often and thus might appreciate a longer name as a clue as to what elements to use.

Resources Required for DTD Development

This section discusses the types of resources that you need to develop or obtain in order to create a DTD and associated formatting environment, or covert any existing documents from their original format into that DTD, or both. This section discusses these resources from the perspective of planning the entire SGML migration process. Other chapters of this book examine these issues in more detail:

✔ Chapter 13 discusses how to analyze your documents and identify the structure that you want to implement in your SGML environment.

✔ Chapter 14 discusses issues in designing DTDs and an associated formatting environment.

✔ Chapter 20 discusses document conversion and related tool development issues in more detail.

SGML expertise

If you're moving to an SGML environment for documentation development, you need to have a certain amount of SGML expertise in order to manage and choreograph this project. You have to evaluate, select, and become familiar with a new software package. You also have to promote a new approach to documentation development among the writers using the new software. Using an SGML documentation development environment changes the way writers view and work with your documentation. Your DTD enforces structural consistency in your documents, requiring that certain elements be present in specific contexts and in a specific sequence. This allows writers to focus on the information that they are creating rather than worrying about what comes next in a document or about specific formatting and presentation issues. However, changing from procedural to descriptive markup (as explained in Chapter 1) is usually a difficult thing for writers to adapt to, especially if they've been working in procedural markup for a long time.

While you are moving to an SGML environment, you serve as a constant advocate for SGML, always ready to explain why moving to SGML is the right thing to do and promoting the long-term benefits of SGML. Therefore, you need to be conversant in SGML terminology and theory, as well as the business and product-quality reasons for moving to SGML.

You must have certain specific types of SGML expertise in order to design and implement a complete, usable DTD and SGML environment. You must

✔ Have a thorough understanding of your document set and the structure that you want it to have. Chapter 13 explains how to analyze your documents, derive their basic structure, and then consider whether you want to use your move to SGML as an opportunity to augment their existing structure.

✔ Have a thorough understanding of the basic components and structure of a DTD, how sets of low-level character entities are included in a DTD, how attributes let you extend the usability of your elements, and how you can define centralized sets of entities that let you enforce standard terminology throughout a documentation set.

✔ Understand what (if any) other groups or software you want to be able to interact with your information and understand their requirements.

There's no shame in not knowing everything when you start such a project. Depending on your project management style, you can use a move to SGML as a chance to bring a group of writers closer together by involving them in the decision, evaluation, and selection processes. Nevertheless, you still need one "expert" on the project who is empowered to make decisions. If you're that expert, make sure you have the SGML expertise to make the right decisions! This book is obviously not the only book on the subject — see Chapter 21 for more information on other SGML guides and references that may be useful sources of information for you.

Documentation tools development

Most writers and documentation groups have a certain set of tools that they use in developing documentation. Aside from the primary software package used to develop documents, they typically use other utilities to perform specific functions, such as pagination utilities used to extract specific pages from formatted output files (such as PostScript) or produce 2- or 4-up versions of formatted output files, archiving utilities that let you save versions of your documents associated with specific releases, and conversion utilities that convert your documents into other formats such as HTML, UNIX man pages, and so on.

Whatever your current documentation toolkit contains, you must be prepared to rewrite these utilities (or purchase SGML-aware versions of these same type of utilities) in order to preserve aspects of your documentation process that are outside the scope of your authoring environment. Moving to a different documentation development environment may make many of your existing utilities obsolete, especially if they were designed around specific aspects of your previous documentation tools.

If you have an existing document set that you want to move into SGML, you will probably have to develop or obtain conversion utilities to convert your existing documents into SGML. Depending on the format used by your current documentation tools, conversion can be a relatively smooth process or a very expensive and time-consuming one. Planning and scheduling the conversion of your existing documents into SGML is discussed in Chapter 20 — at this point, it's just important that you factor the costs and time involved to convert any existing documents into your plan for migrating to SGML. When thinking about scheduling, you also should consider that you can't migrate your documents to SGML until you have a firm idea of the DTD that the converted documents must conform to.

Formatting environment development

If you actually want to print the documents you develop with the DTD you create, you also have to develop a formatting environment for that DTD. As discussed in Chapter 9, different SGML software packages define the formatting associated with a DTD in different ways. Some SGML packages use proprietary applications to associated formatting with a DTD, whereas other packages use standard, software-independent formatting descriptions such as FOSIs, DSSSL, and so on.

Regardless of which SGML package you select, the cost of developing a formatting environment for your DTD is an additional cost that is related to your decision to develop your own DTD. If you opt to use an existing DTD, you may be able to get a formatting definition from someone else who uses that DTD with the SGML software package that you use. Her formatting requirements may be different than yours, but an existing formatting definition will at least give you a starting point.

If you aren't responsible for developing the formatting environment to be used with your new DTD, the person who is should be familiar with the formatting and markup of any existing documents that you have. This familiarity makes it easier to successfully map existing styles or format codes (where possible) into the appropriate elements in the new DTD. See the section of Chapter 13 for more information.

Contracting out DTD development

If you've read the previous sections in this chapter and don't see how you'll be able to develop the expertise or find the time to develop a DTD and its associated formatting environment, you could contract out the development of your DTD with an SGML consulting firm. You should be able to locate a local firm that provides SGML consulting services by calling various computer contracting firms or by contacting the nearest chapter of the Society for Technical Communication (STC), a professional association for technical writers. Assuming that the SGML contractor you locate has substantial DTD development experience, you can reduce both the amount of time it takes for you to migrate to SGML and your costs for the migration (based on what the contractor charges you, of course).

Before selecting an SGML contractor, ask for references from clients whose projects were similar in scope to the one that you're attempting. Contact these previous clients and ask for feedback on the levels of ability, quality, service, and support provided by the contractor. All of these are critical factors in any project, but they are especially important when your future documentation development work is going to hinge on the DTD created by a contractor!

Supporting and Enhancing Your Own DTD

If you create your own DTD, you have to worry about the fact that there are no external sources of information on that DTD — you and the other people involved in developing the DTD are that resource! As mentioned earlier, developing a reference manual for the DTD is a useful exercise during the planning and analysis phase of DTD development. This reference manual can then serve as the specification for the DTD and also serve as the cornerstone of subsequent training for new writers or any other people who will be using documents that are marked up using that DTD.

This section discusses some of the major issues in two different aspects of support for a custom DTD:

✔ Training people to use the DTD and any related software

✔ Fixing problems in and enhancing a custom DTD

At least in the early phases of creating a DTD and an associated formatting environment and migrating a set of existing documents into that DTD, you may feel that your life may never be your own again. Like any software development effort, developing a DTD and an associated formatting description is an iterative process in which you create an initial implementation, fix bugs or issues that surface that you hadn't originally thought of, and then repeat the process. If you are solely responsible for the DTD and the formatting description, you will be a popular person indeed. Well, maybe not popular — let's just say "in demand."

Chapter 14 discusses some techniques for developing a DTD and provides some tips that will help you minimize disruption as the DTD changes while people are actively creating or migrating documents that conform to it.

Training for success

Providing user education is an important part of making your switch to SGML successful. Training helps users get up to speed faster, making them as productive as possible as early as possible. User training also provides an important psychological advantage — if users of your SGML software understand the features and benefits of SGML in terms of both authoring and information management, they are more likely to become partners in your SGML effort rather than simply grudging participants.

Regardless of whether you create your own DTD or use an existing one, you have to develop a process for training new writers (or others) to work with the SGML software package you've selected. You can usually accomplish this by getting multiple copies of the user and reference manuals for the software you've selected. The user documentation for SGML software that provides support for arbitrary DTDs usually provides a fairly generic introduction to using the software package that is independent of the DTD that is being used.

Teaching users to work with a different software package is fairly straight-forward. SGML software's emphasis on structure often makes it easy to educate users on how to use the SGML authoring software. Most graphical SGML software always displays a list of the elements that are valid at the current point in the document. This feature actually takes a lot of the guess-work out of working in an SGML authoring environment, because writers can't insert elements that aren't intended to be used at the current point in your documents.

When you are educating writers on how to use SGML software, remember that writers must change the way they think about the documents in order to use SGML. Changing from procedural markup (telling the software how to format a specific piece of text) to descriptive markup (selecting tags that tell the software the purpose of a specific piece of text) isn't always an easy thing for writers to adapt to, especially if they've been working in proce-dural markup for a long time. The important thing to emphasize to any users of your SGML software is that descriptive markup allows writers to focus on the information that they are creating rather than worrying about what comes next in a document or about specific formatting and presentation issues.

User training for your SGML software and DTD should include the following:

- ✔ An explanation of the features and benefits of SGML, emphasizing its benefits to writers and to the organization. You may want to select a standard SGML reference text (such as this one!) to distribute to writers so that they can familiarize themselves with the basic concepts, syntax, and issues in using SGML.

- ✔ User and reference manuals for the SGML software package that you are using.

- ✔ An explanation of the organization of your DTD, the elements it con-tains, the possible attributes of those elements, and the general entities that are available for use in your documents.

- ✔ A reference manual for the DTD that you are using. Over time (once your DTD has been in use for a while), you should consider developing a user's guide for your DTD and distributing that as well.

- ✔ Printouts of some sample documents that provide examples of the types of tagging used in representative sections of the documents that your company produces.

- ✔ A follow-up session two weeks after the initial training, giving new users a chance to ask questions after they've had a chance to begin using the software and DTD.

Supporting your DTD and formatting environment

If you implement a complex DTD and associated formatting environment and never experience any problems with them or any need to extend them, please let me know so that I can worship you. The fact of the matter is that, just like any development project, the initial implementation of a complex system almost always requires some bug-fixing and enhancements. You should encourage comments and suggestions from users of your SGML software, especially in the early phases of developing a DTD and associated formatting. This encourages team spirit and helps identify problems early. It's much better to find out about them then than on the day when you have to release your first set of documents from the new system!

Though this may be obvious to everyone, it's worth saying — never do maintenance on the live copy of your DTD or its associated formatting description! Once someone has identified a problem and you've corrected it, you have to validate your solution against existing documents to make sure that your solution to the current problem hasn't introduced other problems. Since a DTD defines the structure of your documents, you may create other problems when you fix the problem with your DTD.

Whenever possible, DTD maintenance should involve loosening the content models for various elements rather than making them more restrictive. For example, suppose that your original content model for a figure says that a caption is optional but that you subsequently change the DTD so that a caption is mandatory. Boom! You'd probably have many broken documents. However, if a caption is originally mandatory but you subsequently decide that a caption is optional, you won't have any problems.

Even though loosening content models is a good general rule, there are certainly cases where tightening an existing content model is necessary, even if this breaks your documents. You should try to avoid this whenever possible, but sometimes it's sad but necessary.

Regardless of the changes you make to a DTD, you should always validate those changes against the new DTD before releasing it to the user community for your SGML software. Many SGML software packages provide a command-line, or batch mode, in which you can simply invoke the SGML parser against various documents to ensure that they still comply with the DTD. I generally also like to validate changes to the DTD against sample documents using an SGML parser other than the one in the SGML software package that I'm using, simply as a sanity check. Different SGML parsers are often pickier about different aspects of SGML, and, just like in medicine, it never hurts to get a second opinion! There are several excellent SGML parsers that are freely available, such as nsgmls. See Appendix A for information about where to get source and binary versions of these parsers for your operating system.

Chapter 13

Analyzing Your Documents

● ●

In This Chapter

▶ Basic goals of document analysis

▶ Forming an analysis team

▶ Techniques for successful document analysis

▶ Implications of output formats

● ●

ocument analysis is one of the cornerstones of a successful SGML implementation. In order to create or select a DTD that suits your new and existing documents, you have to understand the structure of those documents. You do this by analyzing representative samples of any existing documents that you have so that you can derive their underlying structures. You can then combine the structures you've identified in different types of documents and determine the components that are shared across those document types and the things that are unique to each document type. If you're producing a single DTD, you need to account for different structures within a single high-level element, such as a book. If you're developing multiple DTDs, you can break these shared components out into separate files that are invoked as a parameter entity by each DTD.

This chapter discusses several aspects of document analysis. After providing some background information about document analysis and who should be involved in the process, I discuss some ways of identifying the basic structure that exists within your documents and how that analysis is critical to the creation or selection of an appropriate DTD. After that, I discuss how the SGML software that you use can influence that analysis and how the output formats that you are targeting can affect structural and formatting analysis.

Document Analysis 101

If you have any existing documents that you want to move into SGML, you need to understand how the existing parts of those documents map into the elements of an SGML DTD. Regardless of whether you're developing a DTD or evaluating existing DTDs, you have to understand the current structure of your documents in order to create an appropriate DTD or determine which existing DTD best matches your existing documents.

When you analyze documents, you identify all the basic units of information that your documents contain and determine how these units are related to each other. As discussed in the "Why a DTD?" section of Chapter 3, SGML is about more than just documents — it's about managing all of the information used by your company and turning frozen sources of information, such as documents, into a reusable pool of information for you or the company you work for. Though most information starts out in documents, not all of it ends up in paper documents — the information in your SGML system may be targeted toward online delivery, database storage, or any other destination. Just as SGML liberates the information that your company uses from a specific software package, it also liberates that information from a specific output format.

Technical writers organize information to help you or your customers use your products efficiently. So even if your documents aren't produced in a structured documentation tool, they therefore contain some structure. Even in a worst-case scenario where your existing documents contain only procedural markup, you can start your document analysis by looking at any parts of your documents that provide insight into their structure. For example, the word processing and publishing software that you use probably provides features, such as a Table of Contents, that shows that structure at some level. If that software uses style sheets, you're probably even better off. As I explain in Chapter 1, style sheets are at least a baby step toward structured documents because they attempt to isolate repeatable elements in your documents and apply a consistent presentation style to those elements. Even though documentation tools that only support style sheets don't actually enforce the structure of those documents or define the contexts in which different styles can appear, they do identify specific portions of your documents and associate them with styles that often have meaningful names, like "Heading 1," "Heading 2," and so on. You can often use the names of various styles to help you lay the foundation of your document analysis.

Assembling a Document Analysis Team

In order to successfully identify the structural components of your documents, you need to involve a number of different people. You need other people's input so that you can get the most mileage out of your SGML effort. Different groups that use your documents often have very different ideas of what portions of those documents are most significant and how the documents are "really" organized.

At a minimum, your document analysis team should include one representative from each group that plans to use your documents or the information that they contain. Including someone from each of these groups helps ensure that you don't overlook anyone's requirements. The document analysis team should include several writers, each of whom is responsible for a specific aspect of the documentation development process, such as authoring, editing, and the different output formats that you are required to produce. If you are going to use SGML software other than authoring and formatting tools, such as database or version control software, you also want to involve someone from each group that is responsible for a piece of that software. The software that you use shouldn't drive the way in which you identify the components of your documents, but insights from the software side can often help crystallize the contents of low-level components of your documents.

You need to involve other people in the process because different groups of people look at information differently. For example, different groups in your company may look at a product part number of 314-255-0001 in the following ways:

- Documentation group: "Part numbers have to be tagged so that we can cross-reference them with more detailed information, such as part descriptions in the catalog."

- Production group: "Part numbers consist of three fields, the first representing the product line, the second the site where they're produced, and the third the revision level of the part."

- Database group: "Part numbers have to have one or more identifiers that serve as a key for records in the inventory database."

In this example, a single element for part numbers would satisfy the documentation and database groups but would leave the production group slightly cranky. By involving a representative from each group, you can take note of these requirements and then make sure that your tagging scheme accommodates everyone.

The Basics of Successful Analysis

Document analysis, like any refining or distillation process, is usually composed of several stages. In the first stage, you clearly identify the purpose of document analysis, provide some background information about SGML so that people know what portions of the documents they're trying to identify, and explain how this information will be used. In the second stage, the document analysis team identifies the basic structural elements of your documents and the relationship between those elements. In the final stage, a subset of the document analysis team takes a closer look at the results of stage two, describing what each structural element of your document is composed of, what elements can be combined into single elements by using attributes, and what portions of you text can be generalized into entities.

Before you have your first meeting of the document analysis team, make sure that you have someone to keep a record of all of the comments, suggestions, discussions, and arguments that occur during your document analysis meetings. This person is no less important than the court reporter at any legal proceeding. Having an accurate record of why various decisions were made will prevent your from reinventing the wheel each time the same issue surfaces, especially if reaching consensus required a compromise among the perspectives of different members of the analysis team.

Verifying that the team is complete

I find that the first step in successful document analysis is making sure that you actually have representatives from all of the groups that will be affected by your move to SGML. For this reason, the first meeting of a document analysis team should focus on making sure that everyone is there who needs to be there. You can make sure that no one is missing by dedicating the first meeting to identifying all the types of information that your company uses, the users of that information, and the tools that those people use to produce and access that information. For example, it might be easy to initially overlook different groups who produce information for your company's web site. Also, over time, companies tend to accumulate tools and procedures like a snowball rolling down a hill. If you want to be successful in moving your company to SGML, you want to make sure that everyone can use the new system that you have selected and that your new SGML software doesn't cut people off from information that they currently use and depend on. Neglecting the needs or concerns of some groups of people not only affects their productivity but may also alienate them and make them resistant to using tools and document models that they didn't help to develop. Including everyone that you can in the document analysis process helps to develop some personal involvement in the results of your analysis work. Allies are always a good thing, especially if you are still making a case for your move to SGML!

Educating the document analysis team

In order to successfully identify the structure of your documents and the elements that comprise it, the members of your document analysis team must at least be familiar with the basic principles of SGML. They have to know what they're trying to do in order to do it; the idea of structured documentation may be new to many people. At the same time that you want to make sure that the team understands the concepts of structured documentation, you don't need to turn them all into SGML experts — at least not right away! In the early phases of document analysis, you don't want your discussions to get bogged down in topics such as whether you really need four types of list elements or whether you should have one list element with an attribute that identifies its type. Don't rush things — you'll come to the element/attribute discussion soon enough!

To make sure that the members of your team understand what they must do, you must make sure that they understand several basic aspects of SGML:

- ✔ SGML separates the structure of a document from how the elements of a document are formatted.

- ✔ An SGML DTD defines the structure of a document and the context in which the components of that structure can appear.

- ✔ One or more formatting descriptions accompany a DTD; each formatting description defines how a specific output format (printed documents, online information, database records, and so on) should be produced.

These basic concepts should be enough to let the members of your analysis team identify the building blocks of your documents without getting them bogged down in details. You must also make sure that all the members understand that document analysis will take quite some time. The more time you spend analyzing your documents, the more information you end up with about your documents. The amount of time you spend analyzing documents is a good predictor for the success of your move to SGML and the usability of the information that you encode in SGML.

Basic structural analysis

When you begin analyzing documents, you first must identify the different types of documents that you currently produce and select a representative example of each. The entire team has to examine each of these types of documents for two reasons: first, because different types of documents are usually organized differently; and second, because various types of documents usually share a significant number of low-level components even though their high-level organization may differ.

As a simple example, user guides and reference manuals usually have different numbers of heading levels. User guides frequently provide introductory material for certain types of sections — chapters may begin with an "About This Chapter" section that summarizes the goals of the chapter, provides a local table of contents for the chapter, and provides a list of related chapters. Reference manuals, which may simply contain sequences of reference pages, usually don't contain such a section. However, a software reference manual may contain an introductory page in each chapter that lists the functions, datatypes, or commands that the chapter contains. At a much lower level, both of these types of documents contain paragraphs of text, different types of itemized lists, figures and tables, and so on. During your document analysis, you should determine at what level you can weave all of these document types together with these common threads.

After you've identified the different types of document that you will have to analyze, you should spend some time identifying the audience for each of these documents and how members of that audience actually use the documents. You may want to consult members of your company's customer support organization, for they may be able to provide insights into current aspects of your documents that your customers don't like or things that users of your documents wish were present but which currently aren't. As discussed later in this chapter, defining the current organization of your documents is only part of a successful SGML implementation — defining what should be there but isn't is equally important. After all, you're designing a new system — do it right or do it over!

Now it's finally time to start looking at each type of document! I find that the table of contents is the most useful place to begin analyzing a specific document, because that usually shows the highest-level structure of a single document.

How you actually work your way through each type of document depends on the tools that you have available. I like to have document analysis meetings in a room with a large whiteboard and use sticky notes (such as Post-It notes) to record different structural elements that team members identify. You can stick these on the white board as you go along, and then draw arrows on the whiteboard to show the relationship between the elements that you identify. When you use sticky notes, you also have enough space to record alternate suggestions for what you call each of these levels, because the different groups that use your information may have very different notions of what a structural element represents. Even something as trivial as what to call an element that contains the name of the person who wrote a specific document can be a point of contention, because different groups use different jargon that's specific to their fields. The difference between an author and a byline may be meaningless to a software developer, but it may be significant to a technical writer and a marketing communicator. If you're the lucky leader for the document analysis meetings, you want to stress that your primary goal is to identify the structure of your documents — assigning permanent names to the elements of that structure can come later!

I don't mean to be <BOLD>, but . . .

When people talk about analyzing an existing documentation set, they sometimes forget that analyzing the formatting of that documentation set is a separate issue that can actually contribute to successfully identifying all of the elements that comprise your documents. The formatting of an existing set of documents certainly expedites document analysis, because examining how things are formatted, especially within paragraphs, often lets you identify different things that should be represented by different elements or attributes of single elements.

Analyzing the formatting of your existing documents is an interesting exercise for two reasons:

✔ If your SGML application has to support some or all of the same output formats as

your current documents, analyzing the formatting associated with the styles in your current documents can provide information about the formatting you want to associate with the elements in a DTD and their attributes.

✔ If you use the same formatting for many different paragraph or word styles in your current documents, you may want to consider whether you actually need to differentiate between all of the things that you currently format in the same way. You may be able to collapse some of these into single elements in a DTD that you are developing or avoid using certain elements in an existing DTD in favor of some other element to simplify the development of your formatting definition.

Elements without context have no place in your analysis!

Identifying the elements that make up the structure of your documents is only one part of the document analysis process — the other is explicitly identifying the context in which those elements can appear. In a standard document, certain elements can only appear within certain other parts of a document. For example, in a book, sections typically have to appear within chapters, and subsections have to appear within chapters. Other elements, such as titles, can appear within any of these document divisions, but have different characteristics based on the division

in which they appear. As you analyze your documents, the context in which each structural element can appear is a critical part of the information that you must record. Whoever is writing your DTD will need this information in order to correctly define the structure of your documents. This structure provides an SGML parser with the information it needs to validate a document. Without context information, your documents have no real structure, and your documents are just a linear collection of chunks of information.

Remember that you can't analyze all your documents in an afternoon — successful document analysis typically requires many meetings, especially when you get to the lower levels of your documents. You can usually knock out the high-level structure of your documents in a single meeting. Once you've identified the structure of your documents to some level and adjourned a specific meeting, you can use drawing software packages, such as those used to develop organizational charts, to record structural information. After each meeting, you can transfer the day's results in a drawing package, from which you can print copies for reference at the next meeting. Depending on the complexity and size of your documents, you want to break your transcriptions of this structure into some number of different pages, each of which describes the structure of a certain part of a document at a certain level. You can then cross-reference these drawings so that people can easily follow the flow of that structure from one sheet to another.

As you identify each structural element of your documents, you should also record the semantic meaning of that element within the context of a document. You can simply define a "title" as a "series of alphanumeric characters and whitespace that identifies the contents of some section of a document." You should record information about your expectations of the content and meaning of various parts of your document so that you can accurately use this information later, when creating a DTD or mapping structures in your documents into an existing DTD.

Advanced structural analysis

At some point in the analysis process, you may want to make attendance at further meetings optional. As you reach a certain level of detail, you may notice that members of the original analysis team are starting to yawn frequently, have begun to doodle, or are playing Doom on their laptops during your meetings. This is a good sign that you may have crossed over to a level of detail that's meaningful only to writers who will actually be using your DTDs or other groups who will be implementing and supporting some parts of the SGML software that you've selected. At this point, you should make attendance optional for the other members of your analysis group or perhaps ask them to begin analyzing a different type of document at the highest level.

Here are some of the aspects of document analysis that may be too detailed for some members of the group:

✔ Developing a list of the items in your documents that should be represented as entities. These items should be important to the documentation and marketing groups, because product names and other tag phrases have a way of changing at the most awkward times. However, software or hardware developers may not really care about these items. If I had a nickel for each time I've heard the phrase "well, you can just query/replace that throughout the docs," I'd probably be writing this book on a Cray.

✔ Enumerating the types of characters that can appear in various elements. Probably only writers, marketing communications folks, whoever is writing or selecting your DTD, and the people who are supporting or developing your SGML software care about these characters. The last group may not be obvious until you consider that certain SGML applications need to know the types of data contained in various elements. A database system is a perfect example, because you need to know how to declare different fields in its records — it would certainly be frustrating to generate a document from an SGML database, only to discover that you're losing certain characters because the report writer has different assumptions about field contents than what they actually contain.

✔ Identifying the different levels at which you want to be able to cross-reference information. As introduced in Chapter 5, elements that you need to be able to refer to must have ID attributes, and elements that refer to those elements must have IDREF attributes. Writers especially care about these things, but any potential users of your documents may also care because identifying the elements that have ID attributes determines how detailed the cross-references in your document can be.

✔ Identifying different types of elements that can be collapsed into single elements with attributes. The number and types of elements that you have and how you implement different types of elements is certainly important to writers and marketing communicators, but it is also important to any other group that actually needs to use your SGML data.

I've seen the future and they is us

SGML liberates the information that your company uses from the constraints of a specific publishing system. It also liberates that information from the standard document model because (as introduced in Chapter 2 and discussed in Part V of this book), SGML lets you access information using many different types of software packages, not just publishing software. For these reasons, many people never consider how they might use that information in the future. It's hard to create specific plans for ways of using information with software that you don't have yet, but it's important that the structure that you identify in your documents is flexible enough that it can be easily adopted for use with new tools.

You can "plan for the future" by brainstorming with your document analysis team about any assumptions that you may be making during the analysis process. For example, if your documents are currently targeted toward a specific industry or agency that requires that you use a specific DTD, are you accidentally building the structure of that DTD into the analysis process? As mentioned earlier in this chapter, you should try to do your initial document analysis in as much of a vacuum as possible, without considering any existing DTDs that you may want to use so that you can understand the current structure of your documents. This step is critical to selecting or creating an appropriate DTD. If you are required to use a specific DTD, you can subsequently look at ways to adopt your documents to that DTD, investigate whether you can extend it (if necessary), and look for other ways to preserve any information that is important for your business but which may not be provided in that DTD.

If you're creating a DTD, you need to consider whether you are building assumptions about your current customers or product lines into the structure you are identifying. If you're creating a DTD, you can always extend it in the future to handle additional items, right? Right — you can extend the DTD, but this may have a ripple effect across other groups in your company. For example, if parts of your SGML data are stored as (or extracted to) records in a database system, adding another field that has to appear in a certain position may blow your database software out of the water or give your MIS or database groups a month-long migraine. Once again, you can't anticipate requirements that don't exist yet, but you can make sure that the results of your document analysis project include as few built-in assumptions about your data as possible.

As mentioned earlier in this chapter, your company's customer support group can help you identify aspects of your current documents that your customers don't like, as well as things that users of your documents wish were present but which aren't.

An Example

This section provides a simple example of a single entry in a parts catalog to show how you might analyze its structure. Suppose a catalog entry contains the following:

002-56899-001R   Jaguar XJ6 Hood Ornament   **$29.95**

You might want to map this entry into the following components:

✔ **Entry:** 002-56899-001R   Jaguar XJ6 Hood Ornament $29.95, consisting of

✔ **Part Number:** 002-56899-001R, consisting of

- Country of Origin: 002
- Jaguar part number: 56899
- Revision level: 001
- New or Refurbished: R

✔ **Description:** Jaguar XJ6 Hood Ornament

✔ **Price:** 29.95

In SGML, this might look like the following:

```
<ENTRY>
<PART-NUM SOURCE="Manson Auto">
<COUNTRY>002</COUNTRY>
<JAG-NUM>56899</JAG-NUM>
<REVISION>001</REVISION>
<TYPE>R</TYPE>
</PART-NUM>
<DESCRIPTION>Jaguar XJ6 Hood Ornament</DESCRIPTION>
<PRICE>29.95</PRICE>
</ENTRY>
```

By identifying this level of information in a simple catalog entry, you can search your catalogs at many different levels — how many parts are refurbished, how many parts are from a specific country, and so on. Note that the PART-NUM element has a SOURCE attribute that doesn't even appear in the description. This is an example of future planning — though the SOURCE attribute doesn't appear in the catalog, someone may find it useful to identify parts from a specific source.

When analyzing documents, I don't encourage people to think of the elements that they're identifying in SGML because, since doing this can defocus the analysis team and confuse members of the team that are new to SGML. However, for this example, I thought it was useful to show how this information might appear in SGML and also to provide an example of how you might analyze a piece of an existing document and discover that there was additional information that you wanted to capture.

Identifying Output Formats for Your SGML Documents

You also need to consider the output formats that you will produce for the new system. Aside from giving you the chance to restructure and standardize your documents, moving an existing document set to an SGML application also provides you with an opportunity to reexamine and modify the ways in which you deliver that information to its users. For example, if you will still be producing printed documentation, the fact that you're using a new package to produce those documents gives you a chance to modify their formatting, layout, and form factor (size and shape). You will probably have to create a formatting definition to accompany your new DTD, so you may as well consider changing the look of your documents.

Today, there is a whole world of information beyond simple printed documentation. Although identifying all of the ways in which you want to be able to deliver information from your SGML implementation isn't purely a part of identifying the current structure of your documents, it is an important part of designing the content model for the information that you are storing in SGML. Different output formats place different demands on your information; each format has to somehow be codified in your SGML documents. An especially important aspect of producing information for output formats such as online documentation is the level at which you associate IDs with different elements so that you can jump to them in hypertext documents. The elements and levels at which you support IDs also determines how you can cross-reference them in printed documents.

Chapter 14

Writing a Usable DTD

● ●

In This Chapter

▶ Figuring out how many DTDs you need

▶ Creating readable, modular DTDs

▶ Working with a top-down design

▶ Testing your DTD

▶ Using version control to track changes to your DTD

● ●

Don't let the existence of this chapter scare you — most SGML users will never have to write a DTD! However, if you aren't working in an industry that forces you to use a specific DTD and you believe that no existing DTD meets your needs, writing your own DTD may well be the right thing to do. Trying to make different documents look the same and ensure that they contain the same types of information causes many migraines for documentation managers and writers who inherit existing documents. A custom DTD can enforce rules of structure and content that can save you and your company lots of aspirin, especially when you work with large document sets.

To design an accurate and usable DTD, you must have a good structural and content analysis of your documents (see Chapter 13). This chapter provides general suggestions for structuring, writing, and commenting your DTD. The hard part — actually writing the DTD — is still up to you. If you follow the guidelines discussed in this chapter, you should end with a well-designed and maintainable DTD. Even if you have to write the DTD, you should err on the side of caution and document and annotate the DTD as you create it because you may not be the sole person responsible for maintaining that DTD in the future. Even with DTDs that I've written, I sometimes find myself wondering "Why did I do that?" Though it may seem trivial, you need to document and comment your DTD as you go along. Yesterday's brainstorm can be today's sandstorm if you don't record the reasons why you made various structural and design decisions.

Always remember that you can't write a successful DTD in a vacuum — like the document analysis process, you need suggestions and feedback from anyone else who has to use the DTD. Make sure that you involve others in the DTD development process as much as possible, even if you just have them attend regular status meetings that describe the hierarchy of your DTD. Getting other people's input throughout the DTD development and SGML adoption process makes it less likely that they will point fingers later, and you minimize the chance that you may overlook the requirements or concerns of any group that will use your DTD.

I haven't used the SGML Magic icon to identify specific tips or considerations in this chapter because if you're writing a DTD, you're either an SGML wizard or at least a sorcerer's apprentice!

Creating One DTD or Several?

When you decide to create your own DTD, you must decide whether a single DTD can satisfy all your documentation requirements or whether you need to create different DTDs to reflect the different types of documents that you produce. Your document analysis should provide much of the information on which you base this decision, but you also should consider maintenance, usability, documentation tools, and scheduling constraints.

Even after completing the document analysis process, you may think that different types of documents cry out for different DTDs. However, remember that many widely used public DTDs, such as the DocBook DTD for software documentation, provide the SGML structures required for many different types of documents. If you use a single, multipurpose DTD, you simplify maintenance issues because you need to be an expert only on that DTD. You also simplify support issues because everyone uses the same DTD, and you simplify documentation tools issues since the documentation tools need to know only about a single DTD. However, a multipurpose DTD is bound to be more complex than a DTD that describes a simple type of document. A multipurpose DTD can therefore be more difficult to maintain and more difficult for writers to use, because multipurpose DTDs usually contain a much richer set of elements than single-purpose DTDs. DTDs that are both multipurpose and relatively simple run the risk of becoming incapable to accurately describe the content of your documents at an appropriate level of detail. The HTML DTD is a good example of this sort of problem.

Writers using a multipurpose DTD need to understand which types of elements can be used in each type of documents. You can minimize confusion by producing accurate documentation for each type of document described in the DTD. You can use these documents in training and in reference materials for anyone working in your DTD.

You also need to consider your current document development schedule when deciding whether to create one DTD or several DTDs. If you're adopting SGML for your documentation development work, have a large set of existing documents, and already have large numbers of upcoming document deliverables, you have my sympathy! Your task is not impossible, but you may face a lot of pressure and potential problems for the writers, your existing schedule, or both. Whenever possible, try not to let yourself get into this situation. If you've proposed a move to SGML that is not driven by corporate or industry requirements, try to develop your DTD in parallel with existing document development, and schedule the actual conversion for shortly after a document or product release. By doing this, you give yourself the time to develop an optimal DTD, fine-tune any conversion utilities that you have to develop, and help to eliminate the chance that problems in your DTD or SGML software will affect your document delivery dates.

It should be clear that a multipurpose DTD is always much more complex to create and maintain than a DTD that only reflects the structure of a single type of documents. Creating several distinct DTDs, however, can be very time-consuming. When creating multiple DTDs that each describe a different type of document, you have to focus on centralizing elements, entities, and attribute definitions that are used by more than one type of document, even if those documents are all defined in a single DTD. This process is known as *modular design*. You can use it to help minimize the amount of design work you have to do and create maintainable DTDs. A good design and implementation always takes more time than one that's simply hacked together. Remember, however, that *if you don't take the time to do it right the first time, make sure you budget the time to do it over*. For some tips on creating portions of a DTD that you can share between multiple DTDs, see the section called "Creating modular DTDs" later in this chapter.

If a DTD that you are creating is going to be used by writers as soon as it's available but you need to support multiple types of documents, you may want to consider creating a DTD for each type of document and then subsequently merging these into a single DTD. When you take this approach, try to make sure that you don't build structural relationships between different types of elements in each separate DTD that may make it hard to combine these into a single structure.

Combining DTDs after they're already in use can be difficult. As an alternative, you can create a single DTD that contains empty definitions for different types of documents and then flesh out each of the definitions for each type of document in turn. For example if you are creating a single DTD that defines the structure of both a book and a technical paper and you want to define the structure of the technical paper first, you might begin your DTD like this:

```
<!ELEMENT doc  -- (book | TechPaper)>
<!ELEMENT book -- CDATA >
<!ELEMENT TechPaper -- (title-block, abstract, body)>
...
```

This code forces you to share structure between these types of documents even if you aren't ready to define each document type simultaneously. If you use this code, make sure that no one writes a book using this DTD — I suspect that they'd encounter problems once you actually began defining the structure of the book!

Organizing and Commenting Your DTD(s)

This section discusses how you can efficiently write and organize a DTD, provides more detail about increasing the readability and maintainability of a DTD, and reiterates the benefits of doing it right the first time. See Chapter 12 for some general issues to consider when deciding whether you should write your own DTD.

Creating modular DTDs

Even if you're creating a single DTD, you want to consider whether your organization may need to have multiple DTDs in the future. No SGML implementation comes with a crystal ball. But with a little time and some foresight, you can make some design decisions now that will simplify subsequent development of other DTDs. You may even make it easier to maintain the DTD you're currently developing.

Whether you're creating a single DTD that defines the structure and content of multiple types of documents or creating multiple DTDs that each represent a specific type of document, you want to have some way of centralizing elements, entities, and attribute definitions that are used by more than one type of document. As I mentioned earlier in this chapter, this process is known as *modular design*. It's easy to see why you would want to centralize entity declarations, because these are usually definitions for common characters or character strings (such as product names) that all your documents use. Similarly, centralizing the definition of elements that are used in different types of documents makes it easy to find and refer to them. Some examples of elements that are building blocks for different types of documents are things like paragraphs, figures, graphics entities, tables, and lists.

If you're creating a single DTD that supports different types of documents, centralizing element and related attribute definitions can be as simple as putting these common elements in a well-commented portion of the DTD that identifies these as building blocks of different types of documents. However, if you're developing multiple DTDs or believe that you might need to do so in the future, you can use SGML's parameter entities to share these declarations. Parameter entities are introduced in Chapter 4 and are also discussed in Chapter 6 as a way of reusing and sharing information.

As a quick refresher, you can use parameter entities to define parts of a DTD that can be shared between DTDs. If you're familiar with the C programming language, parameter entities are much like the #include statements in C programs — they tell an application, such as a compiler or SGML parser, to locate a specific set of standard definitions and include it in your program. There are two types of entities — *general entities* that can be used in an SGML document, and *parameter entities* that are used in DTDs. SGML applications locate entities by looking up the public or system identifier for each set of entities using whatever entity manager the SGML software provides. An entity manager can range from something as simple as a text file that maps the public identifier for a set of entities, to a file on your computer system where that set of entities can be found, to something as complex as a database system where the pubic identifier is a one-to-any key that allows you to retrieve sets of entity definitions. For more detailed information about entities, see Chapters 4 and 6.

An example here might be worth a thousand words! The simple TechPaper DTD developed in Chapters 4 and 5 has the following structure:

```
<!ELEMENT TechPaper -- (title-block, abstract, body)>
<!ELEMENT body -- (section)+ >
<!ELEMENT title-block -- (paper-title, author,
    affiliation, date)>
<!ELEMENT (paper-title | author | affiliation |date) --
    CDATA>
<!ELEMENT abstract -- (body-text) >
<!ELEMENT section -- (section-title, body-text,
    subsection*)>
<!ELEMENT subsection -- (subsection-title, body-text)>
<!ELEMENT (section-title | subsection-title) -- CDATA>
<!ELEMENT body-text -- (paragraph | list)+ >
<!ELEMENT paragraph -- (#PCDATA)>
<!ELEMENT list       -- (list-item)+>
<!ATTLIST list type (alpha|bullet|none|number) "none" >
<!ELEMENT list-item --   RCDATA>
```

In this DTD, the `<BODY-TEXT>` element is a low-level building block of the different types of sections in the DTD. Assuming that other DTDs share these same building blocks, I can break these out into a shared set of element definitions:

```
<!ELEMENT body-text -- (paragraph | list)+ >
<!ELEMENT paragraph -- (#PCDATA)>
<!ELEMENT list       -- (list-item)+>
<!ATTLIST list type (alpha|bullet|none|number) "none" >
<!ELEMENT list-item --   RCDATA>
```

If my SGML software uses a catalog file to locate entities, I can then put these element definitions in a separate file, called `shared.dtd`, for which I then create a public identifier that I register with the entity manager used by my SGML software. This public identifier declaration might look like the following:

```
PUBLIC "-//WvH//ENTITIES Shared Elements//EN" "/usr/
wvhentities/shared.ent"
```

The TechPaper DTD would then look like this:

```
<!ENTITY % shared PUBLIC "-//WvH//ENTITIES Shared Elements/
/EN">
%shared;
<!ELEMENT TechPaper -- (title-block, abstract, body)>
<!ELEMENT body -- (section)+ >
<!ELEMENT title-block -- (paper-title, author,
affiliation, date)>
<!ELEMENT (paper-title | author | affiliation |date) --
CDATA>
<!ELEMENT abstract -- (body-text) >
<!ELEMENT section -- (section-title, body-text,
subsection*)>
<!ELEMENT subsection -- (subsection-title, body-text)>
<!ELEMENT (section-title | subsection-title) -- CDATA>
```

You can use parameter entities to modularize your DTD so that you can easily use the elements defined in each parameter entity in different types of documents. If you use parameter entities, however, you may be frustrated when you try to find the declarations for shared elements if you're new to a specific DTD. As you're reading the DTD, if you encounter elements whose declaration you can't find in the DTD, you have to go back to any parameter entities that were included earlier in the DTD and search through each of these to find the elements you're looking for.

TECHNICAL STUFF

Naming conventions and the reference SGML declaration

As mentioned in Chapter 4, the element names in the sample TechPaper DTD don't conform to the default SGML declaration that limits those names to eight characters or less in length. When the SGML standard was written and the default values for various SGML constructs were assigned, computer memory was a precious thing. I'm not an advocate of wanton growth in the memory requirements of computer programs, but I really think that nowadays, when you can get 16MB of memory for less than $125, using a few extra characters in the names of the elements in an SGML DTD isn't a big deal. This is especially true when a few extra characters can make the difference between elements called `<TBL-CAP>` and `<TABLE-CAPTION>`. The system on which

I'm writing this book (you can guess which one!) takes 163MB of disk space for the operating system alone and needs at least 16MB of memory to avoid thrashing between Free Cell and Solitaire. I really think I can afford a few extra characters to create usable element and attribute names.

Your decision about whether you stick to the eight-character names hinges on two things: how kind you want to be to users of the DTD(s) you write, and whether the SGML software you're using supports changes to the basic SGML declarations. If you want to be kind and your software supports it, I say go for it! For more details, see "Using meaningful element and attribute names" in Chapter 12.

When using shared elements via parameter entities, I often use a combination of comments and naming conventions for those elements to make it easier to find them. For example, I often assign shared elements a prefix that identifies them as shared elements and then associate a comment with each parameter entity reference that makes it clear which entity they're associated with. For example, the beginning of the TechPaper DTD could look like the following:

```
<!-- shared elements have the prefix "s." -->
<!ENTITY % shared PUBLIC "-//WvH//ENTITIES Shared Elements/
          /EN">
%shared;
```

The file containing the shared elements would look like this:

```
<!-- Shared elements common to multiple DTDs -->
<!ELEMENT s.body-text -- (s.paragraph | s.list)+ >
<!ELEMENT s.paragraph -- (#PCDATA)>
<!ELEMENT s.list       -- (s.list-item)+>
<!ATTLIST s.list type (alpha|bullet|none|number) "none" >
<!ELEMENT s.list-item --  RCDATA>
```

Using this model, I also have to modify the basic TechPaper DTD to refer to these elements by these names. You have to work a bit more to use this naming convention, but you can easily identify which elements are shared and where those shared elements are declared.

When choosing various naming conventions, you have to balance the convenience of this sort of implicit cross-referencing with the difficulty that writers may have in remembering and using these naming conventions. I find this sort of thing to be useful, especially since much of today's graphical SGML software automatically provides users with a list of the elements that are valid at any point in the document.

Structuring your DTD for readability

Several basic factors contribute to whether a DTD is readable: the number of comments it contains; how you format the DTD; and how you organize the elements, attributes, and entities that your DTD contains or uses. As mentioned throughout this book, comments and white space in a DTD are *a good thing* — SGML parsers ignore them, and they provide an easy way to communicate your thoughts and intentions with other users or maintainers of the DTDs you write. DTD formatting can be WYSIWYG!

If you use parameter entities in your DTD, remember that you can't refer to an entity before it has been declared. For this reason, you should organize entity declarations at the beginning of your DTD from simplest to most complex, using comments to separate sections of character entity declarations from shared entity declarations. When you do this, you minimize the chance that you will refer to something in one parameter entity that hasn't been defined yet. (Note that there is no such limitation on element declarations, which can appear in any order.)

Interestingly enough, I suggest organizing element declarations in a DTD in exactly the opposite manner — from the top down, rather than from simplest to more complex. When referring to a DTD for confirmation of what elements to use or how things are generally structured, I think that people are most likely to be looking for elements based on the context in which they are used, and I find that context is usually easiest to determine by reading a DTD from the top down, rather than from the bottom up. (See the next section, "Starting at the Top," for a discussion of a related topic, designing a DTD.) For much the same reason, I always group attribute definitions with the elements those attributes are associated with. This makes it easy for me to answer questions about the type of content or intent of an attribute because I can always find either of them by searching for the element they are associated with.

Even though a top-down DTD is my favorite way of organizing a DTD, many others feel strongly about other approaches. For example, many people seem to find it easier to organize element definitions alphabetically. This organization makes it easier to find a specific element declaration, because you only have to know the alphabet (and not the context in which an element is used) in order to find its declaration. Many people have similarly different feelings about how attributes should be organized in a DTD. Many people like to centralize attribute declarations, grouping them together in a separate portion of the DTD. Though I like to group them with the elements that they are associated with, I find it difficult to do when a single attribute is associated with one or more elements. Even though I may tend to bloat my DTDs, I usually define separate attributes for each element whenever possible, and I therefore rarely encounter this problem.

Starting at the Top

Writing a DTD is much like any other logical exercise, such as writing a computer program. SGML DTDs have to follow SGML syntax, just like computer programs have to follow the syntax of the programming language that they're written in. Just as computer programs define the flow of control from the main program, to procedures or subroutines, and back again, SGML DTDs describe the flow of information in a document from the highest level of the structure of a document, through repeatable groups of sections, subsections, paragraphs, and so on.

After you analyze your documents, discussed in Chapter 13, you should have numerous insights into the content and structure of any existing documents that your DTD will have to support, as well as the context in which different parts of that content can appear. When creating a DTD, I suggest starting with the highest-level elements in your DTD and working your way down to lower levels of document structure. However, make sure that you don't fall into the trap of releasing preliminary versions of your DTD before you've accurately mapped out the entire structure of the elements identified during your document analysis, especially if writers are actually using these early versions of your DTD to write documents. These "early adopters" may turn out to be "early complainers" if changes to your DTD during the development process cause problems with documents that people are actually working on. This is not to say that early adopters won't find problems in your DTD and that fixing those problems might not break the documents they're working on, just that you should carefully plan your changes so as not to cause problems for anyone who is using early releases of your DTD. Every company has people who like to live on the bleeding edge — use them as a resource!

If users begin writing documents using a very liberal version of your DTD, they may find that they can't validate their documents against later versions of the same DTD. This situation occurs because top-down design usually uses fairly loose placeholders for lower-level portions of the document structure. As you fill in the structure of the lower levels of the document, you may build in structural requirements that documents that follow your previous, "more relaxed" DTD don't follow. Many DTDs under development experience this problem; it usually occurs when you discover that an element you originally identified as optional should actually be mandatory. As much as possible, you should try to design the lower-level elements of your documents such that subsequent development of the DTD relaxes their content rather than making it more specific. Making a mandatory element an optional one is easy, but making an optional one mandatory may require that you revisit existing documents and fix them. Always trying to loosen content models rather than tighten them is an easy design decision to suggest but is a hard thing to anticipate — unfortunately, you may not learn this lesson until you experience such content problems a few times.

If you find yourself in this situation and you are familiar with a pattern-matching application such as Perl or the sed and awk utilities available on UNIX systems, you can usually write a small script or command file that searches SGML documents for patterns of text that may be affected by the structural changes you've made to the DTD. Writers working in your DTD can then use these utilities to scan their documents and fix these types of problems using a text editor before actually loading the documents into your SGML software. Your utilities can even insert templates for the missing structural elements, eliminating the need for people to fix the documents manually. Even if your SGML implementation is a team effort, remember that your users' patience is limited. Thorough document analysis and good up-front DTD planning help you minimize the number of times you have to develop tools to help resolve this sort of problem. Another good tool for doing this sort of thing is the query or transformation language provided by DSSSL — because DSSSL uses an real SGML parser to read your SGML files, it provides a truly robust way of dealing with cases where you want to automatically add elements based on context.

As you write a DTD based on the results of your document analysis, you frequently uncover problems in your original analysis. You may discover elements that have the same content, grab-bag elements that actually define types of content that you want to distinguish, and elements with mixed content models that weren't originally identified as such. See "Mixing and matching content models" in Chapter 4 for more information on mixed content models and ways of resolving them

You may encounter elements that contain the same types of information but which were originally specified as separate elements after you analyze your documents. After all, you may be new to the document analysis process. The members of your document analysis team may be used to thinking of parallel elements in different parts of a document as distinct elements. For example, if you work from an existing set of documents that were developed in a non-structured documentation tool, you may define separate elements for different types of headings. In your previous word-processing or publishing package, you probably had to have different styles for these elements, because they all had special formatting characteristics. However, in SGML, these elements are really the same thing because you can distinguish among them based on the context in which they appear.

Sometimes you may run into what I call *grab-bag elements,* which are elements that are often overloaded with content models that describe different types of elements. If you find that you have an element whose content model is suspiciously complex or which actually describes two different types of content that you want to be able to distinguish, you should consider separating it into two distinct types of elements.

Test Early, Test Often!

When writing a DTD, you need to validate its structure as often as possible, especially if people are using your DTD while you are still enhancing or fine-tuning it. You should never work on the "official" copy of a DTD that people may be using — instead, work on a private copy that you can release to users when you're confident that it is correct and contains some extra features that writers may need in their documents.

Whenever possible, you should also validate your current DTD against a sample document. If you are converting an existing set of documents into SGML, you may have converted or produced small sample documents during the document analysis process. If so, you should use these samples to test your DTD after making any major changes to it. If not and you are not writing the conversion utility, you should work closely with the developer of that conversion utility to guarantee that you can get samples as early as possible in the DTD development process. If, as I suggest in Chapter 13, you produced a reference document for your DTD during the document analysis process, you can also ask a writer to use a text editor to develop a small sample document using the reference document as a guideline. You can then use this sample document to test your DTD and to verify the results of the document analysis process.

Tracking Changes in Your DTD

You may want to use a software version control system when writing a DTD. Version control systems usually work by using a check-in/check-out model for tracking the changes between different versions of a program or other text file. Since DTDs are text documents, you can adopt most software control systems to work with them.

To use a version control system, you typically initialize it by registering the current version of the file that you want to put under version control, in this case your DTD. This is known as *checking in* your file — what this does is establish a reference point that the version control software can use as a basis for comparison with subsequent versions of your file. You then check a copy of your file out (just like at the library!), modify it, and check the new version back at various points in the development process. Each time you check a new version back in, the version control system assigns it a new version number, compares the contents of the new file against the previous version, and keeps a record of the changes. If you ever make a change that breaks your DTD, you can simply check out the version with the previous version number and start over.

At a minimum, you want to check in a version of the DTD that corresponds to each version that you've made available to users of the DTD. I like to check in versions after each major change that I have validated using an SGML parser. Though I then have many more versions than I would if I perform less frequent check-ins, I have an easier time backing out a specific change.

Version control systems let you check out a copy of any version of a DTD that you've checked in, and they can also produce reports that highlight the differences between different versions of a DTD. You may need to check out an older version (known as *rolling back* to that version) if you've made some changes to the DTD that broke documents that people were working on. You can quickly reinstall an older version so that people can keep working while you identify what went wrong and resolve the problem.

You also can use version control systems that produce summaries of changes between different versions of a DTD to track the progress of your DTD development work or to produce status reports for your management. These status reports may contain more information than you need, but you can always cut out the details and extract a high-level summary.

In most cases, you need to modify only the characters that the version control system uses to delimit comments in the files it manages in order to use the version control system with SGML. Most version control systems embed comments in the files that you check out in order to track the version number and other high-level changes. Since most version control systems are used to manage changes in the source code for programs, you need to "teach" them the comment characters used in SGML.

Chapter 15

Customizing an Existing Document Type Definition

Chapter 12 discusses issues to consider when determining whether to write your own DTD or use an existing one. These issues boil down to whether an existing DTD meets your needs or requirements, and whether you can afford to write and support your own DTD. If you're working in an industry where SGML is widely used, you should at least evaluate the DTDs that other companies in your industry are using. Even if these existing DTDs aren't exactly perfect for you, you may be able to use them as a starting point for your DTD. If you can extend an existing DTD, you've already reduced your costs in migrating to SGML because you don't have to do all of the DTD development work yourself. Similarly, you'll probably also save money when developing a formatting environment for your DTD, since these may be already available for existing DTDs (depending on whether you're using an SGML software package that others in your industry are using). You may be able to further reduce the long-term costs of migrating to SGML by leveraging existing books or training materials, or by hiring writers who already have experience with that DTD.

This chapter discusses strategies for customizing existing DTDs to meet your requirements. I explain how using an existing DTD changes the way in which you analyze your existing documents and discuss how using an existing DTD changes the type of development you'll have to do, including developing a formatting environment for your extensions. I also suggest some effective ways to package and share extensions to an existing DTD.

Planning for Customization

Using an existing DTD as a starting point for your SGML migration effort makes a lot of sense in industries where SGML is already in popular use and where standard DTDs are therefore already available. Some of the publicly available DTDs discussed in other chapters of this book are explicitly designed for customization. For example, the Davenport Group, the maintainers of that DocBook DTD, have a document called the *Customizer's Guide for the DocBook DTD*. The fact that this document even exists should show how frequently people modify that DTD! (You can get SGML or HTML versions of this document from the URL http://www.ora.com/davenport/dbdoc/index.html.)

If you are exchanging information with other groups or companies and you want to modify an existing DTD, you have to focus on making it easy to exchange your documents with those companies or agencies who use the original DTD. Whenever you modify the files that make up an existing DTD, you should create your own public identifier for the new DTD so that the parties that you exchange documents with can easily identify the fact that you are using a modified version of a standard DTD.

Customized DTDs that are based on other DTDs are often referred to as *variant* DTDs because they share much of the same evolution as an existing DTD.

Types of customization

You can customize an existing DTD in three basic ways:

✔ By producing a DTD that is a *subset* of the existing DTD. This DTD uses the syntax and elements used in the original DTD but may eliminate groups of entities or families of elements that you don't want to use in your documents. You can use the original DTD to parse documents produced with a DTD that is a subset of an existing DTD, but you may not be able to use the variant DTD to parse documents produced with the original DTD. Because documents that conform to the original DTD can use entities and elements that no longer exist in your DTD, those documents may not conform to your DTD.

✔ By producing a DTD that includes *extensions* to the original DTD. *Extensions* are entities, elements, and attribute definitions that are not available in the original DTD but which are present in yours. You can therefore use the variant DTD to parse documents that conform to the original DTD, but you can't use the original DTD to parse documents that conform to the variant DTD. Because your documents use entities and elements that are not present in the original DTD, those documents no longer conform to that DTD.

✔ By redefining entities or elements or declaring extensions to the existing DTD in the DOCTYPE statement in each document that you produce using your variant DTD. Each of your documents then contains a complete list of any changes that you have made to the spirit of the original DTD. Documents produced using your modifications can be parsed against the original DTD because they provide all of the information necessary to identify and define your changes to the original DTD.

A primary motivation for extending an existing DTD is to identify or preserve structural or semantic content in your documents that you feel is valuable but which wasn't provided in the original DTD. You can extend a DTD in many different ways, from adding attributes to existing elements that identify subtly different types of content, to adding new elements that support the additional structure you feel that you need. You may create a subset of an existing DTD in order to make it easier for writers to work with a DTD by eliminating structure and families of elements than writers may find confusing, which they might use when they probably shouldn't, or which may simply be irrelevant to your documents.

When using any of these models for customizing a DTD, you need to remember how DTDs and local declarations are parsed. SGML parsers read a DTD sequentially, with the exception of any local declarations made in the DOCTYPE statement. Local declarations are read first, and you can therefore use them to override declarations that appear later in the DTD. Remember that it's not illegal to define the same entity or element multiple times — if you do so, the first declaration is used as the one true definition, and subsequent declarations are discarded. You can use local declarations to extend a DTD as long as those declarations don't depend on any entity or element declarations that are defined later (in the DTD itself), which would therefore be undefined when the local declaration is read.

The next two sections discuss modifying portions of the prolog for your documents. The document prolog was discussed in Chapter 4 — as a quick refresher, it is the portion of an SGML document that identifies the DTD you're using, and which contains the declarations of any elements, attributes, or entities that are local to a specific SGML document — in other words, which are not part of the standard DTD, but are only associated with the current document:

```
<!DOCTYPE foobar PUBLIC "-//Elvis//DTD MyDTD//EN" [
<!-- local modifications in prolog... -->
]>
```

Producing subset DTDs

You can produce a DTD that is a subset of an existing DTD in one of two ways. You can produce a DTD that includes only certain modules from the existing DTD (assuming that it is a well-designed DTD that has parameter entities that you can selectively include or eliminate). For example, the

DocBook DTD uses a parameter entity named dbhier to hold element definitions that describe the hierarchical structure of a document, and it uses another parameter entity called dbgenent to hold other general element declarations. If you don't want to use the general entities from the DocBook DTD, you can produce a DTD that excludes these parameter entities. (You also have to make sure that none of the elements in the dbhier entity use elements that are subsequently defined in dbgenent.) The DocBook DTD actually supports these types of modifications by using marked sections, but you could simply create your own DTD from it by including only those parameter entities that you wanted to use from the DocBook DTD.

You also can produce a DTD that is a subset of an original DTD by providing your own definitions for entities and elements in your variant DTD before invoking the modules that provide the original definitions of those entities and elements. Some SGML parsers issue warnings if they encounter element declarations that you've pruned from a DTD by redefining their parent, but you can ignore these warnings; everything will be just fine.

Producing DTD extensions

If you are making substantial extensions to an existing DTD, you probably want to turn the original DTD into a parameter entity that you invoke in your new DTD:

```
<!ENTITY % techpaper-dtd "-//WvH//DTD TechPaper v1.0//EN">
%techpaper-dtd;
```

In this case, any entity or element declarations that you want to override in the existing DTD must appear before you invoke the original DTD as a parameter entity. Any extensions that you want to make to the entities and elements in the existing DTD should follow that DTD. I call this the *superset* method of creating a DTD because the existing DTD is now a proper subset of your enhanced DTD.

You also can produce extensions to an existing DTD by adding sets of modular extensions to the DTD using parameter entities that identify files that contain the extensions to the DTD. I suggest that you avoid this method whenever possible because it offers the most potential for confusion. Even if you've created your own public identifier for the variant DTD and provided comments that identify your extensions, people looking at the DTD may still overlook your additions or may be confused simply because the DTD looks so much like the original DTD.

Using local DTD declarations

You can produce both subsets and extensions of existing DTDs by using local declarations in the DOCTYPE statement to override the definition of existing entities and elements or to add the definitions of new entities and elements. You have to do this in each of your documents. Here is an example of this method (using the TechPaper DTD as an example):

```
<!DOCTYPE TechPaper [
<!-- new or over-riding declarations go here -->
]>
```

Why can't I change a DTD?

If you are thinking of modifying a DTD that you must use, you first need to determine whether your contract permit you to modify or extend that DTD. If not, then any subsequent discussion of how to extend that DTD is moot, and you will have to make your new and existing documents conform to the existing DTD. Though this sounds harsh, some industries don't allow you to deviate from an existing DTD for good reasons:

✔ The companies working in that industry may already have formatting tools in place that are not easily modified. In this case, you may be able to use a subset of an existing DTD because you aren't adding any new elements for which formatting information must be created.

✔ The elements and structure in an existing DTD might be necessary to guarantee that your documents comply with industry requirements. If an existing element is defined as a series of one or more mandatory elements and you change the meaning of that element so that it simply has some type of character content, your documents may no longer provide all of the information that the industry requires.

The fundamental goal of SGML is to facilitate information interchange, not just between different companies, but also between different software packages. As disappointing as it may be, any changes that you make to an existing DTD may break this model unless the companies you work with and the SGML software you use can handle these changes.

The document analysis process and customized DTDs

If you work in an industry or on a project than mandates the use of a certain DTD but permits extensions, your document analysis process changes radically from a document analysis process in which you evaluate different DTDs or create your own. Since you already have a DTD, you first need someone on the document analysis team to become familiar with that DTD. As you analyze your documents, you first focus on mapping structural elements in your existing documents into the elements provided in the DTD.

As you compare your existing documents to the structure provided by the existing DTD and find portions of your documents that don't exactly fit that DTD, you have several choices:

✔ Determine whether you can eliminate certain types of information present in your existing documents so that the documents you produce will exactly conform to the existing DTD. This is the easiest method for facilitating document interchange with other groups or companies that use an existing DTD, but it's also the most painful since you eliminate parts of your documents that you obviously felt were useful at one time.

✔ Determine whether parts of your documents don't appear to fit because the content model in the existing DTD is more complex than the one that you use. This isn't really a problem, per se, but may identify parts of the existing DTD that you can eliminate to make it easier for writers to work with a DTD. If so, you should keep a running list of these types of elements, and then use these elements to help you produce a subset of the original DTD. You should actually try to avoid producing a subset of the original DTD whenever possible, because documents that conform to the existing DTD would no longer conform to yours. If you feel that you have to take this approach, consider making these types of changes to the DTD in the local declarations section of your DOCTYPE statements. Doing this prevents documents that conform to the original DTD from no longer conforming to your version of it because all of your changes are local to a document and not in the DTD itself. Centralizing your extensions simplifies exchanging documents with other groups or companies who may depend on the structure described in the original DTD.

✔ Determine whether elements in your original documents that don't exactly fit are just different flavors of elements in the existing DTD. If so, you may be able to make them fit by defining additional attributes for the existing elements and then using specific values for those attributes to preserve the intent of the portions of your original documents.

✔ Determine whether the elements that don't fit are actually structurally and semantically distinct types of content that you need to preserve. If so, then you will probably want to keep a running list of these and use this list as the foundation for a set of extensions to the standard DTD.

You should make all of these decisions a part of the permanent record of your document analysis process and make sure that you thoroughly comment any changes that you make to the existing DTD. The next section describes some ways of organizing any changes that you make to the DTD so that they're easy to identify and understand. The last two sections of this chapter discusses ways of making sure that you supply your changes to any other groups or companies that need to work with your documents.

Centralizing Your Extensions

If you make only a small number of changes to an existing DTD, you can centralize those changes by declaring them in the local declarations section of each document that you produce. If your changes simply redefine things such as the values of various entities or the content model for an existing element that already exists in the DTD, you should just list all of these changes in the local declarations section. By doing this, you ensure that any groups that you exchange documents with will get your changes without having to modify the copy of the DTD that they use.

Making local changes to each of your documents is exactly the sort of problem that SGML is supposed to solve by standardizing structure and content models in your documents. However, if you have a very small number of documents, this is a realistic solution. If you have large numbers of documents, a better solution is to create a "wrapper" DTD that includes your definitions and then invokes the standard DTD. Though you'll have to create a new identifier for this DTD (and supply it to any organizations that you exchange documents with), this is a solution more in keeping with the principles of SGML.

If you redefine large numbers of entities, elements, or attributes in an existing DTD, listing all of these in the local declarations section of each document is extremely tedious. You may want to centralize these in a single file that you can include as a parameter entity in the local declarations section of each of the documents that use your extensions. You have to make sure that you provide this file to any groups or companies that you exchange information with, and you also have to explain any changes that they need to make to their entity manager so that they can locate these files. If you declare your parameter entity as a SYSTEM entity, they may not have to make any changes to their entity managers because they may be able to simply put the file containing your extensions in the working directory for each document that uses them. This depends on how the SGML software they are using works. If you declare your parameter entity as a PUBLIC entity, they may have to add the definition for your entity to their catalogs (or whatever method their entity managers use to locate public entities). If you use a PUBLIC entity, you allow them to keep a single copy of your extensions somewhere on their systems but require some changes to how their SGML software is configured.

Whenever you modify an existing DTD directly, you should centralize your changes in separate files that you can include as parameter entities, either in existing documents, in DTDs that make up a superset of the original DTD, or in the original DTD itself. You can then work with smaller numbers of files, and you make it easier for people that use your documents to identify your changes.

If your modified DTD is a superset of your existing DTD and includes the original DTD as a parameter entity, you should still centralize the new declarations for your DTD. If you redefine any existing entities, elements, or element attributes, you must place their declarations in the new DTD before you include the parameter entity that represents the original DTD. For clarity, you should place the new entities, elements, and attributes after the parameter entity that represents the original DTD. Here is an example:

```
<!DOCTYPE BigTechPaper "-//WvH/DTD TechPaper 1.0 Variant//
EN" [
<!-- redefinitions of items in the existing DTD -->
% redeclared;
<!-- the original DTD itself -->
% original-dtd;
<!-- subsequent additions -->
% new-items;
]>
```

This example doesn't show the definition of each of these parameter entities. I have included this example just to show the structure of a superset DTD.

You should avoid directly modifying the files that make up an existing DTD whenever possible. If you need aspects of the DTD's structure, consider extending that DTD with the superset method. However, sometime you may find that you actually want to modify the existing DTD itself. If so, remember the following caveats:

✔ Unless you remember to change the public identifier for the DTD, people you're sharing your documents with may not discover your extensions until a document that they receive from you causes their SGML software to complain or crash.

✔ Even if you change the public identifier for your new version of the DTD, the names of most of the files that make up your existing DTD are the same as those in the original DTD. People therefore have to do more work to locate your changes.

✔ If there are changes to the DTD on which your extension are based (such as a new version, minor bug-fixes, and so on), you have to reintegrate your changes into the new set of files that you get with the new DTD.

Whenever possible, do not modify the files for an existing DTD!

If you absolutely feel that you have to modify the files that make up an existing DTD, use marked sections to identify those sections and use a parameter entity to INCLUDE or IGNORE those sections. The default value for this parameter entity should be IGNORE so that you can verify that documents that are supposed to conform to the original DTD do so; you should set the value of this parameter entity to INCLUDE in the local declarations portion of their DOCTYPE statements in documents that require your extensions. For more information about marked sections and related ways of using parameter entities, see "A Document for All Seasons" in Chapter 6.

Making Your Extensions Available to Others

If you've extended an existing DTD, that DTD won't be very useful to people who work on your documents, even if they use the same base DTD, unless you can provide them with the files they need to match your changes to the DTD. This section summarizes the more common types of customized DTDs and lists the types of files you may have to provide with each in order to let other people work on your documents.

If you've modified your DTD by listing all of your changes in the local declarations section of each document that uses the DTD, you don't have to provide other groups who use your document with anything other than the documents themselves.

If you've modified a DTD using parameter entities in the local declarations part of the DOCTYPE statement or in the DTD itself, you have to provide them with any files associated with these parameter entities. If you declared your parameter entity as a PUBLIC entity, you should also provide them with a copy of your catalog file (or whatever method their entity manager uses to locate public entities).

If your modified DTD is a superset of your existing DTD and includes the original DTD as a parameter entity, you have to make sure that you provide to people that you work with all the files that they need in order to be able to work with your new DTD. These files include

- The main file for the new DTD, containing the public identifier for that DTD.
- Any modules that you created and which are included in your new DTD as parameter entities.
- Templates for any changes to the entity manager that your new DTD requires. These templates can save other parties that use the same SGML software package that you use a substantial amount of time when they use your DTD.

Sharing Extensions That Require Formatting Changes

When thinking about adding extensions to an existing DTD, you need to consider whether those changes will require additional development in the formatting environment used by an SGML software package. You always need to do additional development when you add new elements or attributes that have formatting implications, regardless of the output format. Adding new attributes doesn't always mandate formatting changes, because new values for an existing attribute may just be intended to communicate additional meaning to downstream applications such as databases. Adding new elements may only require slight formatting changes, especially if you've simply added some new semantic tags that you plan to format in the same way as existing elements in the DTD. Creating a subset DTD usually doesn't require any formatting changes because you are eliminating groups of tags for which formatting is already defined rather than adding new tags.

When sharing modified DTDs with other groups or companies, you should always provide them with documentation for your extensions. If your changes to a DTD are extensions for which formatting will have to be defined, you should say so in the document that describes your extensions and explain how you format them for the various output formats you support. If the group or company you are exchanging documents with is lucky enough to use the same SGML software package that you use and has the same output format requirements, you can simply provide it with a copy of your formatting environment in whatever format (FOSI, DSSSL, and so on) that your SGML software package uses.

Part V
Using SGML in Business

The 5th Wave   By Rich Tennant

"NAAAH - HE'S NOT THAT SMART. HE WON'T CHECK HIS SYNTAX, FORGETS
TO DECLARE HIS ENTITIES, AND DROOLS ALL OVER THE KEYBOARD."

In this part

This part of the book discusses various ways that SGML is used in business, providing examples of ways in which SGML can be cost-effective while increasing productivity, efficiency, and the usability of the information in your documents as an information resource for your company.

The first chapter focuses on different approaches to electronic publishing, including today's biggest buzzwords, the World Wide Web. There are many forms of electronic publishing, not all of which specifically have anything to do with SGML. For completeness' sake, I discuss each, but focus on how SGML and structured documentation can make it easier for you to publish your information on the Web. HTML and its probable replacement, XML, are both just implementations of SGML — so you're already half-way to a good Internet or intranet publishing solution if your documents are currently in SGML!

The next two chapters focus on different tools that can help you store, track, manage, and find information in SGML documents. These are document management systems and different types of databases. Actually, the boundaries between these two sometimes blur because many document management systems use object-oriented databases to store your SGML documents. In each of these chapters, I provide general information about these types of software and then discuss specific examples of tools that you can use to better manage and access the information in your SGML documents.

Chapter 16

Electronic Publishing and SGML

· ·

· ·

*T*his chapter discusses electronic publishing, one of the hottest topics in the documentation world. Simply put, *electronic publishing* is the general term used to describe any way of delivering your documents online or on some form of computer media such as CD-ROM, floppy disk, or tape. You can publish your documents electronically in several different ways. Of these different approaches to electronic publishing, the Internet and the World Wide Web most quickly spring to mind.

The explosive growth of the World Wide Web over the past few years has provided companies with an opportunity to make their product information available in an entirely new medium, usually with substantially lower costs than traditional venues such as the printed page. In this chapter, I use the phrase *Internet publishing* as a way to differentiate between making electronic versions of your documents available on the Internet and simply making them available electronically or on a network that is only local to a single organization (called an *intranet*). As a huge, worldwide pool of information, the World Wide Web is infinitely searchable, as opposed to paper documents — if you need more information than a single issue of a printed document provides, you have to get another issue or go to a central repository, such as a library, where you can search for other issues or sources for the information that you want. On the Web, you're already floating in that central repository — all you have to know is where (and how) to look for more information.

The World Wide Web is not the only means for electronic publishing; it's just the most obvious and perhaps the sexiest at the moment. Simply making your documents available on CD-ROM can substantially reduce your publication costs, make your documents more accessible to more people, and make your documents more portable in the literal sense, because you can stuff an entire document set on CD into your shirt pocket or purse. This chapter discusses how electronic publishing changes the way you view your information, lists some alternate ways of electronic publishing that are already in use, explains some ways of getting there from where you are today, and examines some future directions for the publishing industry. Today's vast migration of documents from the printed page does the ancient Chinese curse "May you live in interesting times" one better — we truly live in exciting times!

This chapter provides a lot of background information about electronic publishing, much of which is not specifically oriented toward SGML — until you take into account the fact that HTML, the most popular format for electronic publishing today, is an SGML application. Beyond this fact, however, SGML's emphasis on software independence and document structure provides the underpinnings of converting your documents into any electronic format. The many ways in which SGML can help prepare your organization for electronic publishing and simplify the production of electronic documents can be a strong selling point if you're still considering moving to SGML. Remember our SGML mantra: SGML makes it easy for you to re-use the information that you already have!

Throughout this chapter, I use the term *customers* to refer to anyone who wants to use the documents that you produce. If you are working for a nonprofit group or government agency, the term may not seem appropriate at first, because the people who use the information you produce may not normally be expected to pay for it. By customers, I mean anyone who uses information is a consumer of that information and is therefore a customer in some sense, regardless of whether you paid for it.

Formats for Electronic Publishing

Before discussing the costs and benefits of electronic publishing, I want to examine some of the different ways in which you can deliver your documents online. Understanding the electronic publishing formats that are available will help you make decisions about the formats you may want to consider supporting.

There are three basic approaches to electronic publishing:

✔ Making printable versions of your existing documents available online. You can provide text versions of your documents with your products or versions of your documents in the languages used by different types of printers, such as PostScript or PCL (the Printer Control Language used by HP printers and their clones). Although this is electronic publishing in the strictest sense, it really doesn't replace your printed documents — it just provides your customers with the ability to print their own versions of your documents.

✔ Converting your existing documents into a format that your customers can view and use online. You can generate HTML versions of your current documents and use tools that take your existing documents and produce versions of those documents for online use. There are two camps in this approach to electronic delivery: tools that post-process formatted versions of your documents and tools that use the source code for your original documents. Both of these approaches produce online versions of your documents that are searchable and which provide many different types of hyperlinks and cross-references in your documents. The distinction between these two approaches can get muddy at times!

✔ Redesigning your documents for electronic delivery. If you've ever used a help file for a Microsoft Windows application, you can see that such documents are designed very differently from documents that are intended to be printed. Documents that are designed for online use typically consist of hundreds or thousands of small topics that are woven together using complex hyperlinks.

In this chapter, I focus on the second approach, which is the approach that best suits organizations that have existing document sets that they want to deliver electronically. The first approach, delivering printable versions of your documents, doesn't really change a company's orientation toward print media. The third approach, redesigning everything so that it's usable only online, eliminates the possibility of printing these documents so that they're usable in any meaningful way. People usually employ this approach in addition to having some printed documents because pure electronic delivery provides an interesting *bootstrapping problem*. This phrase comes from the idea of pulling yourself up by your own bootstraps; it is used to describe situations where you can't use an existing system unless that system is already available. For example, if information on how to install a software product is only available in an online document, you can't read that information until after you've installed the product, at which point you no longer need the information.

Depending on your commitment to electronic publishing, the second approach can require redesigning your documents to some extent, but it provides you with the best of both worlds — people who want to buy paper versions of your documents can still do so, and people who prefer to use those documents online can do so and feel that your online documents actually provide value above and beyond the printed versions.

The next few sections explain different ways of making existing documents available online and discuss the benefits of each.

Delivering simple text documents

The classic README files that are found on every floppy, tape, or CD for a software product are a simple example of the Neolithic era of electronic publishing. They provide a way to make information available to users online, and though they are trivial to prepare, they can provide users with late-breaking information that couldn't make the cut for inclusion into the printed manuals.

If you can extract simple text versions of your existing documents from your current word-processing or publishing system, you're already 90 percent of the way toward a cheesy solution for electronic publishing on your company's intranet or on the Internet itself. Slam an HTML header on a text file, paste on a few HTML "pre-formatted text" tags, and your document can go online. Unfortunately, this approach to electronic publishing is much like the old Monty Python skit in which they make a fish out of a bird by stapling some fins and "adding" a tube that it can use to breathe underwater — few people would actually call this a fish! In the same light, people who see electronic versions of your documents that are prepared by wrapping them with trivial HTML tags will take them very seriously, except as sources of information.

However, there is actually a good rationale for simply putting text versions of your documents online in this fashion, at least as a starting point. In the first place, you can make information available online that wasn't available online before. Sure, maybe it doesn't use Java or feature rotating GIFs of your company's logo, but the information is online, is searchable, and most importantly, is available to anyone who has a browser.

Putting text information online is certainly a good first step for internal use within your organization, and it can even be a good long-term solution for legacy information that may not be able to justify the costs involved in producing a fancier version. Luckily, this approach to just "getting there from here" is less necessary today than it was a few years ago.

Generating or exporting HTML

Most modern word-processing and publishing packages allow you to generate HTML directly from your raw documents, embedding semantic tags (such as different types of heading tags) as they export an HTML version of your document. Although this process doesn't convert your existing documents into documents that are designed for electronic publishing, it does produce better-looking documents that are more Web aware and which are easier to use because they contain some font and formatting changes to indicate different types of information.

The HTML generation features of most word-processing and publishing packages provide higher-quality HTML documents than the "wrap a text document with HTML tags" method mentioned in the previous section. By default, most HTML export mechanisms preserve much of the formatting in your original documents by letting you associate styles in your existing documents with HTML tags that provide the same sorts of features. Some of the more intelligent HTML export mechanisms also produce a table of contents for your documents, generate appropriate hyperlinks for table of contents entries and cross references within your documents, and even produce a hyperlinked index.

Generating HTML versions of your documents may be a cost-effective solution to electronic publishing. You can immediately make your documents available on your corporate intranet or on the World Wide Web. Making your documents available within your company via your corporate network is usually a no-brainer, but making your document available on the Internet via the Web often requires a corporate mandate, because different groups within your organization may view this with different degrees of delight and alarm:

- ✔ Customer support groups usually see this as a huge win, since they can guarantee that customers with Internet access can always use the latest and greatest versions of your documents. They can also ensure that both they and the customer are looking at the same versions of a document, because both parties can point their Web browsers at exactly the same Web page. Making everything available on the Internet also eliminates the "I don't have that manual" problem, because everything is always available on the Web. (Modulo Web server outages!)

- ✔ Documentation and production groups may view Internet publishing as something that cuts into revenues from sales of your printed documents. Actually, as I discuss later in this chapter, any form of electronic publishing can often turn your documents into a revenue source rather than a cost liability. Interested? Many companies that publish their documents on the Internet don't make it easy for people to download the entire document set, which typically means that people who use these documents regularly buy one or more copies of your electronic document set. Because paper documents are still popular with many people (myself included!), customers may typically buy additional paper copies of your documents. For more information about the costs and benefits of electronic publishing, see the section later in this chapter entitled "Costs and Savings in Electronic Publishing."

✔ Legal groups typically view Internet publishing with much hand waving, alarm, and whimpering about potential liability. Making your documents available on the Internet increases the number of people who can access them, including your competitors, who could potentially re-engineer parts of your products if they have in-depth information about how your products work. However, your competitors can probably buy your documents directly from you or get someone else to buy them. Legal folks also tend to worry about whether making your documents available on the Internet implies any increased liability for errors or omissions in those documents. My answer to this is usually "You obviously don't understand." Any errors or omissions in your documents are already there. Letting more people identify them doesn't change things. What it does change is the number of potential customers who now have the ability to develop products that interact with (or require) yours.

✔ Sales and marketing groups almost always view Internet publishing as a huge win. They no longer have to send sample versions of your documents to potential customers. More importantly, potential customers have access to detailed technical information about your products. Anything that can embed a fish hook into the wallets of potential customers and induce them to ask for more information is a good thing.

Depending on the capabilities of the software you use to generate HTML, you may not have to change your documents to any significant extent. You may want to reorganize them somewhat to make the online versions of those documents as usable as possible. For example, if you currently integrate guide and reference material for software products into single documents, you may want to split this material so that it's easier to look up functions without having to know the part of your product that they are associated with. You can also augment your existing documents by providing things that may not exist in your existing set, such as a master index. If you can differentiate between guide and reference information, you should have little trouble producing an alphabetical master index for all of your reference information.

Using HTML as an electronic publishing format also means that you don't have to provide your customers with any special software to enable them to use your documents, because you can assume that they have (or can get) one of the many HTML browsers that are freely available. Though many of the software products for electronic publishing in other formats (discussed in the next section) are moving toward being freely available, more people have Web browsers than have some dedicated application for viewing electronic documents.

Delivering pre-formatted documents online

Moving your documents toward electronic delivery via HTML usually means that you lose some of the formatting and other visual bells and whistles that you've probably created in your documents over the years. This loss can be painful for the people who have invested lots of effort in producing those effects. Also, HTML doesn't really allow your customers to print versions of your documents in a useful form because HTML documents don't have any page numbers. Once you print an HTML document, you can use its table of contents only as an overview of the contents of your document — it no longer provides any useful way of getting to any of the headings that it lists. You can click on a paper document all you want — you're not going anywhere.

Several software packages attempt to bridge the gap between printed and electronic versions of your documents, with varying levels of success. The software packages discussed in this section often have different goals that and are often only meaningful to people who are using a specific word-processing or publishing application. There are usually also two sides to each of these packages — the viewer used to display and use documents that are provided in these formats, and the software used to generate documents in these formats. The following sections provide an overview of these packages and also discuss how to get documents into those formats. This is only an overview of each of these products — for more information about these products, contact the companies that produce them.

Adobe Acrobat

Adobe Acrobat uses the Adobe Portable Document Format (PDF) to distribute electronic versions of existing documents. PDF is a very popular format for distributing online versions of printed documents because it is independent of any specific word-processing or publishing tool. The input format from which PDF documents are produced is the PostScript printer control language, which means that you can produce PDF versions of any documents that you can produce a PostScript version of. PostScript is one of the most popular printer control languages in use today; almost all word-processing and publishing software can produce PostScript. All Macintosh applications produce PostScript because it is the default output format used on the Macintosh. All Microsoft Windows applications that use the standard Windows printer drivers can produce PostScript because Windows provides those drivers on its distribution disks. Almost all workstation word-processing and publishing software can produce PostScript because PostScript printers are the most common type of printers used in workstation environments.

You use the Acrobat Reader software to view, print, and search PDF files. This software is free and is available for many platforms, including DOS, Linux, Macintosh, OS/2, Windows, and the HP, IBM, SGI, and Sun flavors of UNIX. You can also get plug-ins for Web browsers such as Netscape Navigator that let you view PDF documents inside the browser. Because the input format used by Acrobat is a PostScript file, the Acrobat Reader can produce output that looks exactly like your original documents.

PDF documents are produced from PostScript files using the Adobe Acrobat Distiller. If your documents contain a table of contents, the Distiller links the entries in the table of contents to the appropriate points in your documents. The Distiller also does a good job of linking cross-references to the appropriate parts of your documents, whenever possible. You often get better results from a PostScript file that was produced using one of Adobe's desktop publishing tools, FrameMaker or PageMaker, but the Distiller does an admirable job of producing usable online versions of your documents from a PostScript file produced by an application. Adobe also provides the Acrobat Capture package to let you produce versions of your documents that are designed for use on the Web, create indexes of your PDF documents that you can search over the Web, and manage large collections of PDF documents.

Adobe FrameViewer

I'm not sure of the future for Adobe's FrameViewer product, which is a part of its FrameMaker product and was a feature of the FrameMaker package when Adobe acquired Frame Technologies, the original creators of FrameMaker. I've never liked it much, but you might want to use it if you are doing all of your document development in FrameMaker and want a quick-and-dirty way of producing online versions of your documents. If you currently use FrameMaker and want to see what FrameViewer looks like, check out any of its online documentation — it was produced using FrameViewer.

If that doesn't scare you, then you may want to consider FrameViewer as an easy way to move your Frame documents online. FrameViewer takes existing Frame documents and moves them online instantly — it turns the table of contents and any cross-references in your document into hyperlinks into the appropriate parts of your documents. FrameViewer also provides some fairly whizzy search features that let you search your documents for specific words or phrases, providing support for Boolean combinations of phrases ("foo" *and* "bar"). You can use FrameViewer to annotate and bookmark your FrameViewer documents, which is handy if you want to fold over the electronic corner of a frequently accessed part of a FrameViewer document or add notes to clarify different portions of a document. You can also print documents from FrameViewer.

FrameViewer is available for the Macintosh and Windows platforms, as well as for the DEC, HP, IBM, SGI, and Sun flavors of UNIX.

Aside from its interface, the primary drawback of using FrameViewer is the fact that it costs money. If you are delivering your documents to your customers in FrameViewer format, you have to factor the cost of the viewing software into the costs of electronic delivery. On the other hand, it does provide some nice features (the Boolean search and annotation features are pretty cool), so its cost may be worth it to you and your customers.

Corel Envoy

Envoy is Corel's entry into the world of electronic publishing. As much as I'm a fan of Corel WordPerfect as a word-processing package and as an SGML solution, I can't get too excited about Envoy, even though the viewer is free. Outside Corel itself, I haven't found many documents that are provided in Envoy format.

Envoy consists of two parts: the Envoy Viewer, which is freely available, and an Envoy Driver that you install as a print driver in the Macintosh and Windows environments. Like Adobe's Acrobat Distiller product, the Envoy Driver costs money, but you need it if you want to produce electronic versions of your documents from any Macintosh or Windows application. Rather than depending on a specific output format as an input format (as Acrobat does with PostScript), the Envoy Driver is actually a printer driver that creates Envoy output files. These files have an EVY extension, so you should have an easy time recognizing them. Using a print driver to produce Envoy files lets you create those files from any Windows or Macintosh application that supports printing, which should (hopefully!) include them all!

The Envoy Viewer lets you annotate and bookmark Envoy documents, provides searching capabilities much like the Acrobat Reader and FrameViewer, and also lets you print nicely formatted versions of your Envoy documents. Unfortunately, the Envoy Viewer is only available for the Macintosh and Windows platforms, which limits it somewhat as a truly cross-platform solution for your electronic publishing needs. A version of the Envoy Viewer available from Tumbleweed Software extends the Envoy format somewhat, allowing you to embed and use URLs and other World Wide Web features in your documents.

Interleaf WorldView

WorldView is an interesting product that takes a different approach to electronic publishing, combining an understanding of the internal formats used by word-processing and publishing packages with output formats such as PostScript. Using WorldView, you can produce electronic versions of documents in documentation formats such as Adobe FrameMaker, Corel WordPerfect, Interleaf (surprise!), Microsoft Word, and SGML. You can also produce electronic versions of documents from any PostScript or RTF file, which is a nice catch-all if you are using another word-processing and publishing package. You can also produce electronic versions of any documents or drawings in the Hewlett-Packard Graphics Language (HPGL) or *Initial Graphics Exchange Specification* (IGES) formats, which are widely used in *Computer-Aided Design* (CAD) and mechanical engineering environments.

Like Adobe Acrobat, FrameViewer, and Corel Envoy, WorldView consists of two packages: the WorldView software itself that lets you produce WorldView files, and a WorldView Viewer that lets you use those files. When generating a WorldView document, WorldView automatically generates a table of contents and index for your documents and preserves cross-references within a documentation set. WorldView also can selectively update only those documents in an electronic document set that have changed since the last time that collection was generated. WorldView lets you search, annotate, bookmark, and print your electronic documents. WorldView is a truly sophisticated system for producing electronic versions of your documents, providing some sexy features such as support for full-text queries and meta-information about your documents that users can search (such as author, date, department, and so on).

Native versions of WorldView are available for DOS, Macintosh, Microsoft Windows, and the DEC, HP, IBM, and Sun versions of UNIX. Unfortunately, the WorldView Viewer software costs money. Interleaf also provides a Java version of the WorldView Viewer, which extends the usability of WorldView documents to any platforms that support Java, which is a cool feature that largely eliminates any concerns you might have about platform independence.

Interestingly enough, you can also produce Adobe PDF files from WorldView, which means that if you are already using Interleaf for your publishing needs, you can use WorldView to generate PDF files and then require your customers to get the free Adobe Acrobat Viewer to use those files, eliminating the need to license the WorldView Viewer. Rather than viewing this as a way for Interleaf to shoot themselves in the foot, I see this as a great feature — you can use all of the power provided by WorldView to produce electronic documents (which should help WorldView sales) and then use a friendly, widely available package that you may already have, like Acrobat Reader, to view those files. You can even use browser plug-ins that support PDF files to view files produced by WorldView. Silly companies insist that theirs are the only true solutions for electronic and print publishing. Clever companies accept the reality that other people use other tools and provide ways to integrate their software into other environments.

Delivering online versions of SGML documents

Having read the last ten pages, you're probably looking at the title of this book and thinking "What does all of that stuff have to do with SGML?" That's a fair question.

As I mentioned in the introduction to this chapter, widespread focus on electronic publishing is a fairly new idea. Much of the growth in the popularity of electronic publishing concept is directly related to SGML implementations such as HTML. In general, structured documentation simplifies electronic publishing, because it standardizes the organization of your documents, simplifying their conversion into any format used for electronic publishing. Here are some specific ways in which SGML tools facilitate electronic publishing:

✔ Adobe, Corel, and Interleaf all provide SGML tools, which makes it easy for you to use their related electronic publishing tools to produce electronic versions of your documents in the Acrobat, FrameViewer, Envoy, and WorldView formats, respectively.

✔ SGML's core notion of separating the structure of your document from how that document is formatted makes it easy for you to use tools such as the Adobe Acrobat Distiller and Interleaf WorldView to publish electronic versions of your documents from output formats that your formatting environment probably supports, such as PostScript and RTF.

✔ Beyond HTML, some tools let you browse and publish SGML documents directly.

The previous sections discuss tools related to the first two points. The remainder of this section discusses the third point, which is just the tip of the iceberg in terms of electronic publishing and SGML. As SGML gains in popularity as a documentation development and management environment, new tools will continue to emerge that directly support electronic publishing from an SGML environment. See "Future Directions for Electronic Publishing" later in this chapter for information. As HTML continues to mature and as Web browsers continue to grow to meet the requirements of their users (through things like style sheets, support for XML, and so on), SGML will continue to grow as a rich base for electronic publishing.

The next sections discuss some of the tools that are available for direct electronic publishing of SGML documents.

DynaText

The DynaText Electronic Publishing System, available from INSO Publishing Systems, is an electronic publishing system that is designed to work with SGML documents. DynaText and associated software such as DynaTag were originally developed by Electronic Books Technologies and were among the first tools available for electronic publishing using SGML and arbitrary SGML DTDs.

DynaText works through a combination of tools. The primary tools for getting your documents into the DynaText environment are DynaTag, which automates the SGML tagging of documents that you import from other environments (such as FrameMaker, Interleaf, and Microsoft Word), and an Indexer that analyzes native SGML input. These tools create SGML versions of your books that are optimized for use with the other parts of the DynaText Publishing System. Once you have a collection of electronic books, you use the InStEd stylesheet editor to define the formatting associated with the tags in your electronic books. In true SGML form, you can create any number of style sheets for use with your electronic documents. These style sheets are stored separately from your SGML documents, so you can shared them throughout your organization, update them without having to change your existing DynaText documents, and distribute them to your customers if you want to improve the appearance of your DynaText documents without modifying their content. After importing and processing your documents and designing a style sheet, you use the DynaText Browser to view and use your electronic documents. Because they were designed from the ground up as a system for publishing SGML documents, all the tools that make up the DynaText Publishing System support very large collections of documents and also work with documents produced using complex DTDs.

If electronically publishing your SGML documents meets your internal needs but you want to export those documents to customers who may not have the DynaText browser, you can use a companion product, DynaWeb, to export HTML versions of your SGML documents.

DynaText automatically prepares a table of contents for your documents and provides this as the default entry point into your electronic documents. You can also produce tables of figures, tables of tables, tables of procedures. Because DynaText is an SGML tool, you only have to identify the tags that identify that type of information to produce a summary of any specific type of information.

The DynaText browser lets you annotate and bookmark your documents and provides some truly sexy searching tools for locating information in your electronic documents. Beyond standard mechanisms such as full-text search and Boolean searches, the DynaText browser lets you do proximity searches, which locate things like the word "Microsoft" within seven words of the phrase "evil empire," and structural searches, which find all instances of specific phrases within a certain set of SGML tags. The latter feature can help you locate specific procedures or identify table or figure captions that contain a specific word or phrase. You can restrict these searches to a certain chapter, section, or book, or you can open them up so that you can search an entire collection of documents.

DynaText is available for the Macintosh, Windows, and for the DEC, HP, IBM, SGI, Sun, and Unixware flavors of UNIX. When I last looked, DynaText was somewhat pricey, but it does provide a complete solution for electronically publishing SGML documents. Coupled with DynaWeb, DynaText can really provide a one-stop solution for electronically publishing your SGML documents with little documentation tools work on your part.

Panorama

The Panorama Publishing Suite, available from Softquad, lets you electronically publish your SGML documents. Beyond its many products for pure SGML document development, management, and formatting, Softquad also produces many sophisticated tools for HTML development, the best known of which is its HoTMetaL Pro product. Many people view HoTMetaL Pro as the best HTML editor available anywhere. For this reason, it's not surprising that Panorama provides many sophisticated ways of viewing SGML documents, including support for features such as frames that you would typically only think of in terms of HTML.

In addition to sophisticated ways of formatting and displaying your SGML documents, Panorama lets you annotate and bookmark your SGML documents and also provides some nice search features. The most interesting of these is its "hit density" display, which shows you all of the instances of the word or phrase you search for, summarizing how many of these matches occurred in specific portions of your documents. You can use this feature to identify parts of your documents that discuss a specific topic in detail rather than just mention the topic once. Like DynaText, Panorama was designed from the ground up as an SGML publishing solution, and you therefore can use it to create multiple stylesheets that can display your SGML documents in many different ways.

Panorama itself is only available for the Windows platform, but you can use a browser plug-in to view SGML documents produced by the Panorama Publishing Suite using any Web browser. Softquad offers many other SGML documentation tools, including an SGML publishing suite that is tightly integrated with Panorama, simplifying SGML publishing in general and electronic publishing in particular. Softquad's tools are well worth a look if you are committed to moving to SGML and want to make sure that you have a complete set of tools for both electronic and print publishing with little documentation tools work on your part.

Why Publish Electronically?

Now that I've discussed various ways of publishing your documents electronically, I want you to consider why electronic publishing is such a hot topic in the world of documentation today.

Basically, electronic publishing provides substantial advantages over classic print publishing because it can make it easier for your customers to access the information about your products that they need. Even if you are only augmenting your current document delivery mechanisms by adding online formats to the formats that you already provide, electronic publishing provides one more way for people to access information about your products. If you are considering replacing print publishing with some form of electronic publishing as the default way to provide information about your products and services, you have to consider a variety of issues, such as how publishing your documents electronically changes the way your document development group works, the tools you want to use, and so on. In most cases, electronic publishing doesn't eliminate the need for print publishing, but it can substantially change your focus, cost structure, and the way in which you schedule documentation development.

The next sections discuss some general advantages (and the few disadvantages) of electronic publishing. For specific information about how electronic publishing affects your costs and procedures for doing business, see the section later in this chapter entitled "Costs and Savings in Electronic Publishing."

Advantages of electronic publishing

The most obvious benefit of adding electronic publishing to the formats in which you currently publish your documents is that it provides an additional way for your organization and your customers to access information. If you have a large document set, electronic publishing can make it easier for your customers to work with that set as a whole, rather than as a number of individual documents. As discussed earlier in this chapter, most electronic publishing systems allow you to link topics across documents, turning your document set into a single usable resource for your customers.

Electronic publishing can also save you money producing your documents and, if you move existing documentation sets online, can save you the postage required to ship your products to your customers!

People can use and view electronic versions of your documents on systems that your software currently doesn't support (referred to as *other platforms* in this section). You may wonder why I view this as a huge feature because you may wonder why people who can't run your software would want to read your documents. One reason is that many companies use different operating systems for various reasons throughout your organization. For example, sales and marketing people may use Macintosh systems, while your development group may use PCs or different types of workstations. If electronic versions of your documents are available and viewers for your electronic documents are available on each of these platforms, these groups can all view your documents, much like they can all use the old paper versions of your documents. There's a big advantage in being able to use tools on a platform that a customer is already comfortable with. For example, marketing people can read your documents online using their Macs, making it easy for them to use your electronic documents as source material or to verify the correctness of advertisements or marketing materials.

Another advantage of having people on other platforms who can use your electronic documents is the fact that your organization may already be working on supporting your products on those platforms. If this is the case, you don't have to do anything special to make your documents available there. If those systems already support the format in which you deliver your electronic documents, you're already home free! Being able to use electronic documents on many different platforms is one of the advantages of using a purely cross-platform delivery format such as HTML, but free viewers for formats such as Adobe's PDF are available for most platforms.

Drawbacks of electronic publishing

Like anything, electronic publishing has its drawbacks, especially if certain documents are only available electronically:

✔ Electronic documents are highly portable, but they're also useless unless you have the means to read them wherever you are. It's pretty darn hard to read product documentation that comes on a CD when you're riding on a bus or traveling on an airplane (unless, of course, you have a laptop or have substantially better eyesight than I do!).

✔ Electronic documents can be more difficult to use for random access. When I read a manual, I usually find myself flipping through the pages until some interesting phrase catches my eye. Even though most electronic documents are searchable, it's hard to enter all possible interesting phrases into the little window where you can type search strings. Also, when reading a book, I usually find myself reading a bit in one place, using a finger to save that location, skimming ahead, marking another section, flipping back to the table of contents, skipping to the index, looking up another section, and so on. It's difficult for electronic documents to support these kinds of non-linear access to a document.

Both of these issues are important, but they are also becoming less so as hardware technology becomes less expensive and more sophisticated and as software solutions to electronic publishing continue to evolve. Ten or fifteen years ago, you were either a dedicated proponent of technology or a masochist if you lugged a portable computer around with you. Remember portable computers that you could lift only if you worked out regularly and that would fit under an airplane seat with only a millimeter to spare? Today's laptops are light, cheap, and as powerful as most desktop machines. Most software companies equip consultants and field service people with laptops. Product documentation, service manuals, or other information on a CD lets you take a complete set of your documentation into the field where you need it the most, and without hurting your back!

The software used to view electronic documents is also evolving. Reading an online manual is no longer the equivalent of loading it into a text editor and searching for the bit of information that you need. Most software for browsing electronic documents now lets you set bookmarks, annotate existing documents (on the off-chance that they're ever wrong or incomplete), and search for complex topics like "feast *and* famine," rather than just searching for "feast" and then looking for nearby instances of "famine."

As electronic publishing becomes more prevalent, the limitations discussed in this section will become less and less meaningful — however, you still need to consider any limitations and requirements that you're imposing on the people who will be using your electronic documents. As I discuss in the next section, electronic publishing can substantially reduce your costs. If you are a documentation or information professional, you have to serve as an advocate for the users of the information you produce, protecting them against the juggernaut of savings if these savings have implications for how usable your documents are to your customers.

Costs and Savings in Electronic Publishing

Just like publishing information in any form, electronic publishing costs something! The next few sections examine how shifting to electronic publishing or adding electronic publishing to the current set of output formats that you provide affects your costs. I also discuss some of the ways in which electronic publishing can reduce existing costs or provide hidden benefits to your organization.

Documentation costs: tools and training

If you currently only publish documents on paper, you have to decide how you want to make your documents available electronically. You then have to examine whether your current publishing software can export your documents in any format you can use for electronic publishing. If you are considering electronic publishing as a result of moving to an SGML environment, you may be able to factor the costs of supporting additional output formats into the cost of moving to SGML. The section earlier in this chapter entitled "Formats for Electronic Publishing" discusses different ways of making your existing documents available. Regardless of which delivery mechanism you select, you need to consider some basic costs to your documentation group and your writers.

You need different tools to perform different forms of electronic publishing. If the SGML software package you use (or plan to use) doesn't provide automatic support for generating HTML, you either have to develop tools to generate HTML yourself or purchase one of the software packages for electronic publishing that I discuss earlier in this chapter. Developing the tools to do it yourself requires an obvious investment of your time. Even if you're purchasing a commercial package, you have to invest some time in learning to use these tools efficiently. You also have to train anyone who will use this software. You have to budget time for generating and verifying your HTML documents. The silver lining here is that the time required to generate HTML versions of your documents can be substantially less than the time required to produce printed versions of your documents.

Costs and savings in production requirements

Moving to electronic publishing, whether as your primary means for document delivery or simply as an additional format, imposes new requirements on the group that is responsible for producing your documentation and making it available to customers. (I'll call this the *production group*.) If you are selling or delivering electronic versions of your documents to your customers, your production group may have to establish relationships with new vendors and will at least have to create the associated packaging (such as CD artwork and CD packaging such as jewel cases). You have to provide auxiliary documents, such as installation instructions for your documentation, and also installation scripts or programs for your online documents. You don't have to provide any of these things when you just deliver documents that go on a shelf!

You also should consider how publishing documents electronically may save you money. If you make electronic publishing the primary way you publish, you will save lots of money delivering your products to your customers. Unless you have a truly small documentation set, it should be cheaper to send your customers a tape or CD containing an electronic version of your documents than to send them the documents themselves. You also save production costs — tapes or CDs are much cheaper to produce than printed document sets. You can also begin to pass the costs of printing your documents on to your customers because printed documentation may now be an optional part of the product that they must pay for. If printed documents are optional, you can be sure that some customers won't buy them, so you can maintain a much smaller inventory of printed documentation sets. Your per-copy price may rise, because you'll order smaller numbers of documents from the printer, but you can probably just pass these costs on to your customers.

Because you order fewer sets of documents, you don't need as much space to devote to your "product warehouse." If your organization frequently produces new versions of your products, reducing the number of sets of documents that you have to order and stock can also reduce your losses when a new version of your product is released that makes your existing documents obsolete.

Savings in production time

Many people often overlook that fact that electronic publishing can buy your documentation staff a substantial amount of extra time at the end of a product release cycle. Traditionally, you have to send your documents to a printer weeks or months before a product is released. Weeks early can become months early if you also have to translate your documents into other languages. If you're working in an industry where you produce hardware, this may not be that much of a problem because you typically also have to finish your designs long before the product actually goes into production so that you can create dies, tool up for the manufacturing effort, set up the manufacturing lines and delivery mechanisms, and so on. However, in the software industry (unless you've worked for firms that are better organized than any I've ever seen), having to finish documents weeks or months before the product actually ships can be the kiss of death as far as accuracy is concerned. The subtle introduction of "critical" but new "features" as a software product nears completion (often called *creeping featurism* or *feeping creaturism*) can mean that your documents may actually resemble the product that they are supposed to describe.

Moving to electronic publishing as a primary way of delivering information about your products can buy you the extra time that you need at the end of a release cycle to perfect your documents. In most organizations that I've seen that have committed to electronic publishing, products ship with the primary documentation set online and only with release notes and installation (and perhaps configuration) information on paper. Since you can produce a number of CDs in a fraction of the time that it takes to print even a small number of books, the extra time you buy yourself by focusing on electronic publishing is the extra time that you can spend in perfecting your documents, ensuring their accuracy, and enhancing them if necessary.

Web-related expenses

If you make electronic versions of your documents available over the World Wide Web, you have to factor various Web-related expenses into the cost of producing these documents. If your company doesn't already have a Web site, you have to consider how much the hardware and support will cost. You probably need to dedicate a machine to be a Web server and need some MIS expertise to set up and support that server. If you're not connected to the Internet, you have to contract with an Internet Service Provider (ISP) to provide you with a connection. You may also want to register your own Internet domain with the Network Information Center (NIC) so that your customers can easily find your Web server and your documents. These are just a few of the costs associated with setting up and maintaining a Web server — as a general topic, setting up and maintaining a Web server is well beyond the scope of this book. See one of the many excellent books available on setting up and maintaining a Web server for more information.

If your organization already has a Web site, the cost of adding material to that Web site is marginal beyond acquiring additional disk space. However, if your products should turn out to be the next Netscape, you may have to buy more powerful hardware and even upgrade your connection to the Internet to support the increased load on your network and Web server. If your product is the next Netscape, you can probably afford the hardware, but you still need to consider its cost.

Electronic publishing and your advertising $$

You also should consider the amount of additional contact information that you get from making your documents available on the Web. The Web is a tremendous source of free advertising, and you can use it to reach people who may never consider sending in a reader comment card in response to an advertisement for your products in a magazine. If your documents are available electronically, people who are interested in your software can find out about it and get enough information to ask informed questions when they contact your sales or marketing groups. Your Web site may grab the attention of potential customers who might not otherwise have seen how your products could work for them.

 Creating a Web site and exporting electronic versions of your documents can be a valuable way of promoting your products and services to potential customers. It may not be able to replace advertising and marketing, but it can certainly add to their success (and your organization's!).

Savings in product support costs

Customer support groups usually see electronic publishing as a huge win, since they can guarantee that customers with Internet access can always use the latest and greatest versions of your documents. They can reduce the setup time for each customer call because they can ensure that both they and the customer are looking at the same versions of a document by pointing their Web browsers at exactly the same Web page. Making everything available on the Internet also eliminates the "I don't have that manual" problem because your whole document set is right there on the Web.

Making electronic versions of your documents available over the Web can generally reduce the number of calls that your product support group gets regarding your products, especially if you use electronic publishing software that gives your customers additional ways of searching your documents for information. If you've written your own tools to generate electronic versions of your documents, you can do clever things like automatically generating hyperlinked cross-references. For example, if the documentation for a software product identifies each datatype and function reference using a specific style or SGML element, you can automatically turn these references into hyperlinks to the reference page for that datatype or function. Instant value add!

Meet the New Boss — Different from the Old Boss

In the long run, moving a documentation set online has some costs that aren't evident at first glance. The biggest of these is that you may have to rethink or redesign your documentation so that it "works" online.

Traditional paper documents are huge linear arrays of words and characters that provide some shortcuts, such as a table of contents, an index, and cross-references throughout each book and documentation set. This monolithic document model isn't necessarily appropriate for online documents, where you have to consider factors like the amount of time it takes to load a document into whatever software you're using to view it. You need to divide the information into bite-sized pieces that are easily digestible both by the reader and the software you're using to read them, especially when moving existing documents into HTML. Some companies may only have a serial or on-demand connection to the net, in which case loading a single huge document is a task best attempted over lunch or started when you're ready to leave for the day. A slow connection to the information you need isn't really very good for finding the answers to those "I just have a simple question" types of issues.

Today, a single monolithic document still has some advantages. Because all of the information about that product is in that document, it's easier to search because you don't need an auxiliary database or search engine; you can use your browser or other viewing software to search for certain phrases. If you don't find them, they're not in the document. You don't have to worry about whether the appropriate phrases were built into the search database you're using or how good the search software is. As the tools used to produce electronic documents improve, these tools will be less likely to produce single huge documents because they'll be better at automatically chunking the information in existing documents.

As you develop newer documents with electronic delivery and publication in mind, you will probably also find that you are beginning to write and think differently because you know that electronic delivery, with hyperlinks and whizzy search technologies, is one of your target output formats. For example, how you handle an issue as simple as expanding acronyms changes when you publish your documents electronically. In printed books, you often have to expand the same acronym multiple times in different portions of a book because you can't be sure where the reader started reading. In electronic versions of those same books, the first use of each acronym in a chunk of information can simply be a hyperlink to the definition of that term in a glossary or elsewhere. Problem solved! Similarly, you can centralize background information that you might have needed to repeat in different books within a document set. By chunking this information and providing useful links to the centralized location of this background information, you can reduce your writing time and usually reduce the size of your documentation set.

Future Directions for Electronic Publishing

Much of the work being done today in enhancing existing formats and in developing new formats for Internet publishing is related to ways of freeing documents on the Internet from the constraints of the small tag set and limited, hard-wired formatting capabilities provided by HTML. As the Internet expands to encompass more and more facets of our business and personal lives, these trends will continue to provide us with more powerful, more feature-rich ways of publishing documents on the Internet.

The next few sections discuss some of the work being done to produce more flexible formats for Internet publishing and how that work may simplify electronic publishing in the near future.

Enhancing HTML

The HTML standard has evolved substantially since the birth of the Web and the dissemination of the original HTML standard. Version 2.0 provided support for many of the features that we take for granted today, such as tables and additional forms of hyperlinks. Version 3.0 of the HTML standard was obsolete before it had a chance to be officially adopted, and version 3.2 is becoming the official standard as work proceeds on the next specification. For a more complete discussion of HTML, its history, and specific details about future trends in HTML, see Chapter 7 or one of the many excellent books devoted solely to HTML.

Some developers are working to provide richer ways of defining the formatting of HTML documents. Improvements such as support for style sheets are only the tip of the iceberg in that respect — as I discuss later in this section, some of the other proposed standards for Internet publishing have already surpassed HTML both in terms of support for formatting and delivering more flexible solutions for Internet publishing. One of the big drawbacks of HTML and the support that various browsers provide for its tagset is the fact that support for a specific HTML DTD must currently be built into the browser — most HTML browsers don't provide support for arbitrary extensions to HTML, which you might expect to find in actual SGML tools. As I discuss in the next section, the proposed XML standard goes a long way toward providing these capabilities.

Other developers are working toward enhancing the ways in which HTML can deliver information by adding features such as pop-ups and similar features that are required in order to use HTML as the basis for online help systems. Though Microsoft has committed to delivering online help in HTML for its next generation of Windows, we may well find that what we actually get when it arrives is support for XML, with HTML as a supported DTD.

XML

The *Extensible Markup Language* (XML), which I discuss in detail in Chapter 7, is worth discussing here as a future direction for electronic publishing in general. The Extensible Markup Language is a simple dialect of SGML that is designed for use over the Internet. XML frees Web documents from the limitations imposed by HTML by providing them with a way of including, or linking to, information about their structure — their DTD! This information can be accessed through a URL to a centralized DTD on the Web or on your local system, or it can be contained within the XML document itself. XML prohibits some of the more obscure aspects of SGML, such as tag minimization and omission, to guarantee that XML documents are easily interpreted by applications and by humans. XML does not provide information about how Web documents are to be formatted, but it does provide a flexible way of defining the structure of a Web document whose formatting can be described by a CSS style sheet or in DSSSL.

As an actual implementation of SGML, XML is a giant step toward empowering electronic publishers to release attractive and creative documents on the Web. Companies that use XML for electronic publishing can automatically export their existing documents for Internet publishing, regardless of the DTD that they use, since they can also export that DTD. To use XML, you must make sure that your SGML documents do not use tag minimization or omission (or pre-process your documents before publishing them, removing any instances of these features). Because XML uses an actual SGML parser, many of the poorly formatted documents that now "just happen to work" on the Web won't pass muster in an XML environment. This is a good thing! If XML becomes a widely used standard on the Web, newer electronic publishing tools will be developed (such as XML editors that will form a superset of the existing HTML editors) that impose stricter structural requirements on documents that are to be published on the Internet. Internet publishing will therefore converge with SGML development, and everyone will be more aware of the benefits and power of SGML because they all will use SGML!

Futures for electronic publishing in SGML

As mentioned in the previous section, XML is a specific subset of SGML that imposes some limitations on the ways that you can mark up your SGML documents. As SGML software becomes more common, as the machines we use become more powerful, and as Internet publishers become more demanding and more sophisticated, I believe that support for pure SGML (as defined by the SGML standard) is only a browser generation or two away. As I discussed earlier in this chapter, tools such as DynaText and Panorama already provide ways of publishing SGML documents on the Web, and also provide sophisticated support for style sheets. Sounds familiar? I'll say! It sounds exactly like the directions in which current enhancements are moving HTML, and much like some of the core concepts of XML.

Future SGML tools for document development and publishing are destined to provide enhanced support for any formats required for Internet publishing, because no one can deny that this is a hot trend in the documentation industry. As the distinctions between HTML, XML, and pure SGML blur, SGML tool and network browser developers have a unique opportunity to provide software that lets organizations that use SGML instantly publish their documents on the Internet, with no modification and no limitations. Here's hoping!

Chapter 17

Document Management Systems

● ●

● ●

*L*ike any other corporate resource, the documents that you produce for your organization require some amount of management. In the simplest form of document management, you make sure that you have a backup copy of all of the files used to produce the documents associated with each release of your products. Production problems may require that you regenerate a version of a specific document for a specific release. Without a record of which documents were associated with each release and a copy of all of the document and graphics files used to produce each document, however, you have no way of reproducing any of these documents!

Keeping backup copies of all of the files associated with each of your documents for each release of your products is a fairly trivial way of managing your documents, but you may not have an alternative, depending on the format in which your current documentation tool stores its files. For example, you may have to keep copies of the files that make up your documents if your documentation tool stores its files in a binary format and no document management applications are available that work with your documentation tool. Luckily, as I explain later in this chapter, SGML eliminates this concern because SGML files are standard text files.

In this chapter and others, I talk about "text" and "binary" files. A text file is one that you can open with a standard text editor, or display on your screen as readable characters without any special software. I use "binary file" to mean a file that contains information in a special format, designed for use with one or more special software packages, and which you can't just look at. Many software packages use special binary file formats to speed up reading and writing the files that they create and use. For example, a file produced by Microsoft Word and which has the .doc extension is a special binary file created by Word to hold a document. You need Word (or some other word processor) to read that file. A file produced with a text editor, such as edit, SimpleText, or emacs, is a text file.

Beyond simply tracking the document and graphics files associated with specific releases of your products, more sophisticated forms of document management let you track each change to any portion of your documents and provide information about the reason for that change, who did it, and when the change was made. Tracking these sorts of changes can provide valuable insights into the amount of documentation change related to each change in your products. Tracking this sort of information can also help you identify where inaccuracies or stylistic deviations creep into your documents and writers or reviewers who need more training on your products or style guide.

Document management systems are software packages that automate the process of managing large collections of documents and changes to them. They typically work by archiving a copy of all the files used to produce any of your documents, tracking the relationships between those files and any changes to those files, and providing a mechanism for you to retrieve specific versions of those files based on date, version number, or specific changes.

SGML naturally lends itself to document management systems for two basic reasons: first, SGML files are usually stored in text form, which simplifies the task of managing and annotating changes; and second, because SGML's emphasis on structure makes it easy to integrate SGML documents with the database systems that are often used as supporting software for document management systems.

In this chapter, I explain some of the basic goals and principles of document management systems and compare these with the parallel mechanisms to track changes in software source code. I then discuss various approaches to document management and the costs, features, and potential benefits of each.

Managing Changes to Information

Document management is most important for documents that will be maintained and developed for a long time (sometimes known as documents that have a *long life span*). Because these documents will undergo many changes and enhancements during their lifetime, you need to have a way to identify the differences between different versions of the same document. You also sometimes need to be able to return to previous versions of the same document, either to reprint them or to eliminate changes that turn out to be inappropriate. By tracking the changes between different versions of a document, document management systems make it easy to identify and regenerate specific versions of your documents.

As I discuss later in this chapter, document management systems provide many other features that help you manage and analyze your documents. For the time being, however, I want to discuss managing change in your documents. The next two section discuss how software projects manage change and why they don't provide all of the power that you'd like to have in managing documentation projects.

Source code and version control systems

Most software development projects use simple version control systems to manage and track the changes to their source code, which is the set of files containing instructions in some computer language which is then compiled to create a software product. These systems are also referred to as *source code control* systems because they control changes to the code that you use to produce your products. For example, if one developer is working on a specific module, he or she typically tells the source code control system to lock that module, which means that other developers can't accidentally work on the same module.

Source code for documents?

"What does this source code stuff mean to me?" I hear you cry. "I'm not a software engineer and don't even play one on TV!" When I think of source code, I think of it as whatever the input files are that make up any part of a product. The source code for a software product is usually a bunch of text files with extensions such as .c and .h. These files are then compiled to make an executable program.

Similarly, the source code for a document set is the set of files that you wrote, and which are formatted or otherwise processed to create the final copies of your documentation. Therefore, the same principles apply to keeping track of revisions in each — the software and the documentation are (or at least, should be) equally important components of your product.

As I discuss in Chapter 14, version control systems keep track of all the changes to each of your files by comparing them against a reference copy of each of the files that make up your source code or documents. You initialize the version control system's reference copy of each of your files by *checking in* a specific version of each of your files. Checking in a copy of each of your files means that the versions control system makes a copy of each of those files and assigns it a starting version number. This copy of each of your files then becomes the reference point that the version control software uses as a basis for comparison with subsequent versions of your files. After registering a reference copy, you then check out a "new" copy of each of your files (just like at the library!), modify them, and check the new version of each file back into the version control system at various points in your development process. Each time you check a new version back in, the version control system assigns it a new version number, compares the contents of the new file against the previous version, and keeps a record of the changes. If you ever make a change that breaks any of your files or which you want to remove, you can simply check out the version with the previous version number and start over. This process is called *rolling back* to an earlier version of your files.

Version control systems let you check out a copy of any version of any file that has been checked in and can produce reports that highlight the differences between different versions of your files. You can use these summaries of changes between different versions of the source code for your products to track the progress of your software development work and as a source of information for status reports that you need to provide for your management. These status reports may contain more information than you need, but you can always cut out the details and extract a high-level summary.

Using source code control systems for documentation

Most existing source code control systems are not suitable for managing documentation work because the source code (the files that you create using your word-processing or publishing system) for documents is typically stored in binary formats. Though some word-processing systems (such as Microsoft Word) provide revision control on a per-document basis, this is hardly good enough for serious document control — it's simply designed to help multiple authors and reviewers identify changes that each has made. After a few rounds of editing, a Word document that uses revision control begins to look like a Jackson Pollock painting! The fact that you can also forget to turn on revision control in a word document and that you have to make sure that it is turned on in each document that you're working with makes it unsuitable for serious document management.

Source code control systems can actually work quite well with documentation in SGML because SGML files are plain text files. In most cases, you need to modify only the characters that the version control system uses to delimit comments in the files it manages in order to use a version control system with SGML. Most version control systems embed comments in the files that you check out in order to track the version number and other high-level changes. Since most version control systems manage changes in the source code for programs, you need to "teach" them the comment characters used in SGML.

When considering whether to use an existing source code control system to manage SGML documents, you need to know whether it provides all the features that you'd like to have to track and manage changes to your documents. Source code control systems are fine for SGML development efforts, such as DTD development, because you typically work with a relatively small number of files. SGML documents, however, are usually composed of many more files than a DTD, and many source code control systems (specifically on UNIX systems) don't work well with vast hierarchical collections of files unless you use (or have written) a master control program that knows how to iterate over each of the files that make up that hierarchy. Some newer source code control systems, such as CVS, do a better job of managing collections of files, but suffer from another drawback of software version control systems designed for use by programmers — they were designed for use by programmers. They can be cryptic, if not downright hostile, for the rest of us to use!

Source code control systems are also typically designed to do nothing more than track changes to your files — they usually don't provide the extra features that you need in a true document management system. For example, most source code control systems that I've seen don't have any way of tracking the progression of your documents through any sort of process. Surprisingly, documentation typically goes through a much more rigorous cycle of checks and cross-checks (the review process) than the source code for software does. I suppose that this is because (almost) everyone can read English but not everyone can read the source code for a software product. Frequently, the validity of changes to software source code is established by testing the result, not by first examining the source code itself. Now you know one of the reasons why every software company has a relatively large customer support group.

Basic features of document management systems

Real document management systems typically provide many advantages to writers and documentation and project managers. Much like standard source code control systems, document management systems make it possible for multiple writers to work on different parts of a document at the same time. By tracking which writers are working on various parts of a document and managing any changes that they make to those portions of a document, document management systems prevent writers from accidentally overwriting each others changes. Document management systems sometimes also implement access control lists, which define the users that can access and modify various documents.

Beyond simply tracking changes to your documents, many document management systems benefit writers and project and documentation managers by managing the *workflow* of a project, which is the progression of a project through different stages, such as authoring, review, integrating comments, final review, and signoff by responsible parties. Document management systems that provide workflow support let users of those systems check the status of any or all documents at a given time, which can help identify potential bottlenecks that may prevent you from releasing your documents on time. For example, if a set of documents assigned to a particular reviewer are still marked as waiting to be reviewed, you can reassign them to another reviewer or discuss the problem with the manager of the existing reviewer.

Document management systems that support structured documentation systems such as SGML provide additional benefits. Most SGML-aware document management systems understand DTDs and let you manage chunks of information at any level of structure in your documents. These systems let you increase the extent to which you can share and reuse core portions of information across multiple documents. You can even create other documents by assembling them from general chunks of information and applying some semantic glue. Don't underestimate the power of a document management system that understands the structure and organization of your documents. Like a Swiss Army knife, this kind of document management system allows you to perform tasks that you haven't needed to do (or haven't been able to do) but which can add tremendous value to the ways in which you can organize, examine, and extract sections of the information that make up your documents.

Document management systems that support SGML also usually provide features that let you search documents and document components for specific types of information. You can usually search a collection of documents at any level for specific elements, specific phrases, or elements with specific attributes. As mentioned previously, document management systems that support SGML often make it easy for you to reuse different portions of your documents, even helping you produce "new" documents from specific components of your existing documents. Document management systems that provide query and search features make it easy for you to identify portions of existing documents that you want to use. For example, if you want to produce a quick-reference sheet for a specific procedure related to one of your products and the steps in that procedure are tagged with a specific element or attribute, you can use a query feature to identify the steps in a specific portion of one of your documents and extract those steps into another document.

Types of SGML Document Management

Document management systems typically come in two different flavors — those that store your documents as hierarchical collections of files using the standard file and directory structure provided by your computer system, and those that store your documents in some sort of database.

SGML document management systems that use your computer's file system to store and manage the files that make up your documents are often easier for writers to manage because they are usually simpler than document management systems that require a database for storage. This simplicity is a two-edged sword. Document management systems that use the standard file system for storage are easier to learn, work with, and support yourself. However, they usually offer less power than document management systems that require databases to store and manage your documents.

SGML documentation management systems frequently use databases to store your files. The structured nature of SGML documents lends itself well to the ways that data is organized in a database system: records (elements), fields associated with those records (attributes and element content), and pointers to related records (the document hierarchy). Some SGML document management systems use proprietary databases that are optimized for SGML documents. Others simply plug in to existing database systems. If you're evaluating SGML document management systems that rely on a database, you need to identify the type of database support that it requires during the early stages of the evaluation process.

Your organization probably already uses a database system for tracking orders, defects, customer calls, and so on. If you select a document management system that can interoperate with your existing database system, you can probably reduce your costs in moving to that document management system. Of course, you have to consult your organization's MIS group to make sure that your existing database system has enough resources to support the extra load and storage requirements that your document management system will impose! However, you usually only have to purchase some additional hardware, establish a backup schedule for the new databases that you will create, and get the participation of a database manager or programmer.

Document management systems that are integrated with databases put all of the powerful features of a database system at your fingertips as potential tools for providing new ways of looking at and working with your documents. For example, triggers are a powerful feature of document management systems that are integrated with databases. A *trigger* is a database term for the automatic execution of some procedure that occurs when specific parts of a database change. These procedures can be as simple as sending mail to a set of writers who also depend on that information, letting them know that it has changed, or automatically running an SGML parser to validate all documents that depend on the information that has changed. Triggers can prevent last-minute gotchas such as finding that a change to some shared portion of your document has introduced elements that are valid in some of your documents but not in all of the documents that depend on that information. This sort of thing is especially common (and especially painful) in organizations that use multiple DTDs or DTDs that provide several different high-level document structures (such as the DocBook DTD's support for articles and books, each of which has structural differences at some level).

Chapter 18 provides more detailed information about how database systems interact with SGML documentation, discusses integration and support issues, and gives examples of how sophisticated queries can give you more insight into your documents and help extend the reusability of the information in your documents.

Document Management Systems and ISO 9000

In many industries, you must comply with ISO 9000 quality standards in order to do business in many parts of the world. To become certified as conforming to an ISO 9000 standard, your company must undergo an ISO 9000 *audit*, in which a third party examines your current policies and procedures and examines their conformance with ISO 9000 requirements. Aside from the fact that conforming to an ISO 9000 standard means that your company has to produce, track, and archive large amounts of documentation about quality policies, internal procedures, and instructions and requirements for various tasks, your company also has to archive records that prove that the quality control systems that you've implemented are working as designed. But I'm sure that your company does that already. . . .

See the sidebar ("And now a few words about ISO") later in this chapter for background information about ISO 9000 if you're not already familiar with it.

Document management is an important part of ISO 9000 compliance because quality control in the document development process is an important aspect of product development in general. Beyond product-related documentation, ISO 9000 compliance mandates that you provide substantial amounts of internal documentation about your policies and procedures, which you must also manage and control.

Using a document management system to control access to your internal and product-related documents, tracking changes to those documents, identifying the reasons for those changes, and verifying that these changes have all been reviewed are all critical parts of a document development process that meets ISO 9000 standards. Of course, it's certainly possible to do all these tasks with an incredibly convoluted paper trail and a set of rigorously enforced standards for marking up changes in your documents, but the chances of things slipping through the cracks are pretty high.

Preparing for ISO 9000 certification requires a tremendous amount of work at even the most meticulous and anal company. Before considering devoting a large part of your corporate resources to preparing for ISO 9000 certification, consider the following questions:

- ✔ Is ISO 9000 important to your customers, your market, or in parts of the world where you do or plan to do business? Are your competitors applying for ISO 9000 certification?

- ✔ What benefits will your organization gain by implementing a more formal quality system? Will a more formal quality system prevent errors that currently occur repeatedly, or do things already seem to be running smoothly?

- ✔ Have you been asked to gain registration by an important customer or the parent company? Are you getting complaints from customers about the quality of your products?

If you've answered yes to several of these questions, then your organization should consider applying for ISO 9000 certification. The costs of preparing for and undergoing an ISO 9000 audit can be very disruptive. If you are already working under tight deadlines, you might want to wait to apply for certification, but your organization should at least create a plan for gradually implementing policies and procedures that will make ISO 9000 certification easier down the road. Evaluating, selecting, and implementing a document management system can go a long way toward preparing your company, documentation group, and technical writers for an audit that's somewhere on the horizon. As discussed earlier in this chapter, document management systems can actually add a substantial amount of value to the ways in which you can examine, analyze, and reuse the information in your documents. The time required to select and install such as system, and to move your existing documents into that type of system, is almost always time well spent.

Strongly consider moving to a document management system if your company is planning to apply for ISO 9000 certification, or you'd better buy a 55-gallon drum of aspirin. Actually, if you're undergoing an ISO 9000 audit, you or someone at your company will probably need the aspirin anyway. Put it in the lobby, beside a watercooler.

And now a few words about ISO

The International Organization for Standardization (ISO) was founded in 1946 in Geneva, Switzerland to develop quality standards for use in different industries. These standards were developed to increase the confidence that different parties have in the quality control systems used by other companies with which they do business.

The ISO 9000 standard actually consists of five separate standards, composed of *guidance* and *conformance* standards. *Guidance* standards provide suggestions about how to interpret the other standards and information about which of the other standards applies to your industry. *Conformance* standards describe the procedures and policies that you must follow to be able to claim that your business complies to one of these standards:

- ISO 9000-1, a guidance standard that provides a road map to the other standards.

- ISO 9001, the most comprehensive of the conformance standards, defines procedures and policies for all aspects of the production process (design, development, testing, manufacturing, installation, and servicing). This standard is commonly applied to the manufacturing, service, and processing industries — or any organization that actually creates and designs new products or unique services.

- ISO 9002, a conformance standard that is similar to ISO 9001 but which only defines procedures and policies for manufacturing and installation processes — it does not discuss the design process.

- ISO 9003, the conformance standard with the fewest requirements, is typically followed by companies who sell finished products provided by other vendors and only discusses the final inspection and testing processes.

- ISO 9004-1, a guidance standard that provides general information about quality management.

The most interesting aspect of ISO 9000 certification is that the International Standards Organization does not audit and certify firms for ISO 9000 compliance. Independent firms send out goon squads consisting of ISO 9000 auditors to examine and assess your policies, procedures, and their conformance to the appropriate ISO 9000 standard. ISO just writes the rules.

Chapter 18

Database Systems and SGML

• •

• •

Database systems provide a substantial amount of power for organizing and querying structured information. Most databases provide powerful query languages (such as SQL) that make it easy to search portions of a database for specific content or to retrieve data by supplying ranges of values that describe that data.

Storing the content of structured documents is a different story, unfortunately. The difference between the type of storage provided by most databases and the type of storage required by documents (structured or not!) is that the amount of content associated with any portion of a document is highly variable. For an SGML example, although it may be safe to say that a `<TITLE>` element will never exceed 256 characters in length, it is impossible to place any functional limitations on the length of the content of an SGML `<PARAGRAPH>`.

Database designers, however, are clever folks. You can work around size limitations by using different types of database fields and by using database fields to hold pointers to external storage locations which have no size limitations.

This chapter provides background information about various types of databases, discusses various approaches to storing SGML information in those types of databases, and examines some of the ways in which SGML documents impose different requirements on the query languages used to extract information from databases. For more information about databases and their most common application for SGML (document management systems), see Chapter 17.

Different Types of Databases

Two basic types of databases are commonly used: relational and object-oriented databases. The way in which these databases store and retrieve data has some implications on how well they can be used to store, retrieve, and work with SGML documents, which can have arbitrary amounts of content at different parts of their structure.

The next two sections introduce these two basic types of databases and explain how each interacts with SGML data.

Relational databases

The most common type of database used today is the relational database. You can think of a relational database as a two-dimensional matrix that consists of rows representing all of the information about a specific entry (a record, in database-speak) in the database and columns identifying each of the specific types of information (a field, in database lingo) in each record. Because these databases are two-dimensional matrices, they are often called tables. For example, the fields in a table of names might be called "name," "email-address," "city," and "state,"   a record in that table might then have the values "Bill von Hagen," "wvh@gethip.com," "Verona," and "Pennsylvania."

 Database hackers may already be up in arms, thinking that I'm playing fast and loose with database terminology. Perhaps I am! For example, some relational database systems allow single databases to contain multiple tables. Please forgive me — I'm not writing a database textbook; I am just trying to define common database terms in the way that they're most commonly used.

A relational database gets its name because you can define a relationship between two different databases based on the value of one or more fields, known as a key. This field (or fields) is then used to extract specific values from each database, based on the presence of identical values in the specified field or fields. For example, suppose that a table of census data summarizes the population in each zip code. Across town, your local McDonald's uses a table that provides sales statistics for all McDonald's franchises, which also contains a field listing the zip code where each franchise is located. By joining these two tables using the common zip code field, you can produce information about McDonald's sales in each zip code, and how this relates to population density.

Relational databases have been in common use for several decades and are starting to show their age. Relational databases are not very good at dealing with records that contain random amounts of data. As I mentioned earlier, the amount of content associated with any portion of a document is highly variable. It's difficult to place functional limitations on the length of the content of different parts of a document — two different paragraphs can be very different in size!

Another drawback of using generic relational databases to hold items with arbitrary size is that relational databases view each record as a collection of indivisible, atomic objects that can be organized in some sequence. Even strings of characters are usually treated as numerical objects — the operations you can perform on them include standard mathematical operations such as the less than, greater than, and equal to operators. When working with text, this just isn't the right model. Give us real content or give us death!

To get around these problems, most relational databases take one of several general approaches. Some create character fields that simply contain the name of some external storage location, usually a file, that then contains the content that is actually associated with that field. For example, I can create a field called "paragraph," whose value is something like "/usr/doc/guide/para1.sgm." When editing an SGML stored in this form, I have to write specialized database code that retrieves the specified file and allows me to modify it.

Other relational databases use a type of field called memo or blob field to hold random amounts of content. These fields are actually pointers to some external storage device that can hold an arbitrary amount of character or binary data. (The term blob field stands for Binary Large Object and is a uniquely convenient descriptor for these kinds of fields because they literally hold blobs of unparsed data.) You can map records in a relational database to an SGML structure by creating a memo or blob field with the name of each SGML element and then putting each instance of its content into the associated blob field.

When you use either of these approaches, you have to write specialized database code to check these fields for valid content. These approaches can get somewhat hairy if the content of an element stored in this way is something other than CDATA because any other type of content has to be validated to make sure that it follows the content rules defined by your DTD. Storing arbitrary amounts of data in this way also can make it difficult to search these fields for different character strings, which is something that you commonly want to do in a documentation environment. For example, if the fields of your database contain filenames, you have to write custom database code to open the files and to enable you to search the files for a specific sequence of characters. This process can be very slow, especially in large databases, because there's a substantial amount of overhead involved in opening and closing external files. Even in database systems that support blob or memo fields, you can't use all the standard searching functions with those types of fields.

These two approaches show that the designer of a relational database application has to force his or her data to fit the tabular matrix model provided by relational databases. Relational databases have their roots in earlier times when memory and storage were at a premium and large numbers of small, interrelated tables were an efficient model for storing, retrieving, and modifying data. The tabular model doesn't work so well with large records, such as documents, and with free-form data that has to be carefully shoehorned into the tabular model.

Object-oriented databases

Object-oriented is one of today's most popular hi-tech adjectives. If you work in the software industry, you'd be hard pressed to find company literature that doesn't use this phrase at least once. Object storage and manipulation is an exciting way of freeing data from specific constraints and of writing common functions that can easily be applied to many different types of objects.

Object-oriented databases try to mirror the data that they store in a way that is as close as possible to the way in which the user uses that data. For example, I'd be surprised if anyone actually visualized their SGML documents as a series of records that contain specific types of fields. Thinking of an SGML document as a single object that contains other sub-objects is a pretty natural way of thinking about a document. Most object-oriented databases make it easy to define rules for the type of content in different objects and to define rules for the relationship between different objects. Object-oriented databases typically hide how they actually store their data from the users, which is fine, especially when users only want to work with that data and don't really care or need to know how it is stored.

Object-relational databases give you the best of both worlds by providing an object-oriented mechanism for data storage and retrieval, while preserving many aspects of the standard relational database model that allows you to define close relationships between different databases, depending on the content of key fields. For more information about object-relational databases and their relationship to pure object-oriented databases, see any modern textbook on database design. Interestingly enough (and not too surprising), the object-oriented and object-relational databases offered by many standard relational database vendors are actually an object-oriented layer that was written to live on top of an existing relational database.

Object-oriented databases provide some nice mechanisms for defining the relationships between different types of objects in an object hierarchy and for associating specific types of operations with these objects. Different types of objects, referred to as different classes of objects, can each have specialized sets of operations, known as methods, associated with them. For example, objects that contain graphics or even multimedia data can have specialized operations that know how to process and validate their content.

The rules that object-oriented databases use to define the relationships between different objects are well suited to imposing the kinds of structural and content rules that an SGML DTD provides. Object-oriented databases make it easy to store well-organized collections of data that have variable amounts of content at different levels of that structure. Object-oriented databases that support SGML documents need to understand the general structure of a DTD and the rules that it imposes on documents that follow that DTD. It's no big deal to design a database that fits the content model of a single DTD, but designing a database system that understands how to impose the general requirements of any arbitrary DTD is a much more complex issue.

Database Query Languages and SGML

All database systems, regardless of their type, provide a query language that lets users identify data that fits specific patterns or that has specific content. The most common query language used today is the Structured Query Language (SQL), which was first adopted as a standard in 1986 and is still evolving. Advances in database models, such as the advent of object-oriented databases, have required changes and enhancements to the types of queries you can make against a database and the way in which you must formulate these queries.

Most existing SQL implementations don't handle the complex structure of an SGML document very well. To use most of the extensions to SQL that are required for easy use with SGML documents, you have to navigate the hierarchy of an SGML document and work with the potentially complex rules for the content of different types of SGML elements. Luckily, the query languages provided by the database systems that are designed for use with SGML, such as those used by SGML document management systems, provide extensions that explicitly support SGML. For example, the enhanced SQL provided by some database systems that are designed for use with SGML let you specify a DTD (or logical subsection of it) as a part of your query — this provides the query with a way of understanding the structure of the data that it is examining.

The differences between standard SQL and the query languages provided for use with SGML document management systems aren't all that important unless you're already very familiar with SQL. Any document management system that provides an extended, SGML-aware query language clearly documents the extensions that it uses. Interestingly enough, an integrated document query language is an important part of some of the more interesting future directions for SGML, such as DSSSL. For more information on DSSSL, see Chapter 9.

Part VI

How Do I Get There from Here?

The 5th Wave — By Rich Tennant

"NO THANKS. BUT I WOULD LIKE ONE MORE CHANCE TO SEE IF I CAN CONVERT SOME EXISTING DOCUMENTS INTO SGML."

In this part

Assuming that by now you're an SGML convert, this part discusses the software you need in order to use SGML in your organization, and I look at various ways to convert your existing documents into SGML.

There are actually many different types of SGML software, each focusing on a different part of the SGML continuum. Part of the beauty of SGML is that you can mix and match the tools that you prefer or can afford — because they all share a common understanding of SGML documents, you're free to combine software from different vendors to get the SGML solution that's best for your organization. The first chapter examines different types of SGML software (authoring and editing software, formatting software, tools for structural analysis and verification, and different tools) that can help you convert your documents into SGML.

After I've identified the types of SGML tools that are available and discussed some examples of each, I cover an interesting and complex topic — how to get your existing documents into SGML. This chapter provides general project planning tips as well as specific suggestions for determining the best way to import your existing documents into your new SGML toolset and DTD.

This part provides a list of other sources for more detailed information about SGML. These sources include SGML special interest groups, resources that are available on the Internet and over the World Wide Web, Usenet newsgroups and electronic mailing lists that focus on SGML, as well as a list of useful books on SGML (in addition to this one, of course).

Chapter 19

What Kind of Tools Do You Need?

In This Chapter

▶ Looking for authoring and editing tools for SGML

▶ Finding SGML formatting software

▶ Peering at SGML parsers and other analysis software

▶ Trying to find SGML translation software

As I mention throughout this book, one of the biggest advantages of SGML as a solution for your documentation needs is that SGML files are standard text files. Although this might seem obvious (and not too exciting at first), the fact that SGML files are text files makes them very portable, not just between different types of computer systems but also between different SGML applications.

In earlier chapters of this book, I discuss some of the more common "one-stop shopping" solutions for working with SGML documents, such as the ArborText Adept Series, FrameMaker+SGML, Interleaf, and Corel WordPerfect Suite. While you can buy a complete SGML solution in the form of these (and other) products, each of these applications has some features that make it more attractive to its users than the other packages. Some people prefer the user interface provided by Frame; others are WordPerfect or ArborText fans. Some people are more comfortable working with SGML in a non-graphical environment, such as a text editor or a collection of tools that you can run from a DOS or UNIX command line.

Besides the off-the-shelf products discussed in Chapter 11, you can get many SGML tools for free on the Internet. Because SGML files aren't stored in any particular format (aside from as text with embedded markup!), you can use most of these tools with almost any SGML files, as long as you can configure the tools so that they know where to find the DTD and any external entities that you use in your documents.

This chapter analyzes the different software components of an SGML publishing system for printed documents.

Authoring and Editing Software

Authoring (also known as writing) and editing are the most basic parts of any writing effort. You should have a relatively easy time authoring or editing an SGML document because most SGML software provides you with a list of the elements that you can insert at any point in the document. SGML's emphasis on structure and its sometimes cryptic element names can be frustrating when you first start working with SGML because you have to focus on working within a specific structure and can't just tweak elements or pieces of text so that they "look right." You have to come to trust (or at least accept) the formatting environment provided by the SGML application you're using and then just worry about the content of the document.

These next few sections provide short descriptions of some of the more popular SGML software packages for creating and editing SGML documents. For information about how to find public-domain software discussed in this chapter, see Appendix A. For information about how to contact the companies that market the commercial software discussed in this chapter, see Appendix B.

ArborText Adept Editor

The ArborText Adept Series of SGML software, discussed in Chapters 9 and 11, is a commercial product that doesn't have to be used as a complete set of tools. You can also license just the ArborText Adept Editor. The Adept Editor comes with precompiled DTDs for articles, reports, memos, letters, and HTML documents, as well as (as of Version 5.4.1) a precompiled version of the DocBook DTD, version 2.2.1. Newer versions of these DTDs will certainly be provided with newer versions of the Adept products.

ArborText's software handles large SGML documents and DTDs with ease. Many companies license a single copy of the Adept Document Architect, the tool used to compile arbitrary DTDs and create FOSIs for use with the Adept Publisher. After compiling a DTD using the Document Architect, you can install that DTD for use with any copy of the Adept Editor in use at your organization. Any writer can then create documents that conform to your DTD. If you also create and install a FOSI, you can use that FOSI and the compiled DTD to print documents from the Adept Publisher. If your organization already uses SGML software, uses a different set of tools for formatting SGML documents, or produces documents for other organizations that don't need you to provide formatted output, the Adept Editor may be the only ArborText software that you need. The Adept Editor provides a nice, QUASIWYG (what you see is something like what you get) environment for editing SGML documents, providing dialogs from which you can select only those elements that are valid at the point where the cursor is currently located in your editing window.

ArborText's approach fits well within the SGML model of providing different tools that satisfy different requirements. You can use the Adept Editor to create and edit SGML documents. You can use the Document Architect to compile arbitrary DTDs for use with the Adept Editor or to create FOSIs associated with any DTD. And you can use the Adept Publisher to produce printed documents using a DTD that you've compiled and an associated FOSI that you created. The Adept Editor and Document Architect run on most UNIX systems, as well as under various versions of Windows and even on OS/2. The Adept Publisher runs on most UNIX systems, and a version for Windows NT is in the works.

InContext 2

If you work in a Microsoft Windows environment, InContext 2 provides a familiar interface for anyone working with SGML documents. Because of its focus on the Windows environment, InContext 2 is well integrated with standard Windows features such as OLE (Object Linking and Embedding), which lets you paste graphics and other types of data from Windows applications directly into your SGML documents. Using OLE, you can even use existing Windows applications to create specific parts of your SGML documents. InContext 2, for example, uses Microsoft Excel as its table editor, creating CALS tables with a tool that you probably already know! Focusing on the Windows environment is a two-edged sword — it's great if you're working in windows, but pretty much slams the door if you use any other operating system (such as UNIX, for example).

You don't have to use any special tools to precompile your DTDs into some custom format to use InContext 2. It actually works with your DTDs as they are, as text files! If you use some editors such as ArborText Adept Editor, you have to purchase other products to compile your DTDs. Some SGML applications such as WordPerfect come bundled with tools to compile your DTDs. InContext 2 skirts this whole issue and reduces your learning curve by using your DTDs in their native forms.

InContext 2 comes with a style sheet editor that lets you create any number of style sheets for use in formatting and printing your SGML documents. In true SGML style, you can easily switch between different style sheets and provide multiple "looks" for documents that conform to a single SGML DTD.

PSGML

'The time has come,' the Walrus said,
'To talk of many things:
Of shoes — and ships — and sealing-wax
Of cabbages — and kings —
And why the sea is boiling hot
And whether pigs have wings.'
    — Lewis Carrol, *The Walrus and the Carpenter*

What single piece of free software that provides support for editing SGML documents does this passage best describe? GNU Emacs, in combination with Lennart Staflin's most excellent (and free) PSGML package for creating and editing SGML documents! GNU Emacs is a text editor to which you can add extra features by loading sets of extensions written in the LISP programming language. Lennart Staflin has written one of these for working with SGML documents, and it really does all the right things! Am I excited, or what?

GNU Emacs is primarily a text editor. Therefore, it may not meet the aesthetic requirements of WYSIWYG fans, but it does provides a powerful, programmable editing environment for almost any type of text, including SGML documents. PSGML is relatively easy to install, includes an SGML parser, and provides structure-based menus and commands that let you insert only the tags that are valid at the current insertion point. PSGML can work with any SGML DTD, supports entities through a standard catalog, and provides separate windows for editing element attribute values.

GNU Emacs is available on almost every platform you can think of, including every modern UNIX box I've ever seen, VMS systems (if there still are any), Microsoft Windows, the Macintosh, and even OS/2. For UNIX users that can stand the bloat of an editor that chews up about twice the disk space that GNU Emacs does, XEmacs comes "out of the box" with a slightly tweaked version of PSGML, suitable for framing (or use!).

Almost every self-respecting software development firm uses GNU Emacs, which makes PSGML a good choice for use by writers and documentation groups in these environments. You'll still have to provide some way of formatting your SGML documents, but PSGML and GNU Emacs can provide a very complete environment for creating and editing your SGML documents. And it really works! By the way, have I mentioned that it is totally free?

If you've wondered what tool I commonly use to create and edit SGML documents, wonder no further. Of course, I also use GNU Emacs to read mail, read Usenet news, write C code and shell-scripts, but that's the subject of another *...For Dummies* book, for sure. Let's just say that on the day that one can boot GNU Emacs and load vmunix.elc on the UNIX box de jour, I'll be the first in line!

SoftQuad Author/Editor

SoftQuad is a well-established and well-respected member of the SGML community, and the quality of its software shows its commitment and understanding of the requirements of people working in SGML. SoftQuad's model for SGML applications is much like ArborText's, providing tools that satisfy the needs of different aspects of SGML document creation and letting you mix and match these tools as you like. Author/Editor comes with a number of precompiled DTDs, including the AAP, DocBook, and CALS DTDs. Author/Editor provides off-the-shelf support for more DTDs than competing products, such as the Adept Editor.

SoftQuad's RulesBuilder software lets you create, edit, and compile DTDs for use with Author/Editor. It does all the things you want a DTD editor to do, including making it easy to modify the values of SGML declarations and providing automatic rules checking that verifies your DTD as you go, identifying potentially troublesome areas such as ambiguous content models. The RulesBuilder can even identify elements in your DTD that aren't used in any content model, keeping you from overlooking implementation details that you identified as a requirement during the document analysis portion of your move to SGML.

If you work in an environment in which you publish documents only to the World Wide Web or on your local intranet, you can use SoftQuad's Panorama Pro product to automatically create HTML documents, as well as a table of contents and index for those documents. SoftQuad's products are available for use on most UNIX, Windows, and Macintosh platforms.

Formatting Software for SGML

After you've created your SGML documents, you'll probably want to print nicely formatted versions of them at some point. This section discusses various software packages that are specifically designed for formatting SGML documents — they take an SGML document (remember, an SGML document consists of an SGML declaration, a DTD, and a document instance that is marked up in accordance with the declaration and the DTD) and produce formatted or typesetter-ready documents.

3B2 SGML

Primarily used in the newspaper, directory, and magazine publishing industries in the UK, Advent Publishing Systems' 3B2 SGML lets users import and format SGML files using their associated declarations and DTD. 3B2 SGML works with native SGML files and includes an SGML parser that validates your files as it processes them, allowing you to correct your files as needed.

To be honest, I've never seen this tool in use, so I can't really say much beyond the fact that acquaintances in the newspaper field say that this is a well-established tool in its target markets, even though I believe that it only runs in the DOS environment.

DL Composer

Datalogics' DL Composer is one of the few SGML formatting tools aside from the formatting portion of ArborText Publisher to have adopted the FOSI standard. DL Composer takes your SGML declaration, DTD, document instance, and FOSI as input and produces high-quality formatted output. DL Composer runs as a server process, which means that writers can submit documents to be formatted from any PC or workstation. DL Composer, therefore, is ideal for use as a centralized formatter for many networked office environments. However, the fact that it is not interactive can mean that you must iteratively correct any problems you detect in your FOSI by fixing the FOSI, printing a sample section of your document, tweaking the FOSI again, and so on. The DL Composer supports arbitrary paper sizes through 11×17, produces PostScript output, and runs on most flavors of UNIX boxes.

XyVision Production Publisher

XyVision's Parlance Publisher takes an interesting approach to formatting SGML documents by requiring the use of another software package, Exoterica's OmniMark, to preprocess your SGML files so that Parlance Publisher can format them. While this might seem like an odd approach, it's quite useful in cases in which printed output is just an optional publishing format and in which OmniMark may already be in use to produce other mandatory formats. IBM uses Parlance Publisher as the print-formatting engine for its Information Development WorkBench (IDWB) project, which is an integrated set of applications that will form the core of IBM's replacement for its aging BookMaster SGML product. Parlance Publisher is well suited for integration into the IDWB project because you can use OmniMark to produce other mandatory publishing formats, such as HTML.

Like Datalogics' DL Composer, the fact that Parlance Publisher is not interactive means that you have to iteratively correct every instance of any problems you detect in your formatted output by fixing the OmniMark translation scripts, printing a sample section of your document, tweaking the scripts again, and so on. Like Datalogics' DL Composer, XyVision's Parlance Publisher runs on various types of UNIX boxes as a server process, which means that it can serve as a centralized resource for a networked office environment.

Parsers and Other Analysis Software

I have a separate section on SGML parsers because validating your documents is an important part of creating a usable SGML document. SGML parsers read an SGML declaration, a DTD, and a document instance and ensure that the document instance conforms to the declaration and DTD. SGML parsers can also typically produce output in the form of an Element Structure Information Set (ESIS), which is a stream of information about the elements and content in a document that other applications that process data sequentially, such as formatters, use.

The two parsers that I discuss in this section, SP and YASP, can help you identify problems in your SGML documents that other software may overlook. Since they are free and run on a wide variety of different operating systems, they are useful for double-checking your SGML documents. In fact, these two parsers form the core of many SGML environments in use or under development at universities and other research institutions. These two parsers can be used with other free software, such as GNU Emacs and PSGML, to get you "most of the way there" in terms of creating and editing valid SGML documents at very little cost! For example, if you want to publish your SGML documents in HTML, your current SGML application doesn't support HTML as an output format, and you are comfortable with writing your own applications, you can use the regularized output produced by these parsers as input to your translator, giving you HTML versions of your documents at relatively little cost.

SP

James Clark's SGML parser toolkit (SP) is probably the best-known free software package in SGML circles today (as James Clark is probably the best known author of free and sexy SGML software!). SP is a complete SGML toolkit, including nsgmls (an SGML parser) and SPAM (SP Added Markup) and sgmlnorm, two SGML normalizers. An SGML normalizer is an application that takes SGML input and produces output that expands all entity references, includes or ignores marked sections as instructed, and so on. The output from an SGML normalizer is a complete SGML document that you can use as input to a formatter, which therefore doesn't have to know how to locate entities or understand anything beyond how to format the elements it encounters.

SP, nsgmls, spam, and sgmlnorm all understand SGML declarations, arbitrary DTDs, and general and parameter entity references. SP uses the standard SGML Open catalog format, discussed in "How SGML software finds entities" in Chapter 6. All the components of SP understand almost all the features of an SGML declaration, including SHORTTAG and OMITTAG, as well as arbitrary syntax definitions. SP is actually used in some commercial SGML applications because James Clark was kind enough not only to release the source code but also to not impose any restrictions on commercial use of SP. James Clark truly deserves kudos for not only his abilities but also his attitude!

If you're gutsy enough to write your own SGML software, you should note that SP is implemented as a set of C++ libraries that make it easy to integrate portions of the SP toolkit into your applications. SP also supports Unicode and a variety of Asian character encoding standards, making it a viable tool regardless of your latitude and longitude.

YASP

The Yorktown Advanced SGML Parser, colloquially known as Yet Another SGML Parser, is a sophisticated SGML parser originally developed by Pierre Richard at IBM Yorktown, and subsequently enhanced and ported to different versions of Microsoft Windows by Christophe Espert. YASP is the successor to Charles Goldfarb's original SGML parser, ARC-SGML (Almaden Research Center SGML Parser). Like the components of the SP toolkit, YASP understands SGML declarations, arbitrary DTDs, and general and parameter entity references and can produce normalized output that can be used by other applications.

Translation and Conversion Software for SGML

As I discuss in Chapter 20, much of your effort in converting existing documents into SGML revolves around how much information about your documents you can (and want to) preserve. The more structural information that you can extract, either directly from your existing word-processing or publishing package or through the clever use of macros in that system (inserting your own structural keywords throughout the document), the better off you'll be regardless of which translation tool you select, whether you contract out the translation effort, or whether you plan to write your own translation tools.

The public-domain tools discussed in this section, rainbow makers and ICA, provide interesting insights into standard ways of converting documents. Both of these tools are no longer widely used and are not really actively supported. Regardless, they can serve as good starting points for planning your own conversion or even simply as suggestions for how to approach the problem.

ICA: Integrated Chameleon Architecture

The ICA is a public-domain set of tools for generating translators between different documentation markup languages, including SGML. The ICA tools enable you to create translators that convert existing documents in some markup language into an intermediate format, from which you can then generate SGML documents that conform to some DTD. You can also do the reverse — translate SGML documents into an intermediate format and then convert that intermediate form into markup that you can print using your standard tools for formatting your documents. The ICA tools don't do this translation for you — they allow you to quickly create sets of expressions that map one markup language into another and then generate translators (using the standard UNIX lex and yacc tools) that implement these translations.

The ICA distribution includes several sample translators which go from troff and LaTeX into SGML. ICA is the outgrowth of academic research at Ohio State University. The ICA tools run on UNIX systems and require the X Window System, but they are not officially supported on versions of the X Window System later than X11R4. You can read *The Integrated Chameleon Architecture: Translating Documents with Style,* by Sandra Mamrak, Conleth S. O'Connell, and Julie Barnes (ISBN 0-13-056418-4) for more information about the goals and implementation of ICA. You can also use that book as a user's guide to the different components of ICA.

OmniMark

Exoterica's OmniMark is a commercial document conversion utility that provides a powerful programming language for converting documents (as well as other things). Actually, calling OmniMark a utility is much like calling a Swiss Army knife a pocketknife — OmniMark is the sort of tool that will help you complete your original translation or conversion projects, at which point you'll find yourself using it for many other things.

Like the other conversion utilities in this section, you can use OmniMark to convert your existing documents into SGML (or whatever). You need some programming expertise to properly use OmniMark. If you don't have a programmer on your staff and don't plan to become one, take heart in the fact that OmniMark is a well-known utility for these sorts of projects, so you should be able to find a contract firm that has experience and expertise with OmniMark.

OmniMark is a powerful conversion utility that can't adequately be described without providing programming-related details about some of its features. If you don't want to plow through these technical details, just skip to the next section and think of OmniMark's document conversion capabilities as the best things since sliced bread.

OmniMark understands structured documents and provides a very sophisticated pattern-matching language that makes it easy to identify markup in different context and handle them appropriately. OmniMark can convert documents between formats in a single pass, rather than the "preprocessing/translation/postprocessing" approach used by many similar or homegrown tools.

OmniMark supports internal respositories, which are analogous to the data structures used in standard programming languages. These repositories can be related together in different ways and make it easier to do complex transformations. Many homegrown conversion tools or combinations of standard operating system utilities (such as the UNIX sed, awk, and, to some extent, Perl tools) treat their input as a stream of information that they modify as it passes through the utility. OmniMark's ability to assemble internal structures to save selected portions of your input data for subsequent reuse or special processing can save both time and steps during the translation process.

Many people use OmniMark to convert SGML documents into other electronic publishing formats such as HTML. OmniMark's ability to save portions of your input data makes it easy to produce summary portions of converted documents, such as an index or table of contents. OmniMark's ability to recognize structure in your documents is a big asset in chunking, or separating, your input documents into the smaller files that HTML browsers work best with.

Rainbow makers and the Rainbow DTD

The Rainbow DTD is a public-domain set of conversion utilities that is the product of an effort to produce an SGML interchange language for proprietary word-processing formats. Software packages called rainbow makers produce SGML documents that conform to the Rainbow DTD from different word-processing formats such as Microsoft Word RTF, Corel WordPerfect, Interleaf, and Adobe FrameMaker's Maker Interchange Format (MIF). You can use the versions of documents that have been converted to the Rainbow SGML DTD as input to other applications.

Selecting SGML as the target of these conversions makes it easy for SGML users to work with the translated output because you can use existing SGML tools to validate, edit, examine, and further translate files that conform to the Rainbow DTD.

DSSSL Software

Earlier in this book, I discuss DSSSL as one of several new approaches to associating formatting with SGML documents. Though no commercial DSSSL applications are available as I write this book, one very interesting public-domain DSSSL application has already emerged, which should be of interest to anyone who is interested in looking into DSSSL in more detail. This is Jade, James Clark's DSSSL Engine. Remember him?

Jade is an implementation of the DSSSL style language that can transform SGML documents into output formats such as RTF, HTML, and TeX, each of which already has associated formatting tools. Jade can also convert SGML documents that conform to one SGML DTD into SGML documents that conform to another SGML DTD.

Jade uses SP to parse SGML documents and associated DSSSL style sheet information and provides an implementation of the DSSSL style language that is used to produce these output formats. Jade only lacks a transformation language (see Chapter 9) to make it a Swiss Army knife for SGML! Maybe in another few weeks. . . .

Like James Clark's SP toolkit, Jade is freely available with source code and places no restrictions on commercial use. I guess we'll be seeing it in someone's products soon!

XML Software

Like DSSSL, XML is a glimpse of the future for SGML, especially as a potential enhancement (or replacement!) for HTML. Some interesting (and free) XML software has already started to appear — by the time this book is available, there will probably be even more!

Lark

Lark is an XML processor that attempts to achieve good trade-offs among compactness, completeness, and performance. Lark is currently limited to reading the entity and element declarations in the current document, but (beyond that) implements the XML specification and reports violation of XML's notion of well-formed documents. You can get a copy of Lark and related documents from `http://www.textuality.com/Lark/`.

NXP

NXP is a public domain XML parser, written in Java, that is currently available in beta (almost ready for prime time) form. NXP supports public identifiers, catalogs, and parameter entities. You can get a copy of NXP (and more information about it) from the URL `http://www.edu.uni-klu.ac.at/~nmikula/NXP/`.

Jumbo

JUMBO (Java Universal Markup Browser for Objects) is a Java-based browser for XML documents. JUMBO provides a set of Java classes for viewing XML applications and can be used as a single application or as an enabling technology, supporting applets downloaded from a server to another Java-enabled browser. You can get a copy of JUMBO from the URL `http://www.ccc.nottingham.ac.uk/~pazpmr/jumbo/`.

TECHNICAL STUFF

What's better than coffee in the morning? 100% pure Java!

No doubt you've heard lots about Java in the press recently. This isn't surprising, because Java is one of the most exciting developments in computer science ever! Java is a system-independent language that runs within a virtual machine on your local computer system. The Java virtual machine must be implemented for a specific hardware platform, at which point any computer system can run any Java application. Sound exciting? Java is already in wide use on the Internet as a way of writing applications that can run on any computer system — browsers such as Netscape Navigator and Netscape Communicator include free Java machines that can run any existing Java application inside your browser! Even Microsoft's Internet Exploder grudgingly provides support for Java, though Microsoft is hard at work adding proprietary extensions to gate the promise of Java.

Java is the key to creating applications that run anywhere, regardless of your operating system. Scary to some, but promising to everyone else, Java is the first hint at a system-independent way of thinking about and writing applications. For this reason, it's not surprising that many XML applications are written in Java. You might as well define the future in its own terms. Would you write a web browser or e-mail application in COBOL? I thought not!

Chapter 20

Translating Existing Documents into SGML

*T*his chapter helps you start thinking about how to move your existing documents into SGML. If you've already decided that SGML is right for your business and you're ready to move forward — congratulations! Now I just have to get you there.

Unless you work for a new company without any existing manuals or you're moving to SGML as a chance to rewrite your whole document set, you have to design a plan to convert your existing documents into SGML. In this chapter, I discuss things to consider when selecting the best strategy for converting documents, how to select the approach that works best for your company, and some software packages that make your life easier when converting documents.

In this chapter, I use the term *desktop publishing package* to refer to any software package used to write manuals, even if it runs on a mainframe. The desktop publishing package you currently use may be something you inherited from previous writers or documentation managers, or it may be the only package that runs on your computer system. You always can find a way to convert your existing documents into SGML — the only question is how much work it will take. The important thing to keep in mind throughout the process is that SGML will make things easier for you in the future. You'll be free to make better use of the information stored in your documents, to change desktop publishing packages, and to enforce styles and print formats automatically. Freedom is within your reach!

How Documentation Software Stores Information

Most desktop publishing packages store the manuals you write in their own internal formats. Using a special internal format makes a desktop publishing package faster because the programmers who wrote the package know the details of the format and can take advantage of it. For example, the files created by Microsoft Word let the programmers at Microsoft store text, formatting, and revision information in a single file. Microsoft Word has functions and routines that are optimized for reading, writing, and updating each type of information.

Your desktop publishing package stores information in one of two ways:

✔ Binary files, which are files that can't easily be read or edited by anyone without that particular desktop publishing package because the binary format of those file is only known to the application that created them

✔ Text files, which are files that can be read or edited with your desktop publishing package or in a text editor

Besides being faster to read and write, binary files can often be more compact because they can store information more efficiently. They don't have to follow any special rules of legibility or readability because no one can read them without a desktop publishing package.

Few desktop publishing packages automatically store documents as text files, but most allow you to create text files from your documents. Text files are usually slower to read or write because they usually try to present formatting and style information in a readable way.

If you're wondering why I'm discussing text files at this point in the book, it's because most desktop publishing packages can read and write them in one way or another. The ability to create some sort of text file provides an escape hatch from any desktop publishing package.

Even if your current desktop publishing package can't create useful text files, you can usually trick it into doing so. You can use a print driver designed for a simple text printer or line printer and then tell your word-processing or desktop publishing package to write its output to a file. You can do this on almost every system I've ever seen. I hope you never have to do it, but. . . .

Converting Existing Documents into SGML

Converting a set of manuals from one format to another is a big task, but it's never impossible. Many desktop publishing packages come with conversion utilities, usually called *filters,* that let you read and write documents in the formats used by different word-processing and publishing packages. Conversion filters strain out any proprietary parts of your documents, replacing them with the appropriate markup for the target word-processing or publishing package. *Import filters* let you read documents written in other formats. *Export filters* let you write documents in other formats. The formats that your desktop publishing package can create files in are known as the *export formats* that your package supports.

Determining the formats your desktop publishing package supports

The first thing to consider when planning a documentation conversion project is whether the SGML software that you are going to use can read any type of files that your current desktop publishing system can write. As discussed in Chapter 19, this should be one of your considerations when selecting an SGML package. The remainder of this chapter assumes that you aren't so lucky and that you're going to have to work to get your existing documents into SGML.

If your current desktop publishing package can write files in a format that your new SGML package can read, the only question is whether this is the best way to convert your documents. If your documents already contain structural information that identifies parts of the document, such as chapters, sections, and lists, and the common format that both packages can read doesn't transfer this information, you have to re-enter all of that information after you get the documents into your SGML package.

There are two keys to selecting an optimal interchange format:

- ✔ Is there a format that your original desktop publishing package can export and which your SGML software can read?

- ✔ If your current package supports more than export format (and you have some sort of structural information in your documents), which preserves most of that information?

If your desktop publishing package doesn't store its files in an ASCII format, you must find out whether it provides export filters. An ideal export format is SGML, but few desktop publishing packages are that advanced. If yours is, you can stop reading this chapter now — you're home free! The next best thing is an export filter that can write files in an ASCII format that you can then convert into SGML. Converting manuals from a binary format to SGML is usually very difficult because you rarely know the details of the binary format.

Selecting a format for converting your documents

If your desktop publishing package provides different export filters, you should select the one that will make it easiest to convert your documents into SGML. To make this selection, you need to discover which filter creates files that provide the most information about the structure of your documents. Since SGML focuses on the structure of a document and the relationship between its parts, you can simplify the conversion process by starting with files that provide similar information about structure.

It's usually easy to convert manuals that are written in desktop publishing packages that use style sheets. Style styles often use descriptive style names to associate the purpose of parts of your documents with specific formatting information. For example, it's usually easy to convert manuals into SGML from desktop publishing packages that identify different levels of headings, different types of lists and paragraphs, and so on, because SGML tags identify much of the same type of information.

For example, most desktop publishing packages can write standard text files without any markup because text files are usually the lowest common denominator for exchanging information with any other software package. However, converting documents into SGML using text files without any markup at all should be your last choice because you cannot tell easily the different parts of the documents apart. Headings look exactly like paragraphs which look exactly like any other part of the document. Even if your headings are numbered, you can't easily tell them apart from parts of a numbered list.

Many desktop publishing packages provide a common ASCII export format known as Rich Text Format (RTF), which is a markup language created by Microsoft. RTF files usually contain both structural and formatting information; how readable these files are depends on the desktop publishing package that created them. RTF files identify different parts and styles in your document by enclosing them in curly brackets ({ and }). Commands that contain stylistic and formatting information begin with a backslash (\). For example, the RTF command to create a new paragraph is \par.

RTF files contain a lot of information that you may not want to worry about, such as font and color information, version information, and so on. However, if your desktop publishing package can create RTF files and doesn't support any export formats that give you more information about the structure of your document, you may want to use RTF for your documentation conversion.

How can you save yourself some time?

One way to save yourself some time during the conversion process is to do as much pre-processing as possible in your original documents. For example, most documentation systems will let you selectively replace elements in the documents. If you can identify stylistic elements of your current documents that you know show a map to elements in your target SGML documents, you may be able to replace the stylistic tags in your current documents with the opening and closing tags that will work in your SGML documents.

Any such pre-processing that you can do in your original documents will pay off when you convert your documents into SGML. In general, anything that you can do to make the conversion simpler before actually converting your documents is both a time- and money-saver when it actually comes time to convert your documents into another format. This is doubly true because the people who are familiar with the styles and structures in your existing documents are immediately familiar with those documents. They are probably not as familiar with the SGML format that you're headed toward (Unless you're luckier than I've ever been!)

Identifying Special Requirements in the Conversion Process

After you've selected the format that will make it easiest for you to convert your existing documents into SGML, you have to identify any special requirements for the conversion. You're probably most interested in how quickly and efficiently you can convert everything, but you may save time later by taking a little bit of time to plan the conversion.

Deciding how many times you'll have to convert your documents is a very important step in planning a conversion. If this is a one-time, one-way conversion, you'll save lots of time and effort. However, if you still need to provide your documents in the format used by your current desktop publishing package, then you have to either build this into your plan or maintain parallel copies of your documents in both formats. Some good questions to ask yourself are

✔ Does any other group in the company use your documents directly? For example, does any other group in your company actually use the word-processing or publishing files for your documents without your having to print or specially prepare these files for them?

✔ Does your documentation group already use tools that require a specific input format?

It's easy to overlook such requirements in the excitement of moving to SGML, but many companies (especially software companies) use internally developed applications that depend on the format of the files produced by their existing desktop publishing packages. For example, many companies use custom applications that can extract information for online help directly from their documentation sets.

When planning to convert documentation, you should let everyone in the company (at least at a certain level) know that you are planning to change the format in which your documents are stored. If people know that the conversion is happening, they can plan for it; but there's nothing worse than a last-minute surprise when you're trying to release a product. If other groups in your company have such requirements, selling them on your conversion to SGML is usually easy. Because SGML provides a lot of information about the structure of your document and the purpose of different parts of it, it's usually easier to extract selected parts of an SGML document than it is to extract that same information from any other documentation format. If you can show other groups how converting the documents can help them use the documents more efficiently, you'll probably pick up a few backers from other departments.

Doing It Yourself or Contracting It Out

The next step in planning the document conversion process is figuring out who's going to do the work. Here are some primary questions you need to ask yourself at this point:

✔ Do you have an easy way to migrate your existing documents into SGML?

✔ Will you have to add a lot of structural information to your documents when converting them to SGML?

✔ Will you have to update any internal applications or processes to use SGML?

✔ Is your document set large?

✔ Are you going to have to maintain support for your documents in the format used by your old desktop publishing package?

If you answered "NO" to the first question, but "YES" to all the others, you'll want to start thinking about who can help you convert your documents!

Many companies have MIS personnel or programmers who provide internal support for the different software packages used throughout the company, such as your desktop publishing package. If your company has such personnel, you may be able to enlist these people's help in the conversion process. If any of the writers in your company's documentation group have this kind of experience, you're even better off using them because they know both the desktop publishing package and the documents.

However, if you don't have access to these kinds of resources and the conversion process is going to require some work, you may want to consider hiring someone to convert your documents. The vendors who sell different SGML packages usually have experience converting existing document sets into their products. If they don't have experience with your specific desktop publishing package (or want too much money to help!), they should be able to recommend another firm that can help you or some software that you can use to do the conversion yourself.

As with most projects, you can boil down the basic issues in deciding whether to do the work yourself into these:

- ✔ How well can you do the conversion without enlisting outside help?

- ✔ Do you or your company have enough resources and expertise to do the conversion yourself?

- ✔ How quickly can you do the conversion compared with hiring a third party to do it?

- ✔ What trade-offs are acceptable between just getting the conversion done and doing it perfectly?

A big factor in deciding whether you should do the conversion yourself is the DTD that you use in your SGML documents. If you have developed your own DTD or use one that is uncommon, you will have to train whoever will convert the documents about the structure and content of the DTD. If someone in the documentation group has the skills to do the conversion, you're in luck! However, if you have to train someone in the MIS group about SGML, DTDs, and the meaning of each tag in your DTD, you may find that the time it takes to bring someone up to speed isn't worth the time you save by hiring a third-party to do the conversion, especially if it's already familiar with SGML.

Doing it yourself

If you or your company have the personnel to convert your documents, can do a good job converting documents, and have the time, then you probably should do it yourself. After all, you know your documents better than anyone else, and your people are (hopefully!) used to working together. I refer to this as an *internal conversion* since you convert without depending on any outside help.

When planning an internal conversion, you must determine acceptable trade-offs between a quick conversion and a perfect one. You should consider these basic questions:

- ✔ Is it critical to do a perfect job of converting your documents in a way that requires no manual intervention?

- ✔ Is it better to get it done quickly in a way that requires some editing and cleanup?

Like any job, the last 20 percent takes 80 percent of the time. If you develop your own tools to do the conversion and you manage to substantially improve the conversion as you work, you have the luxury of re-converting documents that you've already converted once. However, if you have the personnel, it may be more efficient for you to do the bulk of the conversion quickly and then devote some resources to fine-tuning the converted documents.

The format that you use to convert your existing documentation can help decide how to divide your time between developing the conversion tools, converting the documents, and fine-tuning the converted documents:

- ✔ If your documents contain a lot of pure formatting markup (some text is bold, some text is italic, and so on) and you can't identify easily the reason that different phrases are marked up, you may want to plan to spend a fair amount of time cleaning up the converted documents.

- ✔ If your documents contain a lot of pure formatting markup but there are only a limited number of terms that are marked up in this way, you can convert combinations of formatting markup and specific phrases into SGML tags around those phrases. Doing so increases the time spent developing the conversion tools but produces higher-quality converted documents.

- ✔ If you made extensive and consistent use of styles in your documents, you win!

Regardless of how the previous few points stack up, you should assign different people to different aspects of the conversion process so that each person develops an area of expertise, is familiar with issues in his area of responsibility, and to ensure that no one is doing double work. For example, if you have separate guide and reference documents, you may want to assign a person or small group to translate each type of document. You may also want to assign a person or small group to the task of loading converted documents into your SGML package and verifying the results of the conversion. Doing so helps ensure that different people become experts in different aspects of the conversion process, thereby minimizing the chance that multiple people "discover" the same problem independently or solve the same problem in different ways. The conversion process quickly becomes frustrating for the people who develop the conversion tools if different people keep reporting the same problems to them.

If your company uses an online bulletin board system, ask your system administrator to create a bulletin board where you can keep a record of conversion problems, solutions, and issues. Doing so helps minimize the chance that people will re-invent the wheel and also helps you keep track of any outstanding issues.

Doing the document conversion internally has some fringe benefits of which you may not be aware:

- ✔ It forces you to analyze the structure of your documents and how they are marked up. This analysis can provide unexpected dividends by helping you find ways to simplify the tagging that you use, make your documents more consistent, or simply find errors never caught by writers, reviewers, or editors.

- ✔ Developing expertise with some conversion utilities usually helps you identify other things that you can use these utilities for. For example, you may discover that you can use the conversion utilities to extract selected portions of a document for reuse elsewhere in your company, for conversion into SGML and publication on the World Wide Web, and so on.

There are various newsgroups for writers available on the Internet. If you plan to convert your documents, you may avoid some conversion problems by posting a request for people to share their own conversion experiences. Hearing other people's experiences also can help increase your confidence that you can do it.

Hiring a third-party for the conversion

If you're going to hire a third-party to do the conversion, you should create a list of requirements for the conversion. Make sure that you create specific milestones to ensure that the conversion is done correctly and on time. If the firm you plan to hire has done similar projects for other companies, talk to people from those companies to make sure that they are happy with the results. Discuss any problems that they had and how they were resolved.

Your conversion milestones should include verification and acceptance steps as the contractor converts each document. Doing so guarantees that your documents are converted accurately and in the way that you agreed. As you proceed through the conversion process, you may discover ways that the conversion can be improved. You need to consider whether these improvements should require that all of your documents be converted again.

If the firm that you hire to do the conversion is developing a custom application to do the work, make sure that you determine how and where the work will be done and whether you retain the rights to its application. This boils down to whether you hire the firm to do the conversion, develop the conversion software for you, or both. If possible, you want the firm to do the conversion on your computer systems, because this guarantees that all of the software used in the conversion process runs on your systems. Whenever possible, try to keep a copy of the conversion software and make sure that you know how to use it. After converting all of your current documents into SGML, you may find that you need to convert other documents that weren't part of your original plan. You'd be surprised (perhaps not) in how many documents crawl out of various corners after you've converted a documentation set to a different format and desktop publishing package.

If the conversion requires third-party software, make sure that your contract identifies who buys the software, who gets to keep it, and how long you can use it. Many people use commercial products that understand different export formats and can interpret their structure to convert documents. These packages are commonly referred to as *parsers*. When using this type of tool, the firm that you hire to do the conversion actually just develops high-level software that relies on the input, analysis, processing, and output capabilities of the commercial parser. If the parser you use is licensed for a specific period of time (some software only runs for a year or so, after which you have to buy a new license), make sure that you will not need to use the conversion software after the license has expired.

Documentation conversion software

Many different packages can help you convert documents from one text format to another. As mentioned previously, many of the desktop publishing packages that support SGML come with import filters that help you convert documents from other desktop publishing packages. See Chapter 20 for an overview of common desktop publishing packages that support SGML and their import capabilities.

Most software packages for document conversion let you specify the following:

✔ **What defines a tagged region or command in your input file**

For example, tagged regions in RTF files begin with a left curly bracket and contain one or more RTF commands, each of which begins with a single backslash and ends with a right curly bracket. Tagged regions in an input file in troff format consist of lines that begin with a period or backslash characters followed by a two-letter command.

✔ **How to map tagged regions in your input file to SGML elements in the DTD you are using**

This usually consists of a huge list that contains all of the commands that can be found in the files you export from your desktop publishing package and the tags in your new SGML DTD that they correspond to.

This section provides an overview of some of the more common software packages that can help you convert existing documents into SGML. This section helps you select tools to use in the conversion process if you are doing the conversion yourself. Third-party firms that handle document conversion usually already have selected the tools that they like to use.

For a more detailed list of tools that are available for document conversion (and for information on where to obtain these software packages), see Steve Pepper's site on the World Wide Web, "The Whirlwind Guide to SGML Tools and Vendors." The URL for this site is http://www.falch.no/people/pepper/sgmltool/guide.htm.

System utilities

If you are a programmer or have access to one to help you with the conversion, you first should consider whether you need to buy any extra software to help with the conversion. If you convert your documents by using an export format that provides a lot of information about the structure of your document, you may be able to use utility programs that are already on your computer system to convert the documents into SGML. Examples of such structured export formats are those used by Ventura Publisher, Frame's MIF, or semi-structured markup languages such as troff, Scribe, or LaTeX, as discussed in Chapter 1.

The system utilities you can use for document conversion depend on the type of computer system you are using. UNIX systems provide utilities such as awk, sed, and yacc to help you convert and parse input files. OS/2 and VM systems provide utilities such as REXX that you can use to convert documents. You may also be able to find public-domain applications, such as perl, that are available for the system you're using — nowadays, it's probably hard to find a system that perl hasn't been ported to! In general, any utility that you can find that provides pattern-matching capabilities can be an asset to you during a document conversion. You can also write your own, which guarantees job security but which may cause you maintenance headaches for the rest of your life.

If you use RTF as the export format from your existing desktop publishing package, you probably don't want to use system utilities to do the conversion. There are two main reasons for this:

✔ Though RTF is structured, it is not always easy to read or parse. RTF files tend to be huge blobs of text and RTF commands with linebreaks only when necessary. Text within a single RTF command frequently spans multiple lines. You can handle these cases with most system utilities, but each additional case makes the conversion "just a bit more complex." Eventually, it becomes "just too complex."

✔ Better tools for RTF input and processing are already available for free.

This last bullet is a powerful argument. If you are using RTF as the format to get your documents into SGML, see the next sections for information on the Rainbow-maker and OmniMark tools.

Commercial tools

Many companies sell software that is designed to help convert documents from one format to another. As mentioned in the introduction to this section, these tools usually let you define the tags in the export format produced by your desktop publishing package and then let you identify the tags in your SGML DTD that these tags correspond to. This section does not list any conversion utilities that require a specific SGML software package. (Your vendor probably told you about those when you bought its package!)

The following is a list of some commonly used commercial packages for documentation conversion. See Appendix A or the World Wide Web for information on how to contact the vendors who market these products.

✔ **DynaTag,** from Electronic Book Technologies, Inc. EBT is a well-known vendor of SGML-based authoring, editing, and online help software. This software only runs on UNIX or Microsoft Windows systems.

✔ **FastTAG,** from Interleaf. Interleaf is a well-known company whose desktop publishing software provides optional support for SGML. FastTAG is well known as a powerful conversion package — it was so well known that Interleaf acquired the company that originally marketed it!

✔ **OmniMark,** from OmniMark Technologies Corporation. OmniMark is the best-known conversion software in the documentation industry, is well-respected by anyone who has ever used it, and is extremely powerful. OmniMark runs on almost any popular computer system, from mainframes to micros.

Public-domain and shareware tools

Public-domain tools are software packages that are freely available on bulletin boards, FTP sites, or World Wide Web sites. These tools are frequently developed by academic or non-profit groups, or by programmers who simply want make a contribution to the software community by donating the tools that they have developed. Many public-domain tools are only available as source code in a specific language that you must then build for your system, or require other software to be able to use them. For example, any public-domain tools that are available for UNIX systems are either only available as C source code that you must then compile or as perl command files (scripts) that require that the perl interpreter's presence on your system before you can use them.

Shareware tools are software packages that are freely available on bulletin boards, FTP sites, or World Wide Web sites, but that you are eventually expected to pay for. Payments for shareware packages are usually made by the honor system — nothing but your conscience prevents you from using most shareware software forever without paying for it. Shareware packages usually give you a fixed period of time to use the software before you have to pay for it. This trial period is intended to give you time to verify that the tool meets your needs before you pay for it.

As you might expect, there are more public-domain and shareware translation tools available than there are pure commercial ones. Keep in mind that each of these was developed by someone else, usually for a specific purpose, and that authors may not support their tools actively. Therefore, the tool may not do exactly what you want, and you may not be able to ask anyone questions about how to use the software. When using public-domain or shareware packages, the motto *Caveat Emptor* (Let the buyer beware) is more applicable than ever, especially when the price is little or nothing!

The following is a list of some well-known public-domain or shareware packages for documentation conversion. See Appendix A or the World Wide Web for information on how to find copies of this software.

- ✔ **ICA**, the Integrated Chameleon Architecture, is a set of public-domain tools that you can use to translate between different documentation format. To do this, you first translate your existing documents into a generic format from which you can then generate different output formats, including SGML. ICA was originally developed at Ohio State University and can only be used on UNIX systems that run the X Window system. It's an amazing tool but requires lots of work to get anything working.

- ✔ **Rainbow-makers**, produced by a project sponsored by EBT, provides free applications that translate documents from different formats used by desktop publishing packages and word processors into a special DTD, the Rainbow DTD. Once your documents are in SGML using the Rainbow DTD, you can convert them to the DTD of your choice. Rainbow-makers are available to produce SGML documents from RTF, Frame's MIF format, and the internal format used by Interleaf. Rainbow-makers are available for PC and UNIX systems.

- ✔ **Xreplace32** is a 32-bit Microsoft Windows utility that makes it easy for you to graphically define ways to convert files. Xreplace32 is a shareware application.

Chapter 21

Getting More Information about SGML

● ●

In This Chapter

▶ Contacting SGML societies and special interest groups

▶ Life on the news stand — SGML periodicals

▶ Finding general Internet resources

▶ Reading newsgroups and mailing lists

● ●

As SGML grows in popularity, you can find more and more resources of information about SGML. Reference texts and other books about SGML can provide background information about SGML, help you plan and implement SGML solutions, and help you with many other aspects of using SGML. However, you may not be able to find the answers to all your questions in books.

What if you, for example, want to compare and contrast different SGML software packages and figure out how to do specific tasks with those tools? The documentation for each SGML tool may be of some help, but everyone knows that product documentation can't cover every possible scenario.

If you have a connection to the Internet, you can search the Web for information on SGML. You'll be surprised at how often you'll actually find the answer! Having all this information at your fingertips may spoil you, and you may expect to find the answer to your questions as soon as you think of them. However, you still have to put forth some effort in order to find information on the Web.

This chapter discusses some of the more common sources for additional information about SGML. For those of us who like to read, I list SGML-related periodicals and some of my favorite books on SGML. For those of us who are wired, I provide summary information about popular Internet sites with substantial amounts of information about SGML and about how to subscribe to various electronic mailing lists and Usenet newsgroups that discuss SGML.

SGML Societies and Interest Groups

Beyond the users groups associated with using specific software packages, you can find a number of general SGML-oriented organizations. Also, a number of special-interest groups focus on specific aspects of adopting and using SGML. The list of SGML-related organizations given in this chapter is not complete, but they should provide you with an idea of the types of organizations that exist. For a more up-to-date list, see Robin Cover's SGML page (`http://www.sil.org/sgml/`) or any of the other SGML Internet resources listed in the "Internet Resources" section of this chapter.

Electronic Publishing Special Interest Group

The Electronic Publishing Special Interest Group (EPSIG) was originally created to further develop and promote ISO 12083, the Electronic Publishing Standard. As electronic publishing technologies have continued to emerge and evolve, EPSIG has begun promoting all forms of electronic publishing. In general terms, the EPSIG attempts to use electronic publishing technologies to make information more accessible to and usable by the general public.

EPSIG offers different membership levels (all of which cost something) and publishes a quarterly newsletter called the *EPSIG News*. For more information about EPSIG, send e-mail to `epsig@aol.com` or visit the EPSIG Web page at `http://www.gca.org/epsig/`. You definitely should check out the EPSIG if you are interested in electronic publishing.

If you're interested in electronic publishing, you may also want to investigate the online Journal of Electronic Publishing, produced by the University of Michigan Press. This is a free archive of relevant articles that examine trends in electronic publishing. For more information, see the URL `http://www.press.umich.edu/jep/`.

International SGML Users' Group

The International SGML Users' Group (ISUG) is a worldwide group devoted to promoting the use of the Standard Generalized Markup Language and related formats such as XML and DSSSL and to providing a forum for exchanging information about SGML. The fact that the group doesn't think that the boundaries of the United States are the edge of the planet is most certainly a good thing because much of the excitement about SGML comes from outside the United States and many interesting SGML tools have been and are being developed outside the U.S. SGML is in common use in the United Kingdom and Europe. Companies from outside the U.S. have many excellent SGML software packages. If you're doing a serious evaluation of SGML software, you're only short-sheeting yourself if you overlook them!

Like the SGML Users' Group, ISUG publishes a quarterly newsletter containing information about SGML developments, SMGL software, and internal issues. You can find a number of back issues at `http://www.sil.org/ sgml/isgmlug/pubs.htm`.

For more information about the International SGML Users' Group, see the URL `http://www.sil.org/sgml/isgmlug/`. You can use the URL `http:// www.sil.org/sgml/isgmlug/apply.htm` to submit a membership application.

SGML Open

SGML Open was founded in 1993 to further the development and implementation of SGML applications. SGML Open is a nonprofit group sponsored by most of the best-known firms in the SGML publishing industry. Because it is sponsored by most of the powerhouse firms doing SGML application development, SGML Open serves as a place to discuss technical issues and enhance existing SGML standards so that SGML applications can better interoperate. Interoperability is especially important in the world of SGML, where the whole idea is that SGML provides a system- and software-independent way of preserving your organization's investment in the information it creates and uses.

SGML Open has sponsored and produced a number of technical and white papers on different aspects of adopting and using SGML that you can order online. You can get more detailed information about SGML Open and any of its publications by going to its Web site at `http://www.sgmlopen.org/` or by sending e-mail to `info@sgmlopen.org`.

Its snail mail address is

SGML Open
7950 Hwy. 72 W.
Suite G201
Madison, AL 35758
Tel: 205-772-2355
Fax: 205-464-9470

SGML Periodicals

Because SGML is an approach to documentation, you shouldn't be surprised that some excellent printed publications focus on SGML. Even though online sources of information about SGML are more numerous than printed ones, you can still find useful information on printed pages! Of course, SGML makes it easy to re-use this information via different approaches to electronic publishing.

This section lists some of the major SGML publications that provide usable, general information about SGML. I do not discuss various product-specific newsletters, such as Adobe's, because those are understandably biased toward a certain approach to SGML.

SGML Users' Group Newsletter

The *SGML Users' Group Newsletter* provides product and industry news, a calendar of upcoming events, and informative articles that often contain case studies in SGML implementation. It is published quarterly by the International SGML Users' Group. For more information, you can send e-mail to kp@dps1.co.uk, or send snail mail to

SGML Users' Group
Database Publishing Systems, Ltd.
P.O. Box 361
Swindon
Wiltshire SN5 7BF
UNITED KINGDOM
Tel: 44-793-512-515
Fax: 44-793-512-516

<TAG>: The SGML Newsletter

<TAG>: The SGML Newsletter is a monthly publication for SGML users with any level of expertise that provides product and industry news, as well as many interesting features about different aspects of SGML. Many issues of *<TAG>* contain case studies in SGML implementation, articles about related standards such as XML or DSSSL, and a calendar of upcoming SGML trade shows, conferences, or other industry events. Find out when the SGML glitterati will be in your neighborhood!

Seriously, *<TAG>* is an excellent publication that is always worth reading. *<TAG>* is not only an excellent source of industry information, but it also provides many hands-on tips that can save you time and effort in your SGML work. Each issue of *<TAG>* contains an "SGML Tips and Techniques" column, often by a guest author, that discusses a specific SGML issue in detail. This column alone is well worth the price of a subscription!

For more information about *<TAG>*, see its Web page at `http://tag.sgml.com` or send e-mail to `tag@sgml.com`. You can browse a large number of back issues of *<TAG>* from its Web site, which is handier than piling them up in your garage or attic. You can also contact *<TAG>* by phone, at 303-680-0875, or by fax, at 303-680-4906 (in the United States).

Internet Resources

In Chapter 8, I discuss some centralized sources of SGML information on the World Wide Web, specifically those that provide DTDs that you can download. Not surprisingly, many more sites on the Web can provide you with information about SGML. I would need an entire book to list them all, but this section provides some starting points for SGML-oriented surfing.

Background information about SGML

Several Web sites provide good background information about SGML and related topics. Many of these sites also provide information about specific SGML products and services provided by the companies that host the sites. You can find some good introductory information at the following sites:

- *An Introduction to SGML* (by Benoît Marchal) at `http://www.brainlink.com/~ben/sgml/`

- *Internet Publishing* (from Interleaf Corporation) at `http://www.ileaf.com/cyberpaper.html`

- *SGML: An Introduction* (from InContext Corporation) at `http://www.incontext.com/products/sgmlinfo.html`

- *SGML: Getting Started* (from ArborText Corporation) at `http://www.arbortext.com/wp.html`

- *Standard Generalized Markup Language* (from SGML Open) at `http://www.sgmlopen.org/sgml/docs/general/sgmldesc.htm`

- *The SGML Primer* (from SoftQuad Corporation) at `http://www.sq.com/sgmlinfo/primbody.html`

These are only the tip of the iceberg as far as free information about SGML on the Web goes. For specific sites that provide different types of detailed information, read on!

SGML Web page

As I discuss in Chapter 9, Robin Cover's centralized repository for SGML information (`http://www.sil.org/sgml/sgml.html`) is probably the ultimate Web site for finding out anything you want to know about SGML. This site includes links to SGML archive sites on the Web that you can access using your browser, through GOPHER, or simply through FTP. It provides an extensive SGML bibliography and a calendar of upcoming SGML events, including conferences, seminars, tutorials, and workshops. The site also has links to collections of information about public and commercial SGML software and links to most academic and government projects that are SGML related. This site is probably the first place you should look for any information about SGML!

Whirlwind Guide to SGML Tools and Vendors

Steve Pepper's Whirlwind Guide to SGML Tools and Vendors is a centralized collection of information about SGML software that's currently available, either commercially or as public-domain software. Located at `http://www.falch.no/people/pepper/sgmltool/`, this site provides an exhaustive list of SGML software and vendors, divided into a number of different categories based on how those tools are used. This site also provides some good background information on SGML applications and the categories into which different SGML tools have been divided. Chapter 19 of this book only skims the surface of available SGML tools and provides some general categories into which SGML tools can be divided — the Whirlwind Guide to SGML provides much more information at a much greater level of detail! This site is hosted by Falch Infotek AS, a leading Norwegian vendor of SGML tools and consulting services. Just hosting this site is a tremendous service to the SGML community, as is the tremendous amount of work that Steve Pepper has put into developing and maintaining this site.

SGML Open Web site

The SGML Open Web site at `http://www.sgmlopen.org` is a great site for finding out what's happening in the world of SGML. SGML Open is a consortium of SGML software vendors whose goal is to further the acceptance and use of SGML throughout the known world, so you shouldn't be surprised to find a lot of truly useful information here. Besides an extensive (and frequently updated) calendar of upcoming SGML events, this site provides an extensive collection of white papers on different aspects of SGML, including case studies, document conversion, and some good general information on getting started with SGML. You can also find many technical papers that explore specific topics such as CALS, entity management, and SGML data interchange.

Newsgroups and Mailing Lists

The exponential growth of the Internet has provided two simple avenues for asking specific questions of a group of interested parties and getting an answer back in your lifetime: electronic mailing lists and Usenet newsgroups.

Electronic mailing lists are what the name suggests — collections of addresses to which mail on a specific topic is forwarded. You can usually subscribe to electronic mailing lists in one of two ways — either directly, which means that mail you send to the list is instantly copied and sent to every subscriber on that list, or by subscribing to collections of messages (known as a *digest*) that are electronically mailed to subscribers on a set schedule (usually once or twice a day). To send a message to an electronic mailing list, you send e-mail to the address for the list, usually on a machine that is known as a *listserver* because it services requests to one or more electronic mailing lists. The server then forwards the mail to the subscribers and bundles the mail into the next digest that is scheduled to be sent. Electronic mailing lists look the same as standard e-mail and don't use any special protocols.

Usenet newsgroups are essentially hierarchical bulletin boards on specific topics that are distributed across the Internet. Interested parties can post messages to a newsgroup and see their messages as well as other people's replies. Most Internet Service Providers (ISPs) carry Usenet newsgroups that you can read using browsers such as Netscape or Internet Explorer or by using software designed for reading these groups. These newsgroups get a lot of posts each day, on many different topics, so you may want to make sure that the software you use to read a newsgroup (called a *newsreader*) supports *threading*, which is the ability to follow specific chains of posts on the same topic. Threading makes it easy to follow specific questions and answers — without it, it's easy to miss an important bit of information on a specific topic that you're interested in!

Due to the volume of daily postings on Usenet newsgroups, most ISPs expire posts after a few weeks, which means that they're deleted from your ISP's local copy of that newsgroup. Don't worry about what you've missed — all of the postings to many Usenet newsgroups are archived at various locations on the Internet. The critical bit of information that you needed isn't gone — it's just been moved, and you may have to do a bit of detective work to find it.

The `comp.text.sgml` *newsgroup*

The Usenet newsgroup `comp.text.sgml` is a great group for asking questions, getting information about what other people are doing in the world of SGML, and for picking up tips and tricks about using SGML. Beyond pure SGML, this group often carries spirited discussions of related topics and new developments such as XML, DSSSL, and so on. James Clark, the author of some truly amazing SGML tools discussed in Chapter 19, is a frequent contributor, as are many other well-known SGML users, implementers, and theorists. You can find collections of older posts to this newsgroup at various sites on the Internet.

In addition to the comp.text.sgml newsgroup, you may find other newsgroups in the `comp.text` hierarchy interesting, especially if you are using a specific company's tools. You can ask detailed questions and get help on specific issues from other users who have asked the same questions from newsgroups such as `comp.text.frame` (for FrameMaker users) and `comp.text.interleaf` (for Interleaf users). The `comp.text.desktop` newsgroup is a good forum for asking general questions about desktop publishing, and the `comp.text.pdf` newsgroup is a good forum for issues related to electronic publishing using Adobe's Portable Document Format (PDF!).

The Davenport Group mailing list

The Davenport Group mailing list is a forum for discussing the DocBook DTD. To subscribe to this mailing list, send e-mail to `listproc@online.ora.com` with "subscribe davenport" in the body of your message. To post messages to this mailing list, send e-mail to `davenport@online.ora.com`.

The DSSSL-Lite mailing list

The DSSSL-Lite mailing list is a forum devoted to a discussion of the issues involved creating a subset of DSSSL (Document Style Semantics and Specification Language) that can be used to supply style information for Web pages. To subscribe, send e-mail to `majordomo@falch.no` with "subscribe dsssl-lite *login@host*," where *login@host* is your e-mail address. To post a message to the mailing list, send e-mail to `dsssl-lite@falch.no`.

The DSSSList mailing list

The DSSSList mailing list is a fairly new mailing list that provides a forum for discussing the DSSSL standard and a place where DSSSL users can exchange questions, ideas, suggestions, and solutions. Because DSSSL is such a hot topic in the world of SGML, this list sees lots of action every day, with some fairly spirited discussions! To directly subscribe to the DSSSList, send e-mail to majordomo@mulberrytech.com with "subscribe dssslist" as the body of your message. To subscribe to the DSSSList in digest form, send e-mail to majordomo@mulberrytech.com with "subscribe dssslist-digest" as the body of your message. Posts to the DSSSList mailing list are archived at http://www.mulberrytech.com/dsssl/dssslist/archive.

The TEI-L and TEI-TECH mailing lists

The TEI-L mailing list is a general forum for discussing issues related to the Text Encoding Initiative, whose Tei and Tei-Lite DTDs are discussed elsewhere in this book. The TEI-TECH mailing list is a forum for discussing advanced issues related to the TEI guidelines and their implementation. To subscribe to one of these mailing lists, send e-mail to listserv@listserv.uic.edu with "SUBSCRIBE TEI-L" or "SUBSCRIBE TEI-TECH" in the body of your message. To post messages to the TEI-L mailing list, send e-mail to TEI-L@uic.edu. To send a message to the TEI-TECH mailing list, send e-mail to TEI-TECH@uic.edu.

Reference Texts

Many excellent books on SGML are available, and many more are being written as I write this book. This section contains a list of some of my favorites. You should be able to order any of these from your local bookstore. Or you can order them through one of the online book stores available on the Internet, such as Amazon Books at http://www.amazon.com.

Here are some great books on SGML:

- *ABCD...SGML,* Liora Alschuler, 1995, International Thomson Computer Press (ISBN 1-850-32197-3)

- *Developing SGML DTDs,* Eve Maler and Jeanne el Andaloussi, 1996, Prentice-Hall (ISBN 0-13-309881-8)

- *Industrial-Strength SGML,* Truly Donovan, 1997, Prentice-Hall (ISBN 0-13-216243-1)

- *Practical Guide to SGML Filters,* Norman Smith, 1997, Wordware Publishing (ISBN 1-55622-511-3)

- *Practical SGML,* Eric van Herwijnen, 1990, Kluwer Academic Publishers (ISBN 0-7923-0635-X)

- *README.1st:SGML for Writers and Editors,* Ronald Turner, Timothy Douglass, and Audrey Turner, 1996, Prentice-Hall (ISBN 0-13-432717-9)

- *The SGML Handbook,* Charles F. Goldfarb, 1990, Oxford Press (ISBN 0-19-853737-9)

- *The SGML Implementation Guide,* Brian Travis and Dale Waldt, 1995, Springer-Verlag (ISBN 3-540-57730-0)

- *$GML the Billion Dollar Secret,* Chet Ensign, 1997, Prentice-Hall, (ISBN 0-13-2260705-5)

Chapter 22

Ten Solid Business Reasons for Using SGML

In This Chapter
▶ How using SGML can benefit your organization
▶ Using SGML to simplify your documentation process
▶ Standardizing your documentation with SGML

*I*n this chapter, I summarize many of the features and benefits of SGML. This chapter provides short descriptions of points introduced elsewhere. If you're considering moving to SGML as a documentation solution and are having problems converting anyone else, you may want to just copy this information and distribute it at your next meeting!

A Software-Independent Solution for Documentation

The Standard Generalized Markup Language (SGML) is just that — it's a standard that is independent of any particular word-processing or publishing software package. If you produce documents that will be used for a long time and go through many revisions, moving those documents into SGML guarantees that you won't be locked into a specific word-processing or publishing package. As new software emerges that supports SGML, or as your current software package adds support for SGML or enhances it, you don't have to waste time and resources moving your documents from one software package to another. Putting your documents into SGML today means that you can still work with them tomorrow, using any software package that supports SGML.

This isn't to say that moving from one SGML software package to another doesn't require any work — it probably will. If you will still be making your documents available to consumers in printed form (even if it's optional), you will probably still have to do some work to develop a formatting environment for these documents. The primary function of your documentation is to contain and convey information — moving to SGML guarantees that this information won't be lost.

Guaranteed Standard Structure in Your Documents

SGML emphasizes the structure and content of your documents, separating this from how they are formatted. The Document Type Definition (DTD) is the structural definition of the elements that your documents can contain and how those elements are related. For example, a DTD can define that your documents consist of chapters, each of which has a title, an introduction, a summary list of what you'll find in that chapter, and a number of sections and subsections. Your SGML software package uses the DTD to enforce those content rules in your documents. For example, writers can't omit the summary list in any chapter, because your SGML software won't let them — it typically either inserts the summary list automatically, or won't validate any document that is missing a summary list. Validation, typically done by parts of your SGML software that compare each of your documents against the rules in the DTD, is a critical step in producing a valid SGML document.

Guaranteed Specific Formatting in Your Documents

After you've produced a valid SGML document using your SGML software, you may want to print it. Although various forms of electronic publishing are all the rage, many people still want paper, even if just during the review phase of your documentation. SGML software provides a formatting environment for your documents that enforces the same formatting rules on the different elements in your documents. SGML eliminates the tweaking that writers often have to do to get a document to look just right, or which they may feel compelled to do for some aesthetic ideal.

SGML transcends word-processing and publishing packages that simply provide style sheets, because those style sheets usually don't enforce where different styles can be used. Style sheets also don't prevent writers from overriding styles or using them in ways that you didn't intend them to be used. SGML eliminates these possibilities.

Increased Lifespan of Your Documents

By freeing you from using a specific word-processing or publishing package, SGML lets your organization continue to use the information in your documents, long after your original word-processing package may have bitten the dust. The information your documents contain is a corporate resource that may outlive a software package or specific approach to documentation, such as print publishing. SGML is an approach to documentation, not a specific set of tools. SGML makes it easy for you to adopt new technologies and apply them to your documents. It's easy to use software such as document management systems and version control systems with your SGML documents, extending or changing these systems as necessary in the future.

Reusable Information throughout Your Company

Because of its emphasis on structure, SGML make it easy to share information between different documents, different groups, and even use that information with software beyond the scope of word-processing or publishing packages, such as databases and document management systems.

For example, assume you have some central background information about your products or related technologies that you want to share between your marketing and technical writing groups. SGML's emphasis on structure makes it easy for you to modularize your documents, building them up from building blocks of information that can be stored in different files or locations. This building-block approach makes it easy for different groups to use only the chunks of information that they need — and because the information is being shared rather than duplicated, it's easier to manage that information, guarantee its correctness, and update as needed.

Increased Productivity

SGML increases productivity by freeing writers from having to worry about the vagaries of formatting, helping them focus on the content of documents rather than their appearance. SGML also increases productivity by minimizing the number of times you have to duplicate or re-write parts of your documents: SGML makes it easy to share information between different documents. By enforcing structure in your documents, SGML also makes it easy for you to publish your documents in multiple formats, such as paper or electronic forms, reducing or eliminating the time required to pre-process your documents for alternate production formats.

Easy Integration with Other Applications

Because of its emphasis on structure, SGML is naturally suited to other structured applications, such as databases. These applications can not only provide a way for you to store your document, but also can provide you with alternative ways of searching your documents for specific content. For example, if your documents are stored in an object-oriented database, you can easily write a query that will locate specific information throughout your document set. This strategy can simplify things for your writers and also for groups, such as customer support organizations, that have to be able to find specific bits of information in potentially large sets of documents.

SGML documents are stored in standard text format, which makes it easy to integrate with document management systems — and even with the version control systems often used in software development environments. Because they are just text documents, any other software that you want to use with your documents doesn't need to understand any specific internal formats used by a particular word-processing or publishing package.

Compliance with Government and Industry Regulations

Many industries, such as the government and aerospace industries, require that documents produced under contract to them be in SGML. This requirement protects industries against charges of favoritism for a specific word-processing or publishing package; it also extends the lifespan of documents because they aren't locked into a specific publishing package. As I mention elsewhere in this book, the technical manuals for some aircraft are in use for 20 years or so. Would you like to bet that a specific word-processing or publishing package used today will be around in 20 years?

Optimization of the Document Production Cycle

By freeing writers from having to worry about formatting and pagination, SGML lets them focus on writing, reviewing, and updating documents. This freedom can save lots of time during the production of a printed version of your document set because the formatting rules for those documents are centralized. Producing proof copies for publication can often be assigned to a small, dedicated group rather than distributing it throughout your technical writing group.

Because of its emphasis on structure, SGML prevents many of the annoying problems that often crop up late in the production cycle. For example, most SGML software flags cross-references that can't be resolved. Many word-processing and publishing packages don't provide such warning, and these things can be tricky to spot in documents — or at least require careful proofing of the final copies of your documents. If you've ever seen a document containing the message "ERROR: Bookmark not defined," you may wish that whoever produced it had used SGML — the authors probably do!

Simpler Conversion to Other Formats

SGML's emphasis on structure in your documents, as enforced by your DTD, helps guarantee that there won't be any surprises in how your documents are organized. For example, unless your DTD allows you to insert a bulleted list inside a table, writers won't be able to insert one there. Regular, formal structure makes it easier to convert your documents into other formats, or simply to generate other formats from your SGML documents.

If your organization focuses on electronic publishing, the production cycle for those documents is often substantially less than for printed documents. Rigorous insistence on well-defined structure simplifies converting your documents into other formats, such as HTML or XML. This simplicity translates into extra time for you to focus on improving the content of your documents.

Part VII
The Part of Tens

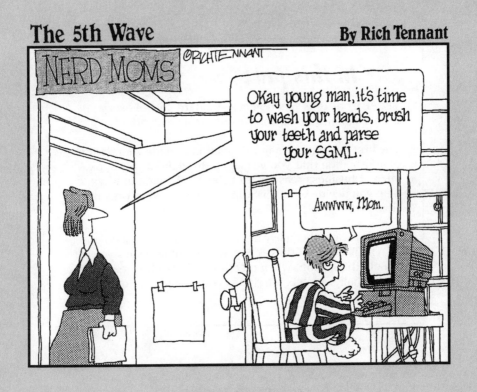

In this part . . .

The "Part of Tens" section is a standard part of every ...For Dummies book, and this one is no exception!

The first two chapters in this section provide summaries of information that you've gained throughout this book, such as business reasons for using SGML and ten ways to help you decide whether SGML is right for your organization.

This part provides fairly detailed lists of issues in creating a DTD. The first of these chapters identifies issues you should think about when creating a DTD — the next is its darker half, which is ten things you should *not* do when creating a DTD.

Chapter 23

Ten Ways to Decide if SGML Is Right for You

In This Chapter

▶ Deciding whether SGML is mandatory or optional

▶ Integrating a move to SGML with your current schedule

▶ Can you afford it? It's not just tools. . . .

*T*his chapter summarizes some of the basic issues in considering moving your documents into SGML (or starting with SGML from the ground up, if you're lucky!). Like any change, SGML has its own set of costs and issues in "getting there from here."

Does Your Industry Require SGML?

If the industry that your products are designed for requires that you submit documents in SGML, this isn't much of a question — you're probably already using SGML. However, if your organization isn't already working in that industry, but intends to apply for contracts in the aerospace industry or with any government agency, you'll have to factor SGML into your plans, at least for the new documents you'll be writing for this project. The question then becomes whether you plan to re-use any of the information in any existing documents you might have. If so, you'll have to factor in how to get these documents (or just the portions that you want to reuse) into SGML. Chapter 20 discusses many of the issues involved in converting existing documents into SGML.

If you're going to be working in an industry that requires SGML, you should plan to migrate any existing documents that you'll still be updating into SGML at some point. Supporting multiple documentation sets and using different documentation tools can be a nightmare. The points that I summarize in Chapter 22 should show you some of the benefits of working in a pure SGML environment.

Do You Have Many Existing Documents in Different Tools?

If you already have one or more large document sets that were produced using different tools, the cost of migrating those documents into SGML goes up because you can't use a single conversion utility to get them all into SGML. However, if you stop to consider the costs of supporting multiple word-processing or publishing packages, you may see that conversion is much cheaper in the long run. Using different software packages for the documents produced by a single organization means

✔ Writers have to be trained to use different packages. Different writers will encounter different problems using these packages, but you'll still have to support all of them.

✔ It is more difficult to move writers from one project to another because different projects may require different tools.

✔ You are at the mercy of multiple software vendors. If the vendor of one of the packages you depend on goes out of business or stops supporting a publishing package that you depend on, you're in for a potentially rough time.

If you have existing sets of documents that you will still need to update, and those documents were produced using different software packages, and you can afford the time and expense of converting them into SGML, go for it! Like any change in an organization, moving to SGML has its own sets of costs and issues. However, what it buys you in the long run is better-organized documents, a smaller set of documentation tools to support, reduced training costs, the ability to easily reuse information across your documents, and independence from a specific word-processing or publishing package. See Chapter 22 for a more complete list of SGML features and benefits.

Are You Changing Documentation Tools?

If you are planning to change documentation tools anyway, you should seriously consider SGML tools. Changing the tools that you use can be motivated by any number of things, from changing the hardware or operating system platform that you are using for documentation or product development, to simply looking for a better approach to managing your information.

Chapter 23 discusses many of the benefits that SGML can provide to your organization — why not use this as an opportunity to adopt an SGML approach to your documentation? You don't even have to convert all of your existing documents into SGML right now, though the previous section provides some good arguments for adopting a single set of word-processing or publishing tools. Still, if new products or product requirements mean that you need to consider new tools, SGML is the right thing to consider. Adopting SGML for new document development means that you will be developing expertise in SGML as well as the new tools that you'll be using. You can probably stage the conversion of your legacy documents into SGML, and the expertise in SGML that you will be developing can help smooth that process.

Do You Plan to Move to Electronic or Web-Based Publishing Soon?

Many companies today are looking for ways to trim costs by focusing on electronic ways of publishing their documents, de-emphasizing paper as their primary format for document delivery. This isn't just a cost issue — as I discuss in Chapter 16, electronic publishing can make it easier for your customers to access your documents, can make it simpler for you to update your documents, and can reduce costs and production time for your documents.

An entire spectrum of approaches to electronic publishing is available today, ranging from converting your existing documents into portable formats, such as Adobe's Portable Document Format (PDF) or Corel's Envoy format, to converting your documents into formats that are immediately suited for use over the Internet or an intranet, such as HTML and XML. These last two solutions are perfectly suited for electronic publishing because they don't require any special software beyond a web browser, which I assume everyone has access to nowadays!

I discuss HTML and XML in Chapter 5. These approaches to electronic publishing are especially well-suited to SGML documentation environments because they are SGML. HTML is as SGML DTD, while XML is a well-defined subset of SGML with specific requirements. If you work in an SGML documentation environment, you often generate HTML or XML directly from your exisiting SGML documents, mapping the elements in your SGML DTD to those in the HTML DTD or to the set of elements used in a specific XML document, and expanding entities as required. This conversion may be more difficult if your SGML tools make extensive use of SGML features such as tag omission or tag minimization (which I discuss in Chapter 4), but you're still closer to HTML or XML than you would be if you were using an unstructured documentation tool.

Do You Have a Hard Time Producing Documents that Resemble Each Other?

Almost everyone who has ever worked in the wacky world of documentation has experienced that sinking feeling that you get when you compare two documents from the same document set and notice how different they are from each other. Obviously, not all documents have the same structure or contents (such as guide versus reference material), but it can be pretty sad when your guides don't resemble each other that closely. Even style sheets, which go a long way toward standardizing the appearance of documents in a document set, can't fully prevent dissimilarities because they don't enforce content or structure.

The reasons for dissimilar appearance are often no one's fault. Newer documents that use enhanced styles will drift from older documents that you may not have had to update. Word-processing and publishing software gets upgraded and may behave differently. Writers come and go in most organizations, often taking their secret formatting magic with them, leaving their successors to wonder "How'd they do that?" or, more often, "Why'd they do that?"

SGML can't protect you from every potential problem in your document sets, but its separation of structure from formatting can help minimize differences between documents that should be similar. SGML can require that specific portions of your documents appear in a specific order, or that they're present in the first place. Moving existing documents into SGML just to standardize their formatting and structure isn't the only reason to move to SGML, but it's a powerful argument. It can also reduce your expenses for antacids late in the productions cycle for a document set.

Do You Repeat Information in Different Documents?

If you have multiple documents that share information, SGML's emphasis on structure can make it easier for you to share that information between them. Of course, SGML tools aren't the only tools that can do this, but they are among the most effective. SGML's structured approach to documentation development is a good fit with sharing chunks of information across documents and also simplifies sharing this information across different output formats or tools, such as databases, Internet or intranet publishing, and so on.

Can You Afford Moving to SGML?

Beyond the costs of the SGML software you purchase, SGML has other costs that you have to consider. For example, if you are planning to develop your own document types, you'll have to budget the costs of someone to develop those DTDs and their associated formatting environment (more about this in Chapter 24!). Other costs in moving existing documents into SGML are the costs of converting large amounts of existing documentation into SGML. As I discuss in Chapter 20, there are several ways to go about this, but they all cost time and money.

If you're already working under tight deadlines for new documentation development, it can be very costly to try to produce new documents while learning new tools. Anyone will take some time to come up to speed at using the new tools. If things are already tight, this can certainly cause writers and editors to spontaneously combust.

Like any project, moving existing documents to SGML has to be carefully planned and staged within your organization. Careful document analysis during the planning phase (which I discuss in Chapter 13) can help you produce schedules that are accurate and reduce the number of bumps you'll experience along the way. But plan to hit a few — there's always that one odd document that you still have to produce that was written years ago, and which you may not discover until you think you're done. Childbirth, even in the documentation industry, is a source of incredible pain but is almost always worth it.

Can You Teach and Support SGML?

One of the subtler costs in moving to a new approach to documentation is the cost to all of your users. They won't instantly be productive in your new tools, which can be frustrating. More important, anyone using your SGML software will have to learn to work in the structured model that SGML provides. This is often more difficult than it sounds because it's hard to break the orientation toward formatting that most writers have spent years absorbing. In the long run, it's obviously worth it, but unlearning the tips and techniques of many years in the documentation industry can take some time and may bring some frustration. As I discuss in Chapter 13, this is one of the best reasons to get as many people involved as possible in planning your move to SGML — people will not only understand what's involved in using SGML but will have had a hand in getting your organization there.

Does SGML Fit in Your Computing Environment?

Many of the more sophisticated SGML tools that are available today require some sort of UNIX environment. Even if these tools follow the client/server model, the servers for these tools often run on UNIX systems. If you believe that SGML is the right solution for you, but your entire computing environment uses Macintoshes or PCs, you will need to consider the costs of adding new systems, new system administrators, and training for users of these new systems to your budget. UNIX system administration is getting easier as new administrative software and standardized administrative interfaces are developed, but it's still not a romp in the park. Also, network-based documentation development and management software will increase the load on your network and your existing servers. Make sure that you involve someone from your MIS or computing services groups when considering and evaluating new software packages!

Do You Need to Integrate SGML with Existing Software?

As a documentation group works with a specific word-processing or publishing package over time, they tend to develop sets of auxiliary tools that they depend on. When considering a move to SGML, make sure you examine each of these utilities to see whether it is specific to your existing documentation tool, or whether it's something you will have to convert to work with your new SGML software.

The best example of these types of utilities are tools that you use to archive the versions of your documents and graphics that are associated with each release of your documents. It's strange to say, but I've seen many organizations that don't have a good plan for archiving the documents that are associated with specific product releases. If your organization does, congratulations! However, an existing archival plan means that you will have to consider how your current archival mechanism can be made to work with your new SGML documents, or whether you should adopt a different mechanism. A good archival mechanism or other form of version control means never having to say "OOPS!," but it won't do you much good if your existing system doesn't understand SGML or can't be made to work with it. Luckily, unless your current archival or version control software is tightly integrated with a specific word-processing or publishing package, this usually isn't much of an issue. As I discuss elsewhere in this book, the fact that SGML documents and their associated DTDs are text documents makes them easy to work with and easy to adopt to most archival or version control tools.

Chapter 24

Top Ten Considerations When Writing a DTD

This chapter summarizes some of the points that you should consider when deciding whether you should write your own DTD. As I discuss in Chapter 12, writing a DTD is a lot of work, but it is the right thing to do under various circumstances. This chapter explores some common issues to think about when deciding if this is one of those circumstances — or when writing a DTD after making that decision.

Does Your Industry Have a Standard DTD?

If your current contract requires that you use a specific DTD, that DTD is probably listed in your contract and may be supplied by the organization you're working for. If you're simply ahead of the curve by being an SGML devotee, a specific DTD may not be a contractual requirement. In this case, you should try to determine if the industry you work in uses a standard DTD — if so you should strongly consider using it. There are probably some good reasons why it's in use in your industry! For example, the DocBook DTD is freely distributable and was designed for use in producing technical documentation for the software industry. Even if you need to develop your own DTD, any existing DTD oriented toward the types of documents used in a specific industry will be a useful reference for you.

If you don't know how to find out about the DTDs in use in your industry, try contacting a SIG or industry society such as the ASME (American Society of Mechanical Engineers). You can also look in one of the SGML reference texts listed in Chapter 21, or contact one of the SGML users' groups listed in that same chapter. Of course, there's always the World Wide Web!

Issues in Extending an Existing DTD

If your contract or industry requires using a specific DTD, you should think very carefully about any extensions that you want to make to that DTD. It's easy to extend a DTD by adding specific element, entity, or attribute declarations in the DOCTYPE statement in your documents. However, if you think you want to do this, you should ask yourself why no one else in your industry seems to need the specific features you want to add. If you have good reasons for adding those extensions, then do so, remembering that these can limit the extent to which you can then exchange documents with other companies that use the same DTD.

If your contract and the industry you work in don't mandate using a specific DTD, you should consider extending an existing DTD to meet your needs. This can substantially reduce your development time but requires careful planning on your part to make sure that anyone you exchange your documents with gets all the information they need to work with your documents.

If you extend an existing DTD and declare your extensions as external parameter entities, you'll have to make sure that you provide other companies who use your documents with the SGML catalog where your parameter entities are defined (or with whatever mechanism your SGML software uses for managing entities). You will also have to provide them with the files containing your declarations, as well as general information about how those elements are formatted in your documents. If you use the same SGML software package as the companies you're exchanging information with, you may be able to simply give them a copy of your FOSI or other formatting environment declaration.

See Chapter 15 for more detailed information about extending an existing DTD.

Top Down or Bottoms Up?

Designing a DTD has to be a good combination of top-down and bottoms-up design. Top-down design means starting from a high-level description of the structure of your documents and working your way down through lower levels of their structure. For example, when doing document analysis prior to writing a DTD, I find that the Table of Contents for your documents is a good starting point.

At the same time that you want to start with the high-level design of your documents and work your way down, you want to make sure that you define the low-level elements of your documents correctly. For example, if you define some low-level part of your documents as simple character data (CDATA) and later want to add some mandatory structure to that element, documents that you're already working with may not match the new, more restrictive content model that you impose.

This is a situation that will probably happen to you one or more times during any DTD development. Not to worry! Being aware of this issue can at least help you minimize the number of times this particular issue bites you, which is progress!

General or Specific Elements?

One issue that you'll hit when designing a DTD is whether to use specific elements in different contexts, or whether to use a single element in each context and let your formatting software figure out how to handle it. A good example of this is a ⟨TITLE⟩ element, which probably occurs in every level of your documents, such as chapters, sections, subsections, and so on. The only thing that really differentiates these different types of titles is how they're numbered in whatever output formats you support (assuming that you number them!).

In general, I prefer to use single elements for simple constructs that appear throughout a document and to minimize their use for structural elements. The ⟨TITLE⟩ element is a good example — if this element is defined as the first tag that appears after each structural element, it's easy to see the sectioning level associated with each title. However, some DTDs use a single element, such as a ⟨DIVISION⟩ to indicate different structural levels in a document. For example, in a book composed of chapters, sections, and subsections, the first ⟨DIVISION⟩ is a chapter-level division, the second is a section-level division, and the third is a subsection-level division. I find DTDs that use this convention to be extremely hard to read and difficult to parse without looking at the whole document — which can be challenging in a huge document set!

There is no specific rule to follow here, except "do what seems right for you based on how you'll be using the information in your documents." For example, if you want to be able to share text between different documents, using what appears as a section in one document as a chapter in another, you might want to adopt the ⟨DIVISION⟩ model mentioned in the preceding paragraph. I find instances of this sort of thing to be rare, but it can happen and may be quite useful in these rare cases.

Designing DTDs for Usability

One of the most important issues in writing a DTD that people can actually use is to give your elements and entities meaningful names! Unfortunately, the declaration in the SGML concrete reference for the maximum length of an element is 8 characters, which is hard to cram much meaning into (as most DOS users would agree!). Short element names are largely a hangover (and I mean that in every sense of the word) from the days when computer memory used to store and process your documents was expensive, and SGML software was primitive, meaning that you had to type in every opening and closing tag. Nowadays, when 16MB costs less than a good dinner, and SGML software usually inserts tag names for you, these issues are less important.

If your SGML software package supports it, consider increasing the maximum length of your element names to something meaningful, like 16 characters or so. This lets you pack meaning into your element names, which makes your SGML documents more readable. However, do this carefully — for example, using <PARAGRAPH> as the name of your basic paragraph element is probably overkill, and will certainly irritate anyone who is writing SGML documents using a text editor. In this case, <P> is probably just fine. On the other hand, using an element named <K> to represent a keyword is probably underkill. I'd vote that <KEYWORD> was much more meaningful, and that the number of keywords in your documents probably isn't high enough that this will wear down any of your writers' fingers.

Using Attributes or Different Elements

Deciding whether to use different elements to represent structurally similar portions of your documents, or whether to just identify these different types of things using an attribute of a more generic element is a tough call. Having too many different elements is a common cause of bloat in your DTDs and can also make it harder for writers to figure out which elements to use for different things. On the other hand, using attributes too often can make your DTD equally hard to use and work with, because every other element has an attribute definition associated with it.

A good rule of thumb that I use to differentiate between when elements and attributes are appropriate is to think about whether the item in question is a structural part of my documents or whether it provides information about a specific structural part of my documents. Lists are a good example of where attributes are useful — a <LIST> is a structural part of my document, while whether a list is bulleted or numbered is really just information about that specific list. I usually create attribute values for lists such as NUMBERED, BULLETED, PLAIN, and so on. An example of related issue where I would not use attributes is to differentiate between things such as keywords, function names, and so on. Some DTDs would view these all as instances of some generic <PHRASE> element, with attributes that identify the type of information the <PHRASE> contains. Since most technical documents, especially in the software industry, could contain many of these in a single paragraph, I'd create different <KEYWORD> and <FUNCTION> elements to heighten readability.

"There's not much difference between those two examples," I hear you cry. That's essentially true. There is no "one true way" of deciding when to use elements or attributes. Some SGML software limits the number of attributes that you can place on a specific element, which can be a factor.

One important thing to remember when using attributes is that, in most cases, you'll want to clearly define the values that different attributes can have. It's easy to make a typo in a free-format attribute value that can cause your SGML formatting software to choke on a specific attribute value because it doesn't know how to handle it. This is not so critical on page 5 of a document but can be quite frustrating on page 505.

Identifying External Data

As I discuss in Chapter 6, SGML's NOTATION attribute type is a powerful way of letting you use data produced by other applications in your SGML documents. The most common instances of such external data are things like graphics, embedded multi-media, and complex mathematical expressions. These are not only outside the scope of many SGML applications but contain data that you don't want to be parsed by your SGML applications. In these cases, you could define a notation attribute for the elements in which these external objects can appear, and let your SGML software handle passing those external objects off to other software that can handle them. This is one of those cases where some knowledge of the formatting engine used by your SGML software can be useful.

When writing a DTD, consider what type of external types of data you may already use (such as GIF, PostScript, or XBM bitmaps), and create a NOTATION attribute for the elements that those objects appear in, such as figures.

Planning Your DTD Distribution

As you begin to develop and enhance a DTD, it will change often. It's important to be kind to your users during these "wonder months" of DTD development. Make sure that you always do at least a minimum amount of testing before releasing your DTD to users. If I had a nickel for each time I'd thought "well, that can't break anything," I could at least take some of my victims out to lunch!

Make sure that you have a central forum for announcing any changes that you make to a DTD, whether it's a bulletin board or mailing list. DTDs that break for no reason are exponentially more frustrating than those that you've at least warned people about. Because some of your changes may break users' documents, it's also important to use version control when developing a DTD! This strategy is especially true when you're making extensive changes but is equally important to allow you to quickly back out changes that are causing problems. Some problems are almost unavoidable, like changing content models, because of oversights in your document analysis process. However, as the author of the DTD, it's your responsibility to minimize the pain of your users and testers.

Minimizing Bells and Whistles

Some of SGML's more magical features, such as LINK, CONCUR, and SUBDOC are not supported by all SGML software. If you will be exchanging documents and your DTDs with other companies that use other SGML software, you will at least want to make sure that you understand the features that their SGML software supports. You may want to minimize the use of fancier features such as these, on general principle.

As I confessed earlier in this book, I'm not a big fan of SGML features such as tag omission and minimization. There are cases where these things are useful, and they can certainly be useful during the conversion process from unstructured document formats. In general, I feel that you shouldn't use these features unless you have a really good reason to do so — and unless you also make sure that users of your DTD understand these features in detail, and when and why they're appropriate. I generally find that the cost of reduced readability that these features provide is much higher than your savings in the number of characters typed.

Designing DTDs for Reusability

If you have to write multiple DTDs, make sure that you design them in a modular fashion, using parameter entities to share entity and element declarations wherever possible. This not only reduces the number of times you have to reinvent the wheel but increases the portability of your documents between those DTDs. It's often harder to try to disassemble existing DTDs than it is to spend some time planning their structure and relationships in advance.

Chapter 25

Ten Common Errors when Creating a DTD

In This Chapter

▶ Common DTD errors and how to avoid them

▶ Investing time now, or paying later

▶ Designing your DTD for the future

*T*his chapter summarizes some of the most common problems people run Tinto when writing a DTD. Not all of these are actually problems with the DTD itself — many of them are maintenance migraines that you will cause yourself if you aren't careful in documenting and commenting your DTD as you go.

Providing Insufficient Document Analysis

Not doing a sufficient amount of document analysis before you actually begin designing your DTD is the biggest source of potential problems in your DTD in the future. These problems can range from designing a DTD that won't support some of the document types that your organization uses, to leaving out critical parts of your documents and having to subsequently make major changes to your DTD. Though the document analysis phase of your DTD design and selection process may be the most time-consuming portion of your move to SGML and may seem trivial or obvious, it's actually critical. See Chapter 13 for more information about document analysis.

Not Commenting

The right time to comment your DTD is as you write it, explaining what you were thinking as you designed and implemented specific elements and their content models. References to the type of structures in your original documents that you are modeling using certain elements and content models can be useful data for the future, and you may no longer remember what you were trying to do by the time that problems arise. Also remember that you probably won't be responsible for this DTD for the rest of your life. Someone else will eventually have to become involved in its maintenance — and will either thank you or curse you, depending on how well your DTD is commented.

Using Poor Formatting or Style

You should take advantage of the fact that SGML parsers don't mind whitespace in a DTD when you write one. Reasonable formatting and the use of whitespace can make a DTD much easier to read and understand.

Similarly, you should think about how to organize the elements and attributes in your DTDs. As I discuss in Chapter 14, I prefer to organize elements structurally and follow them with any attribute definitions for each element. Others prefer to group all the elements and attributes together, organizing them alphabetically. The advantage to structural organization is that the organization of the elements makes it easy for me to visualize the content model for each element; and attributes are immediately visible beside the elements that they're associated with. The advantages of alphabetical organization are that elements and attributes are easier to find in a DTD.

There is no "one true way" to organize things in your DTDs. The most important thing to do is to select the model that works best for you — or come up with your own! The most important thing is to be consistent with whichever model you select.

Adding Unintuitive Elements

This procedure isn't an error so much as a usability issue. As I discuss in Chapters 5 and 24, the readability of documents that are marked up using your DTD can make or break it. Don't put yourself in the position of saving a few characters at the expense of associating some real meaning with the elements in your DTD and their content. DTDs with cryptic element names are frustrating for users and can be more difficult to debug. If you insist on cryptic element names, at least document their purpose in the DTD and provide some mnemonic clues that people can use to visualize their purpose.

Not Using Version Control

When developing a DTD, version control is critical for several reasons:

- ✔ It lets you see exactly what has changed between versions of a DTD
- ✔ It makes it possible for users to tell you exactly what version of a DTD they had problems with
- ✔ It provides a quick way (by rolling back to a previous version) for you to eliminate sets of changes that caused problems for your users

Version control is easy to implement with DTDs and other SGML files, because they are simply text files. If your company doesn't already use a software version control system, you can implement version control by simply saving copies of each release of your DTD and related files, embedding SGML comments containing version numbers. If you don't have access to a software system for automatically doing this, you'll have to be careful to correctly increment version numbers and save copies of all of your files at each release of your DTD. The effort required for this task is nothing besides the effort required to figure out what went wrong if you didn't bother to save this information.

Doing Insufficient Testing

As part of your DTD development effort, you should evolve a sample document that tests each new feature, element, or content model that you add to the DTD. Whenever users discover problems, I typically include those problems in my sample document. This strategy not only makes it clear when a problem is actually fixed, but makes it easy for you to identify regressions in future versions of your DTDs — new features that resolve one problem but cause others to resurface in your documents.

You should also make sure that you involve future users of the DTD in your tests. Element names or contexts that make perfect sense to you may be totally confusing to someone else. An element misunderstood will be an element that will probably be misused.

Using Element Names that Imply Formatting

SGML is based on the idea of separating the structure and content of your documents from how those documents are formatted. Using tags with names such as <BOLD> or <ITALIC> don't buy you anything structurally and deny you the chance to identify the type of content that you're actually marking up. Also, if your local styles ever change, italicizing what used to be bold, you'll have a lot of editing to do!

Using Mixed Content Models

As I discuss in Chapter 4, mixed content models are a common source of ambiguities in your DTDs. Mixed content models are elements that can contain a mixture of #PCDATA and other elements. Whenever possible, avoid this sort of construct or replace it with a content model where your elements can contain #PCDATA *or* other elements.

Not Tightening Existing Content Models

Whenever possible, design your DTD so that the original content models for your elements are as restrictive as possible. Although it is easy to later relax the content models for your elements, further restricting them can cause problems in documents that parsed correctly with the previous content model. This sort of thing can be unavoidable as you discover additional details about the actual structure of your documents — but it's a point to consider when designing a DTD and a common source of problems when enhancing or refining one.

Not Planning for Reuse and Expansion

When writing a DTD, organize it such that it is easy to selectively include or exclude related sets of elements, attributes, and entities. The DocBook DTD provides a good example of this type of organization. Not only will you find it easier to maintain a well-organized, well-commented DTD, but this type of organization lets you reuse parts of your current DTD in other DTDs that you may develop in the future.

For great examples of how to plan for reuse and expansion, see Eve Maler and Jeanne El Andaloussi's *Developing SGML DTDs from Text to Model to Markup.*

Part VIII
Appendixes

The 5th Wave — By Rich Tennant

AFTER SPENDING 9 DAYS WITH 12 DIFFERENT VENDORS AND READING 26 BROCHURES, DAVE HAD AN ACUTE ATTACK OF TOXIC OPTION SYNDROME.

In this part . . .

The appendixes in this book tell you how to find cool SGML software that you can start using right away. If you have an Internet connection, the first appendix lists locations on the Internet and World Wide Web where you can find free or shareware SGML software. The second gives you information about where to contact many of the companies that market SGML software, providing World Wide Web, e-mail, and snail mail contact information.

The third appendix provides you with the easiest way of starting to use some SGML software, reading existing specifications, and looking at existing DTDs — it explains how to access the software and other information that's provided on the CD-ROM that accompanies this book!

Good luck with SGML!

Appendix A
Public-Domain and Shareware SGML Software

This appendix lists some sites on the World Wide Web where you can find public-domain and shareware SGML software. Some commercial SGML software vendors offer demonstration copies of their SGML software — these are discussed in the next appendix. You can typically run these demonstration copies only for a limited time, but they can be very useful in evaluating products or simply seeing different companies' approaches to SGML.

This list only scratches the surface of the free or shareware SGML software that's available on the World Wide Web — to keep this book from being the size of a telephone book, I've just listed specific pieces of free software that I've found especially useful or interesting in the past. For a fabulously detailed list of public-domain SGML software, see http://www.sil.org/sgml/publicSW.html.

DTDParse: A DTD Parser by Norman Walsh

DTDParse is a set of Perl utilities that read an SGML DTD and construct a simple database of its structure. The DTDParse distribution provides several scripts that further interpret this database, letting you identify the context in which any element can be used, or any elements that a particular element contains. DTDParse also provides a utility called dtd2html (no relation to the perlSGML program with the same name, though its purpose is the same) that builds a set of HTML pages which reflect the structure of a DTD.

You can get DTDParse from http://www.ora.com/homepages/dtdparse/.

ICA: The Integrated Chameleon Architecture

As I discuss in Chapter 19, the ICA tools are a set of utilities designed to help you build tools that convert documents from one format to another. The utilities do this by converting their input to a generic format which is then translated to other formats. The ICA require the X Window System, and are not supported on releases of X11 later than X11R4 (though I have built them successfully, with minor tweaking, on X11R6).

You can get the source for ICA from `ftp://archive.cis.ohio-state.edu/pub/chameleon`.

Jade: James' DSSSL Engine

Jade is another excellent tool from James Clark. Jade implements the DSSSL style language and provides output in RTF, TeX, and SGML. Jade can also be used as a simple transformation engine, converting from one SGML format to another.

Jade is actively under development, and is available for various UNIX systems as well as versions of Microsoft Windows. You can get more information about Jade, and the tools themselves, from `http://www.jclark.com/jade/`. Note that Jade includes James Clark's SP package; if you get Jade, you don't need to retrieve separately a copy of SP.

JUMBO: Java Universal Markup Browser

JUMBO (Java Universal Markup Browser for Objects) is a set of Java Classes for viewing XML applications. JUMBO can be used stand alone or can be configured for use with other Java-enabled browsers. You can get a copy of JUMBO from `http://www.vsms.nottingham.ac.uk/vsms/java/jumbo`.

Lark: SGML Parser with XML Support

Lark is an XML processor that is currently under development. Lark does not validate XML documents and currently uses only internal entities and elements declared in an XML document. You can get a copy of Lark and its documentation from `http://www.textuality.com/Lark/`.

perlSGML: Perl Programs and Libraries for SGML

Earl Hood's perlSGML is a collection of Perl programs and libraries for processing SGML documents. The perlSGML package includes dtd.pl and sgml.pl (Perl libraries for parsing SGML DTDs and documents, respectively), dtd2html (a DTD-to-HTML converter and navigation tool), dtddiff (a utility that lets you identify changes between two versions of a DTD), and stripsgml (a Perl utility that lets you remove SGML markup from an SGML document). Of these, the dtd2html tool is perhaps the best known, because it converts your DTDs into multiple files that allow hypertext navigation of the structure of a DTD. The dtddiff tool is also exceptionally useful if you're developing a DTD and need to be able to track changes.

You can get perlSGML from `http://www.oac.uci.edu/indiv/ehood/perlSGML.html`.

PSGML: An SGML Editing Package for Emacs

As I discuss in Chapter 19, PSGML is an excellent addition to your set of SGML tools if you happen to use the Emacs text editor, which is itself a public-domain software package. You can get PSGML as well as its documentation and installation information from `http://gopher.lysator.liu.se:70/1/information/SGML/about_psgml.html`.

Rainbow and Rainbow Makers

As I discuss in Chapter 19, the Rainbow DTD and associated Rainbow makers make up a set of tools that can help you convert documents from various word-processing formats into SGML. Supported formats include WordPerfect, FrameMaker's MIF format, RTF, and Interleaf.

You can get these tools and their documentation from `ftp://ftp.ebt.com/pub/nv/dtd/rainbow`.

SGMLS: Another SGML Parser from James Clark

SGMLS is the predecessor of James Clark's SP SGML parser toolkit. SGMLS is only a parser, but its widely used and is very fast, even when parsing large documents and associated DTDs. SGMLS produces structured output that is designed for use as input to other SGML applications, such as formatters. SGMLS has been ported to many different platforms, so all you really need to get up and running with it is a C compiler. The source code for SGMLS is available from `ftp://ftp.ifi.uio.no/pub/SGML/SGMLS`.

sgrep: A Tool for Searching Structured Documents

sgrep (which stands for structured grep) is a tool for searching text files and filtering input streams based on structural criteria. This tool takes its name from the standard UNIX utility for searching for text strings in files and input streams, and is only supported on UNIX systems.

You can get more information on sgrep from `http://www.sil.org/sgml/sgrep099.html`, and can get the latest version from `http://www.cs.helsinki.fi/~jjaakkol/sgrep.htm`

SP: James Clark's SGML Parser Toolkit

James Clark's new SP parser toolkit, discussed in Chapter 19, is the successor to his original SGMLS parser. SP is both a set of tools for working with SGML documents and entities, as well as a toolkit that provides C++ libraries that you can link with your applications.

SP and its documentation are available at `http://www.jclark.com/sp/howtoget.htm`. You can get SP in source form, or get precompiled binaries for Windows 95, Windows NT, Linux, Solaris, SunOS, and other platforms. As I mentioned earlier in this appendix, SP is included if you get a copy of James Clark's excellent DSSL package, Jade.

YASP: The Yorktown Advanced SGML Parser

Originally developed by Pierre Richard at IBM, this parser has been further developed by Christophe Espert, and has been ported to various UNIX and Microsoft Windows platforms. Like SGMLS, YASP produces normalized SGML output that can by used as input to other SGML applications, such as formatters. YASP is available from `ftp://ftp.edf.fr/pub/SGML/YASP`.

Appendix B
SGML Software Vendors

• •

*T*his appendix lists many vendors of different types of SGML software. For a much larger list, see Steve Pepper's *Whirlwind Guide to SGML Tools,* available at `http://www.falch.no/people/pepper/sgmltool/`.

Adobe Systems Incorporated
Product: FrameMaker+SGML
Description: Document editor, Formatting Environment, Creates DTD Equivalents
Platforms: Macintosh, Microsoft Windows, UNIX
411 1st Avenue South
Seattle, WA 98104
Phone: 206-622-5481
`http://www.adobe.com`

Advent
Product: 3B2 SGML
Description: SGML Formatter
Platforms: DOS
3B2 House
12 Bath Road, Old Town
Swindon, Wiltshire SN1 4BA
UK
Phone: 44-1793-511432
`http://www.3b2.com`

ArborText, Inc.
Product: Adept Series (Adept Editor, Adept Publisher, Document Architect)
Description: SGML Editor, Publishing System, FOSI Designer
Platforms: Microsoft Windows, UNIX
1000 Victors Way, Suite 100
Ann Arbor, MI 48108
Phone: 313-997-0200
`http://www.arbortext.com`

Chrystal Software
Product: Astoria
Description: Document Management System, can be integrated with
Arbortext and Adobe tools
Platforms: (Client) Microsoft Windows NT; (Server) Microsoft Windows NT,
Sun Solaris
10875 Rancho Bernardo Road, Suite 200
San Diego, CA 92127-2116
Phone: 619-676-7700
http://www.chrystal.com

Corel Corporation
Product: Corel WordPerfect Suite 8.0
Description: SGML Editor, Formatter, DTD Builder
Platforms: Microsoft Windows
Corporate Headquarters
1600 Carling Avenue
Ottawa, Ontario K1Z 8R7
CANADA
Phone: 613-728-8200
http://www.corel.com

Datalogics, Inc.
Product: DL Composer, WriterStation
Description: SGML Formatter, SGML Editor
Platforms: (Composer) UNIX; (WriterStation) Microsoft Windows 95 and
Windows NT, OS/2
101 N. Wacker Drive, Suite 1800
Chicago, IL 60606
Phone: 312-853-8200
http://www.datalogics.com

Digitome, LTD.
Product: Intelligent Document Manager
Description: SGML Converter to Folio Views, FrameMaker MIF, HTML, Lotus
Notes, RTF, and Microsoft Windows Help
Platforms: Microsoft Windows
13 Herbert Street
Dublin 2
IRELAND
Phone: 353-1-6621499
http://www.screen.ie/digitome/

GRIF S.A.
Products: SGML ActiveViews, SGML Editor, SGML Notes, Symposia Pro
Description: SGML Browser/Annotator/Printer, SGML Editor, "Lite" SGML
Editor, SGML Browser and HTML Editor
Platforms (ActiveViews) Microsoft Windows, UNIX; (SGML Editor) UNIX;
(SGML Notes) Microsoft Windows; (Symposia Pro) Microsoft Windows
2, boulevard Vaubanm BP266
78053 St Quentin en Yvelines Cedex
FRANCE
Phone: 33 01 30 12 14 30
http://www.grif.fr

InContext Systems
Products: InContext 2
Description: SGML Editor
Platforms: Microsoft Windows
6733 Mississauga Road, 7th floor
Mississauga, Ontario L5N 6J5
CANADA
Phone: 905-819-1173
http://www.incontext.ca

INSO Corporation
Products: DynaText Professional Publishing System, DynaWeb
Description: SGML Editor/DTD Builder/Formatter; WWW Exporter for SGML
Documents
Platforms: (DynaText) Macintosh, Microsoft Windows, UNIX; (DynaWeb)
UNIX
31 St. James Avenue
Boston, MA 02116-4101
Phone: 617-753-6500
http://www.inso.com

Interleaf, Inc.
Products: Interleaf 6, WorldView
Description: SGML Editor/Formatter, Electronic Publishing System
Platforms: Microsoft Windows, UNIX
Corporate Headquarters
62 Fourth Ave.
Waltham, MA 02154
Phone: 617-290-0710
http://www.ileaf.com

Microstar Software, LTD.
Products: Near & Far Author, Near & Far Designer
Description: SGML Plug-in for Microsoft Word; SGML DTD Designer
Platforms: Microsoft Windows
3775 Richmond Road
Nepean, Ontario K2H 5B7
CANADA
Phone: 613-596-5934
http://www.microstar.com

OmniMark Technologies Corporation
Products: OmniMark
Description: Converter from any text thing to anything, including SGML
Platforms: Microsoft Windows, OS/2, UNIX, VMS (!)
1400 Blair Place
Ottawa, Ontario K1J 9B8
CANADA
Phone: 613-745-4242
http://www.omnimark.com

Passage Systems, Inc.
Products: PassageHub, PassagePro
Description: Converts Word-processing files into HTML/SGML/XML; SGML
Converter/Editor/Document Management/Publishing System
Platforms: Microsoft Windows, Sun SunOS, Sun Solaris
1200 Chrysler Drive
Menlo Park, CA 94025
Phone: 415-323-2222
http://www.passage.com

SGML Systems Engineering
Products: SGMLC
Description: SGML Conversion software (SGML into anything interesting)
Platforms: Microsoft Windows
Banwell House
Banwell
Weston Super Mare
North Somerset BS24 6DG
ENGLAND
Phone: 44-1934-822911
http://www.dircon.co.uk/sgml/

SoftQuad, Inc.
Products: Author/Editor, Panorama, Panorama Publishing Suite
Description: SGML Editor, SGML Viewer, SGML Editor/DTD-Builder/Formatter
for the Web
Platforms: (Author/Editor) Macintosh, Microsoft Windows, UNIX; (Panorama)
Microsoft Windows; Panorama Publishing Suite (Microsoft Windows)
20 Eglinton Ave. West, 12th Floor
PO Box 2025
Toronto M4R 1K8
CANADA
Phone: 416-544-9000
http://www.sq.com

TechnoTeacher, Inc.
Products: HyBrowse, HyMinder
Description: HyTime SGML browser (HyTime extends SGML to multimedia
and beyond!), HyTime development toolkit
Platforms: Microsoft Windows
PO Box 23795
Rochester, NY 14692-3795
Phone: 716-271-0796
http://www.techno.com

Xyvision, Inc.
Products: Parlance Document Manager, Production Publisher
Description: SGML Document Management System, SGML Formatter
Platforms: UNIX
101 Edgewater Drive
Wakefield, MA 01880-1291
Phone: 617-245-4100
http://www.xyvision.com

Appendix C

About the CD

Here's a taste of what you can find on the *SGML For Dummies* CD-ROM:

- ✔ A 90-day demonstration version of Corel WordPerfect — other than the time-limit, this is a fully-functional version of all of the tools you need to work with SGML in WordPerfect, including WordPerfect itself, the Corel Logic Compiler, and Layout Designer.

- ✔ A demonstration version of Digitome Electronic Publishing's IDM Personal Edition and its associated documentation. IDM is a powerful software package for generating Windows Help, RTF, and Lotus Notes format files from SGML input files.

- ✔ Sample SGML applications from SGML Systems Engineering, including SGMLC-Lite, a Lite version of their core toolset, Generic SGML Viewer, SGML Normaliser, and SGML Parser.

- ✔ The SP SGML Parser for Win95 and NT PCs.

- ✔ A 45-day demonstration version of HyTime's HyBrowse Browser, an SGML/HyTime-aware browser and educational development system.

- ✔ DTDs such as the TEI-Lite and DocBook DTDs.

System Requirements

Make sure your PC or compatible meets the following system requirements for using this CD:

- ✔ Windows 3.*x* (that is, 3.1 or 3.11), Windows 95, or Windows NT installed on your computer. (Some software, such as WordPerfect, requires Windows 95 or NT 4.0.)

- ✔ If you're running Windows 3.*x:* a 386SX or faster processor with *at least* 8MB of total RAM.

- ✔ If you're running Windows 95 or Windows NT: a 486 or faster processor with *at least* 8MB of total RAM.

- ✔ At least 150MB of hard drive space available to install all the software from this CD. (You need less space if you don't install every program.)

  ✔ A CD-ROM drive — double-speed (2x) or faster.

  ✔ A monitor capable of displaying at least 256 colors or grayscale.

If you need more information on PC or Windows basics, check out *PCs For Dummies,* 4th Edition, by Dan Gookin; *Windows 95 For Dummies* by Andy Rathbone; or *Windows 3.11 For Dummies,* 3rd Edition, by Andy Rathbone (all published by IDG Books Worldwide, Inc.).

Using the CD: Installation Instructions

Installing the bonus software is easy, thanks to the CD interface. An interface, as far as this CD goes, is a little program that lets you see what is on the CD, gives you some information about the bonus software, and makes it easy to install stuff. It hides all the junk you don't need to know, like directories and installation programs.

1. **Put your CD in your computer's CD-ROM drive.**

2. **Windows 95 users: Click on the Start button, and then click on the Run option in the Start menu.**

   For Windows 3.x users: From Program Manager, choose File➪Run.

3. **In the dialog box that appears type:** D:\setup.exe

4. **Click OK.**

If your CD-ROM drive is not called D:\, be sure to use the correct letter for your drive. The first time you use the CD, you will see our license agreement. After you agree to that, the interface will open up and you can start browsing the CD. Follow these steps any time you want to use the CD.

Installing Support Software

Before you can use this CD, you need to install Adobe Acrobat Reader so you can read the Acrobat documents on the CD.

To install Adobe Acrobat Reader 2.1 for Windows 3.x and Windows 95, follow these steps:

1. **Insert the CD into your computer's CD-ROM drive and close the drive door.**

2. **Windows 95 users: Click the Start button and click Run.**

   Windows 3.x (that is, 3.1 or 3.11) users: From Program Manager, choose File➪Run.

3. In the dialog box that appears, type *N*:\ACROREAD.EXE, **where *N* represents the drive letter for your CD-ROM drive.**

4. **Click OK.**

What You'll Find

Here's a summary of the software on this CD, given by descriptive sections for each piece of software.

Corel WordPerfect 8.0

In the SGML Tools category.

For Windows 95 and Windows NT 4.0.

This is a 90-day demo of all of the parts of Corel WordPerfect that are required for you to work with SGML documents in SGML. This includes WordPerfect itself, the SGML DTD Compiler (dtd2lgc), and the Layout Designer. This also includes documentation for Corel WordPerfect in the Corel Envoy electronic publishing format.

For more information about Corel, see http://www.corel.com.

SGMLC Core Components

In the SGML Tools category.

Select the 16-bit version for Windows 3.x, or the 32-bit version for Windows 95 and Windows NT 4.0.

You must install the SGMLC Core Components before you can use any of the other sample products from SGML Systems Engineering.

This is the core set of components used by the other products from SGML Systems Engineering on this CD. This set includes

- SGMLC-Lite, an SGML toolkit.
- The Generic SGML Viewer, an application that lets you see the hierarchical structure of SGML documents.
- The SGML Normaliser, which flattens the structure of an SGML document and expands any entities that the document contains.

> ✔ The SGML parser, which validates the content of an SGML document instance against the appropriate DTD.

For more information about SGML Systems Engineering, see `http://www.dircon.co.uk/sgml/`

SGMLC-Lite

In the SGML Tools category.

Select the 16-bit version for Windows 3.x, or the 32-bit version for Windows 95 and Windows NT 4.0.

You must install the SGMLC Core Components and SGMLC-Lite before you can use any of the other sample products from SGML Systems Engineering.

This is an SGML toolkit used by the other products from SGML Systems Engineering on this CD. This toolkit includes:

> ✔ The Generic SGML Viewer, an application that lets you see the hierarchical structure of SGML documents
>
> ✔ The SGML Normaliser, which flattens the structure of an SGML document and expands any entities that the document contains
>
> ✔ The SGML parser, which validates the content of an SGML document instance against the appropriate DTD

For more information about SGML Systems Engineering, see `http://www.dircon.co.uk/sgml/`

SGML Parser for DOS

In the SGML Tools category.

Select the 16-bit version for Windows 3.x, or the 32-bit version for Windows 95 and Windows NT 4.0.

You must install the SGMLC Core Components and SGMLC-Lite before you can use this product.

This is an SGML parser from SGML Systems Engineering, which validates the content of an SGML document instance against the appropriate DTD.

For more information about SGML Systems Engineering, see `http://www.dircon.co.uk/sgml/`.

SGML Normaliser

In the SGML Tools category.

Select the 16-bit version for Windows 3.x, or the 32-bit version for Windows 95 and Windows NT 4.0.

You must install the SGMLC Core Components and SGMLC-Lite before you can use this product.

This is an SGML Normaliser from SGML Systems Engineering, which flattens the structure of an SGML document and expands any entities that the document contains.

For more information about SGML Systems Engineering, see `http://www.dircon.co.uk/sgml/`.

Generic SGML Viewer

In the SGML Tools category.

Select the 16-bit version for Windows 3.x, or the 32-bit version for Windows 95 and Windows NT 4.0.

You must install the SGMLC Core Components and SGMLC-Lite before you can use this product.

This is an SGML Viewer from SGML Systems Engineering, which shows you the hierarchical structure of any SGML document.

For more information about SGML Systems Engineering, see `http://www.dircon.co.uk/sgml/`.

SP SGML Parser and Toolkit

In the SGML Tools category.

For Windows 95 and Windows NT 4.0. For users who have Windows 3.x, there is also a version of this program for DOS, which will run under DOS.

This is an SGML parser and programmer's toolkit from James Clark. SP is a core component of other public-domain SGML-related software discussed elsewhere in this book, such as Jade.

For more information about James Clark and the other amazingly cool (and free) SGML-related software that he has authored, see `http://www.jclark.com`.

HTML Links

In the Link category.

For use with any Web browser.

This is simply an SGML file that provides shortcuts to many of the SGML resources that I discuss in this book. I found them once — why not save you the trouble of finding them again?

HyBrowse Browser

In the Browsers category.

For Windows 3.x, Windows 95, and Windows NT 4.0.

HyBrowse is an SGML browser and educational development systems that also demonstrates the capabilities of HyTime, a set of multimedia extensions to SGML.

For more information about HyTime and HyBrowse, see `http://www.techno.com/HyBrowse.html`.

Panorama Viewer

In the Browsers category.

For Windows 3.x, Windows 95, and Windows NT 4.0.

Panorama is an SGML browser from the folks at SoftQuad, maker of some popular, commercial SGML applications mentioned in this book.

For more information about Panorama and SoftQuad, see `http://www.softquad.com`.

IDM Personal Edition

In the IDM category.

For Windows 3.x, Windows 95, and Windows NT 4.0.

IDM Personal Edition is a demonstration version of SGML conversion software from Digitome Electronic Publishing. IDM lets you convert SGML documents into other formats, such as Microsoft Word's RTF, suitable for use as Windows Help and Lotus Notes format.

For more information about IDM, see `http://www.nwconnect.ie/ digitome.`

IDM Personal Edition Documentation

In the IDM category.

For Windows 3.x, Windows 95, and Windows NT 4.0.

This is the documentation for the IDM Personal Edition software in Microsoft Word format.

For more information about IDM, see `http://www.nwconnect.ie/ digitome.`

TEI-Lite DTD

In the DTD category.

For any SGML software package.

TEI-Lite is a subset of the TEI DTD, which was designed for markup and electronic publishing of existing literary works.

TEI-Lite WP

In the DTD category.

You must already have installed the demonstration version of Corel WordPerfect SGML in order to use these files.

TEI-Lite is a subset of the TEI DTD, which was designed for markup and electronic publishing of existing literary works. This package includes the TEI-Lite DTD and layout files that you can use to edit and print documents marked up with this DTD using the demonstration version of Corel WordPerfect that is also included on this CD.

DocBook 2.4.1

In the DTD category.

For use with any SGML software package.

The DocBook DTD is the premiere DTD that is freely available for use in marking up and working with technical documentation. As I explain in this book, the DocBook DTD was developed as a collaborative effort of a number of software companies, and is an excellent DTD to use when developing software and other technical documentation using SGML. Version 2.4.1 is the most common version of this DTD in popular use, though Version 3.0 (also included on this CD) is also available and offers some enhancements and corrections.

DocBook 3.0

In the DTD category.

For use with any SGML software package.

The DocBook DTD is the premiere DTD that is freely available for use in marking up and working with technical documentation. As I explain, the DocBook DTD was developed as a collaborative effort of a number of software companies, and is an excellent DTD to use when developing software and other technical documentation using SGML. Version 3.0 is the latest version of this DTD, and offers some enhancements in content models, as well as being somewhat easier to modify.

CALS SGML specification

In the Specs category.

In (government) English, so for use by anyone. You must have installed the Adobe Acrobat Viewer in order to read this documents after installing it.

The CALS (Computer-Aided Logistics and Support, as well as many other expansions!) specification is the U.S. government specification that mandates the use of SGML for government projects, and is one of the documents that really got the whole SGML ball rolling. You want to read this document if you are a U.S. government contractor or plan to apply for a government contract.

Implementation guide

In the Specs category.

In (government) English, so for use by anyone. You must have installed the Adobe Acrobat Viewer in order to read this documents after installing it.

This document explains how to use the guidelines spelled out in the CALS specification to produce documents for government projects. You want to read this document if you are a U.S. government contractor or plan to apply for a government contract.

Markup & style sheet

In the Specs category.

In (government) English, so for use by anyone. You must have installed the Adobe Acrobat Viewer in order to read this documents after installing it.

This explains how to mark up documents so that they conform to the CALS specification, and also discusses formatting (FOSI) and style information for CALS documents. You want to read this document if you are a U.S. government contractor or plan to apply for a government contract.

Adobe Acrobat Viewer

In the Browsers category.

For Windows 3.x, Windows 95, and Windows NT 4.0.

Adobe Acrobat, which I describe in this book, is used in electronic publishing to view documents that have been published using the Adobe Acrobat Distiller.

For more information about the Adobe Acrobat Viewer, see http://www.adobe.com.

If You've Got Problems (Of the CD Kind)

I tried my best to include programs that work on most computers with the minimum system requirements. Alas, your computer may differ, and some programs may not work properly for some reason.

The two likeliest problems are that you don't have enough memory (RAM) for the programs you want to use, or you have other programs running that are affecting the installation or running of the program. If you get error messages like Not enough memory or Setup cannot continue, try one or more of these methods and then try using the software again:

- ✔ Turn off any anti-virus software that you have on your computer. Installers sometimes mimic virus activity and may make your computer incorrectly believe that it is being infected by a virus.

- ✔ Close all running programs. The more programs you run, the less memory is available to other programs. Installers also typically update files and programs. So if you keep other programs running, installation may not work properly.

- ✔ Have your local computer store add more RAM to your computer. If you're a Windows 95 user, adding more memory can really help the speed of your computer and allow more programs to run at the same time.

If you still have trouble installing the items from the CD, please call the IDG Books Worldwide Customer Service phone number: 800-762-2974 (outside the U.S.: 317-596-5261).

Index

• T •

IDG Books Worldwide, Inc., End-User License Agreement

READ THIS. You should carefully read these terms and conditions before opening the software packet(s) included with this book ("Book"). This is a license agreement ("Agreement") between you and IDG Books Worldwide, Inc. ("IDGB"). By opening the accompanying software packet(s), you acknowledge that you have read and accept the following terms and conditions. If you do not agree and do not want to be bound by such terms and conditions, promptly return the Book and the unopened software packet(s) to the place you obtained them for a full refund.

1. **License Grant.** IDGB grants to you (either an individual or entity) a nonexclusive license to use one copy of the enclosed software program(s) (collectively, the "Software") solely for your own personal or business purposes on a single computer (whether a standard computer or a workstation component of a multiuser network). The Software is in use on a computer when it is loaded into temporary memory (RAM) or installed into permanent memory (hard disk, CD-ROM, or other storage device). IDGB reserves all rights not expressly granted herein.

2. **Ownership.** IDGB is the owner of all right, title, and interest, including copyright, in and to the compilation of the Software recorded on the disk(s) or CD-ROM ("Software Media"). Copyright to the individual programs recorded on the Software Media is owned by the author or other authorized copyright owner of each program. Ownership of the Software and all proprietary rights relating thereto remain with IDGB and its licensers.

3. **Restrictions on Use and Transfer.**

   (a) You may only (i) make one copy of the Software for backup or archival purposes, or (ii) transfer the Software to a single hard disk, provided that you keep the original for backup or archival purposes. You may not (i) rent or lease the Software, (ii) copy or reproduce the Software through a LAN or other network system or through any computer subscriber system or bulletin-board system, or (iii) modify, adapt, or create derivative works based on the Software.

   (b) You may not reverse engineer, decompile, or disassemble the Software. You may transfer the Software and user documentation on a permanent basis, provided that the transferee agrees to accept the terms and conditions of this Agreement and you retain no copies. If the Software is an update or has been updated, any transfer must include the most recent update and all prior versions.

4. **Restrictions on Use of Individual Programs.** You must follow the individual requirements and restrictions detailed for each individual program in the "About the Disk or CD" section (Appendix C) of this Book. These limitations are also contained in the individual license agreements recorded on the Software Media. These limitations may include a requirement that after using the program for a specified period of time, the user must pay a registration fee or discontinue use. By opening the Software packet(s), you will be agreeing to abide by the licenses and restrictions for these individual programs that are detailed in the "About the Disk or CD" section (Appendix C) and on the Software Media. None of the material on this Software Media or listed in this Book may ever be redistributed, in original or modified form, for commercial purposes.

5. Limited Warranty.

> **(a)** IDGB warrants that the Software and Software Media are free from defects in materials and workmanship under normal use for a period of sixty (60) days from the date of purchase of this Book. If IDGB receives notification within the warranty period of defects in materials or workmanship, IDGB will replace the defective Software Media.

> **(b)** IDGB AND THE AUTHOR OF THE BOOK DISCLAIM ALL OTHER WARRANTIES, EXPRESS OR IMPLIED, INCLUDING WITHOUT LIMITATION IMPLIED WARRANTIES OF MERCHANTABILITY AND FITNESS FOR A PARTICULAR PURPOSE, WITH RESPECT TO THE SOFTWARE, THE PROGRAMS, THE SOURCE CODE CONTAINED THEREIN, AND/OR THE TECHNIQUES DESCRIBED IN THIS BOOK. IDGB DOES NOT WARRANT THAT THE FUNCTIONS CONTAINED IN THE SOFTWARE WILL MEET YOUR REQUIREMENTS OR THAT THE OPERATION OF THE SOFTWARE WILL BE ERROR FREE.

> **(c)** This limited warranty gives you specific legal rights, and you may have other rights that vary from jurisdiction to jurisdiction.

6. Remedies.

> **(a)** IDGB's entire liability and your exclusive remedy for defects in materials and workmanship shall be limited to replacement of the Software Media, which may be returned to IDGB with a copy of your receipt at the following address: Software Media Fulfillment Department, Attn.: *SGML For Dummies,* IDG Books Worldwide, Inc., 7260 Shadeland Station, Ste. 100, Indianapolis, IN 46256, or call 800-762-2974. Please allow three to four weeks for delivery. This Limited Warranty is void if failure of the Software Media has resulted from accident, abuse, or misapplication. Any replacement Software Media will be warranted for the remainder of the original warranty period or thirty (30) days, whichever is longer.

> **(b)** In no event shall IDGB or the author be liable for any damages whatsoever (including without limitation damages for loss of business profits, business interruption, loss of business information, or any other pecuniary loss) arising from the use of or inability to use the Book or the Software, even if IDGB has been advised of the possibility of such damages.

> **(c)** Because some jurisdictions do not allow the exclusion or limitation of liability for consequential or incidental damages, the above limitation or exclusion may not apply to you.

7. U.S. Government Restricted Rights. Use, duplication, or disclosure of the Software by the U.S. Government is subject to restrictions stated in paragraph (c)(1)(ii) of the Rights in Technical Data and Computer Software clause of DFARS 252.227-7013, and in subparagraphs (a) through (d) of the Commercial Computer–Restricted Rights clause at FAR 52.227-19, and in similar clauses in the NASA FAR supplement, when applicable.

8. General. This Agreement constitutes the entire understanding of the parties and revokes and supersedes all prior agreements, oral or written, between them and may not be modified or amended except in a writing signed by both parties hereto that specifically refers to this Agreement. This Agreement shall take precedence over any other documents that may be in conflict herewith. If any one or more provisions contained in this Agreement are held by any court or tribunal to be invalid, illegal, or otherwise unenforceable, each and every other provision shall remain in full force and effect.

Using the CD: Installation Instructions

Installing the Bonus software is easy, thanks to the CD interface. An interface, as far as this CD goes, is a little program that lets you see what is on the CD, gives you some information about the bonus software, and makes it easy to install stuff. It hides all the junk you don't need to know, like directories and installation programs.

1. **Put your CD in your computer's CD-ROM drive.**

2. **For Windows 95 users: Click on the Start button, and then click on the Run option in the Start menu.**

   For Windows 3.x users: From Program Manager, choose File⇨Run.

3. **In the dialog box that appears type:** D:\setup.exe

4. **Click OK.**

If your CD-ROM drive is not called D:\, be sure to use the correct letter for your drive. The first time you use the CD, you will see our License agreement. After you agree to that, the interface will open up and you can start browsing the CD. Follow these steps any time you want to use the CD.

Using the CD interface

The CD interface has three general regions: the category list, the product list window, and the background. When you first see the interface, the product list window displays instructions on using the CD. The category list, on the left side, lists the categories of software that are available on this CD. When you select an option from the category list, the product window changes and shows you all of the products available in that category. Now you can select a product from the list and get more information about it or install it.

To get more information, click on the Info button. A window will open up, probably your NotePad program, with a brief description of what the program does and any special information you might need to know about installing it. When you are done reading the information, be sure to close the text window, or you will get *text-window build up* and have them pile up all over your desktop. To close the text window, just click on the File menu and select Exit.

To install a program, just click on the Install button. The programs' installers will walk you through the process.

Note: See Appendix C for further instructions on the CD, including contents, system requirements, and troubleshooting.

IDG BOOKS WORLDWIDE REGISTRATION CARD

RETURN THIS REGISTRATION CARD FOR FREE CATALOG

Title of this book: SGML For Dummies®

My overall rating of this book: ❑ Very good [1] ❑ Good [2] ❑ Satisfactory [3] ❑ Fair [4] ❑ Poor [5]

How I first heard about this book:

❑ Found in bookstore; name: [6]

❑ Advertisement: [8]

❑ Word of mouth; heard about book from friend, co-worker, etc.: [10]

❑ Book review: [7]

❑ Catalog: [9]

❑ Other: [11]

What I liked most about this book:

What I would change, add, delete, etc., in future editions of this book:

Other comments:

Number of computer books I purchase in a year: ❑ 1 [12] ❑ 2-5 [13] ❑ 6-10 [14] ❑ More than 10 [15]

I would characterize my computer skills as: ❑ Beginner [16] ❑ Intermediate [17] ❑ Advanced [18] ❑ Professional [19]

I use ❑ DOS [20] ❑ Windows [21] ❑ OS/2 [22] ❑ Unix [23] ❑ Macintosh [24] ❑ Other: [25]_____
(please specify)

I would be interested in new books on the following subjects:
(please check all that apply, and use the spaces provided to identify specific software)

❑ Word processing: [26]

❑ Data bases: [28]

❑ File Utilities: [30]

❑ Networking: [32]

❑ Other: [34]

❑ Spreadsheets: [27]

❑ Desktop publishing: [29]

❑ Money management: [31]

❑ Programming languages: [33]

I use a PC at (please check all that apply): ❑ home [35] ❑ work [36] ❑ school [37] ❑ other: [38] _____

The disks I prefer to use are ❑ 5.25 [39] ❑ 3.5 [40] ❑ other: [41]_____

I have a CD ROM: ❑ yes [42]   ❑ no [43]

I plan to buy or upgrade computer hardware this year: ❑ yes [44] ❑ no [45]

I plan to buy or upgrade computer software this year: ❑ yes [46] ❑ no [47]

Name: _____ Business title: [48] _____ Type of Business: [49] _____

Address (❑ home [50] ❑ work [51]/Company name: _____)

Street/Suite# _____

City [52]/State [53]/Zipcode [54]: _____ Country [55] _____

❑ **I liked this book!** You may quote me by name in future
IDG Books Worldwide promotional materials.

My daytime phone number is _____

IDG BOOKS

THE WORLD OF
COMPUTER
KNOWLEDGE

❑ YES!

Please keep me informed about IDG's World of Computer Knowledge.
Send me the latest IDG Books catalog.

COMPUTER
BOOK SERIES
FROM IDG

NO POSTAGE
NECESSARY
IF MAILED
IN THE
UNITED STATES

BUSINESS REPLY MAIL
FIRST CLASS MAIL   PERMIT NO. 2605   FOSTER CITY, CALIFORNIA

IDG Books Worldwide
919 E Hillsdale Blvd, STE 400
Foster City, CA 94404-9691